IN DISGRACE WITH FORTUNE

A Chronicle of Harlotry

Jean Hendy-Harris

Copyright Print edition 2017 Jean Hendy-Harris
Smashwords Edition2015

All rights reserved. No part of this book may be used or reproduced in any manner whatsoever including Internet usage, without written permission of the author.

Ebook formatting by Maureen Cutajar
www.gopublished.com

Print layout and cover design by Bev Robitai
www.bevrobitai.co.nz

ISBN-13: 978-1978450493
ISBN-10: 1978450494

Autoboigraphy, London, 1960s, sex workers

This third volume of my memoir has been the most difficult to write.

It tells of a period in my life when I became involved in the sex industry, working in a number of London night clubs as a showgirl and hostess and finally in a House of Deviation.

The latter establishment catered to the tastes of those with a variety of sexual fixations that differed substantially from that we regard as normal.

Contents

1. Completing The Trilogy
2. Flesh Coloured Costumes
3. Chasing The Sound Engineer
4. A Showgirl At Last
5. A Force To Be Reckoned With
6. On A White Charger
7. A Lark Arising
8. Troubling Deaf Heaven
9. Once With Friends Possessed
10. An Audience With Madam Sandra
11. Fairy Tale Babies
12. Always Blessed
13. Somebody Has To Do It
14. A House Of Deviation
15. Not Clothed In Scarlet Garments
16. Sweet Love Remembered
17. You'll Have To Give It Up

Completing the Trilogy

The man I had been married to for forty-one years was looking more than disapproving. He had a distinctly negative aura about him, judgmental even. He had just said.
'I think it would be most unwise for you to write such a book.'
And I had said, 'Why? It would after all complete the trilogy. It can't be a trilogy without it.'
There had been a short pause before he added, 'You can't write it because it would hurt people – too many people.'
'Would it hurt you?'
'No – not me, but it might hurt the children.'
'The children are all older than I was when these things happened – and anyway they all know about it.'
He said that our daughter did not know about it and I told him he was wrong because she had known since she was fourteen. Somebody at school had talked about an incident I wrote of in a previous book.
'But *that* book,' he pointed out almost jubilantly, 'was written under a pseudonym!'
I had to admit he was right. But maybe writing under a pseudonym had been an unwise decision in the first place. Most readers knew it was me and thought it was fiction anyhow and it was a long time ago. I wished I still had a copy so I could check exactly what it was I had written. Might it be possible to obtain one via Amazon? Later on I would check.

'She is now thirty-eight years old,' I reminded him, 'Quite old enough to cope with a little bit of emotional trauma.'

'What about her career? Have you thought about how her colleagues would view it?'

'Do you imagine for one moment that the bigwigs of banking are going to actually stumble across it? If they did would they bother to read it? Will the City of London come to a standstill when the news gets around?' I had now stopped trying to control the anger that was rising imperceptibly, little by little. Soon I would be shouting and so would he.

But he was fidgeting with the base of his empty beer glass and staring at the wall of the tiny courtyard as though trying to recall what he should say next.

I filled the ensuing silence with, 'I wrote it once before – as a novel,' and added honestly, 'But only a couple of dozen people have bought it so I think you'll have to come to the same conclusion as I have – no-one is terribly interested.'

'You just can't stop writing about it can you?' he said nastily. I decided to ignore that comment.

He sighed and said, 'If nobody is interested I cannot for the life of me understand why you want to write about it yet again.'

'Because it completes the cycle – like Wagner.'

'Wagner?' He looked at me owlishly. 'Why Wagner?'

'The Ring,' I said, 'Though of course it's completely different. I do understand that before you explain it to me in minute detail. Sets of books – a trilogy for instance are selling well at the moment – that's all I'm saying.'

'I know you won't take any notice of my opinion,' he said, 'you never have. It's not just the children who might be hurt. What about your family? Your brother? Your cousins? Don't you care what they might think?'

'Not much. They're most unlikely to read it,' I told him, 'and I cannot understand why you are so against it.'

'The material is sensitive – the nature of the work was.... improper...' he sighed again and stopped suddenly.

'Maybe that was so *then* – but society has changed. Attitudes have changed. After all, in 1900 or thereabouts it was quite shocking if you had a daughter who ran away to become an actress but if it happened these days nobody would bat an eyelid except perhaps to tell you that the politically correct term is 'actor'. You just haven't moved with the times yourself and that's why you find it unacceptable.'

He remained silent.

I reminded him, not for the first time that morning, that he had chosen to marry me even though I had made him totally aware of the socially unacceptable nature of the work I was involved in. In fact we had been discussing marriage when I first mentioned it during the dinner date at Rules in Maiden Lane.

'You were much more accepting back in those days,' I observed spitefully, 'It's as if you haven't simply failed to move with the times, but actually gone backwards.'

He nodded but barely noticeably and asked me if I was going to change the names of the people involved.

'Well I won't be naming any of the crowned heads of Europe of course,' I tried to be as acerbic as was possible whilst draining my gin and tonic. The ice had melted and the mixture in the bottom of the glass was now unpleasantly warm. Why was it he could only concentrate on the eminent, the notorious or the celebrated?

I told him that most people I had come into contact with had been ordinary, everyday, conventional human beings. After all these years it was quite difficult to recall those who were not but if I was to write about them I would have to try to do so.

'No-one will want to read about the ordinary,' he said unnecessarily and I replied that if that was the case I couldn't understand why he was so against me writing it.

He said that some of our friends might avoid us if they knew the truth about my past and I exploded and told him that they probably all knew anyway, or most of them at least, and that I couldn't ever recall us being hurriedly dumped off Christmas card lists. Unless my perception was totally wrong, after a first flurry of fascination from some of the men, and brief tut-tutting from slightly scandalized wives, the initial interest had rapidly waned.

When I calmed down and had a fresh gin and tonic in front of me, which was more tonic than gin because he had poured it, I said that in any event the past now felt to me as if it had happened to somebody else. It was all so long ago.

'I'm a different person now,' I said, 'I've been a different person for forty years. I married you and became a doctor's wife – I wasn't the worst doctor's wife in Auckland. I thought I was quite good at it.'

He agreed although adding that there were things he might have changed in order to make me perfect. I ignored that remark. 'And once I had children I became a superlative mother.'

He reminded me that our son, currently living in China, would not agree with me and that in fact he had recently told me that I had been a 'smothering' mother. On the other hand he had at the same time described his father as 'distant' and he was never going to forgive either of us for having him circumcised as a helpless infant.

'It was a pity that between us we couldn't get the parenting right for him,' I admitted, 'But then that's only how he sees it now – he might assess things differently when he gets older.'

His father gently reflected that was unlikely in his view as he was already more than forty years old.

I wanted to continue enumerating the advantages of having me as wife and mother as I saw them. 'I was a very good home schooler. Even the Education Department thought I was a very good home schooling parent.'

'Except you insisted on doing it for far too long – the children should have gone back to school long before they did.'

'They had a very good education,' I asserted.

But I knew he was right. I added, tearfully now because I had drunk far too much gin for someone with temporal lobe epilepsy on anti-convulsion medication, 'Well I had to make a few mistakes surely – otherwise I wouldn't be human.'

As he got up from the table, gathering up the glasses as he did so, he leaned towards me and said in a very low voice, 'You have a habit of never taking advice and there are times when it would be better all round if you did. This is one of those times.'

He disappeared inside, into the tiny living room of the diminutive terrace house where we had lived for the past two years. The estate agent had described it as 'city fringe living at its best' and it certainly had advantages over the beach suburb where we had been for the previous thirty-eight years but space was not one of them. What I had liked best about the place when we first looked at it was the little courtyard entrance with its cream stucco walls and large grey paving stones.

Sitting within its walls could transport me almost anywhere in the world, even now, when I felt tearful and angry and furious with myself for being so transparently emotional. The other aspect of the place that initially attracted me was that the little houses, unified in their appearance so that each obediently copied its neighbour, were strangely reminiscent of those depressing rows of working-class terraces in English industrial towns. Houses that I once hated with a vehemence impossible to conceal, and now hankered after.

There were forty such residences in our particular block, a little society that spilled towards the untidy and impersonal city, yet because we were gated and walled from the streets around us, never quite got there.

'It's just a little bit like living in Coronation Street,' I said with great satisfaction in conversation late one night with my daughter in London who had just bought half of a terrace house herself, though late Victorian with a garden that, astonishingly, harboured a family of foxes.

'But not quite as friendly,' I felt forced to add because admittedly my neighbours were far less likely than my favourite soap opera characters to invite me in for cups of tea or share confidences at the drop of a hat.

On the other hand I liked the vaguely impersonal aspect of the place because you could be as anonymous as you might like and yet if you wished others good morning they generally responded appropriately. Best of all, there was always a slight flurry of activity about the alleys and passageways much like the narrow throughways of a Northern English town. At all times of day and night it seemed that residents bustled about the place to-ing and fro-ing from the confines of their homes, perhaps to the bins in the dark and slightly menacing rubbish room beneath the car-park, or to the tiers of mailboxes outside the safely locked front gates. Comforting sounds of other human beings going about their normal business.

In summer echoes of laughter, clinking of beer cans and the tempting aroma of sizzling sausages on barbecues wafted up from surrounding patios. Everyone secure and separate yet each sharing the odd kinship of quasi-village life, recently sprung up in this far-flung city in the Pacific.

It is in the sunshine that Auckland seems to suddenly bloom and once more is a place that has never seemed quite real to me. In the glare of sunlight the ordinary colours of life become unbearable. The green of the trees all at once is radiantly lime or jade or emerald and the blue of the sky almost blinding, the aquamarine of the sea so mesmerizing that I expect a corps de ballet of mermaids to appear on the waves. The heart of the vast untidy city perches unequivocally on the very edge of the harbour enabling the thousands of summer tourists to tip directly from their cruise ships into the main street, still blinking with surprise as they do so.

A dreamscape of a surreal metropolis where suburbs stretch mile upon mile, whilst still hugging the ocean, each neat avenue etched with starkly iconic palms and ferns and cabbage trees. And towards the midst of the city the visitor becomes aware of the surprising myriad of volcanoes, some said to be extinct but others only sleeping, on whose slopes homes have been built, whilst nearby, inexplicably, sheep and cows calmly graze close by to office blocks and churches. For all this, as far as the inhabitants are concerned, it is a place where eccentricity is frowned upon and conformity is greatly valued although the parameters of convention differ greatly from those of Paris, New York or London.

Ninety-year-old women in bathing suits and rubber caps, all armed with rolled up towels, exit beachside homes and cross main roads each morning to swim for half an hour or so. Their bodies are sagging though slender, strangely yellow-brown, skin like rawhide. Slowly being picked off by the inevitability of death this particular breed of antipodean womanhood is breathtakingly assertive, forceful and uncompromising. They have reigned above their families relentlessly until desperate daughters-in-law, now ageing themselves have after decades of tyranny finally managed to banish them to beaches where they can swim to their hearts' content, attend watercolour classes and take up Yoga or Pilates. Most of them still hold driving licences and drive vehicles in odd colours like hot pink or tangerine which they navigate with determination into small spaces, at times whilst still in their swimsuits. From time to time, they board buses with folded umbrellas as weaponry to attend summer sales at department stores or lunch in hotel restaurants with grandsons or nephews. Dementia does not dare to visit them and despite their great ages they are perfectly capable of stripping a neighbour's plum tree and producing two dozen jars of jam or initiating a support group of over-eighties for pelvic floor exercises to improve bladder control.

The city's beaches have until recent years remained surprisingly empty even in summer except for dog owners and groups of children intent upon school projects involving rock pools. Unlike other coastal areas of the world where the population spills onto the sand at the first sign of sunshine, the people of Auckland don't appear to notice their local stretch of shoreline or most of the time choose to ignore it. This merely adds to the feeling that both the place and its hinterlands are not quite real but simply poised uneasily in a half-remembered dream.

This was the place I had come to over forty years ago, the city I had found so difficult to settle into because it differed drastically from the one I had left. In London at the first hint of summer warmth the lake at The Serpentine in Hyde Park is at once barely visible through the sunbathers crammed side to side and every grassy area nearby is host to groups of mothers with small children or office workers on lunch breaks. The vast emptiness of Auckland's blindingly lush parks was both unnatural and unnerving. In the intervening years this has changed and babies in tri-wheeled pushing devices career about the parks steered by jogging mothers. But in the early nineteen-seventies infants did not know what a push chair was and were simply transferred from cot or cradle to the back seat of a car to be driven to whatever their destination happened to be.

Somehow over the decades I had learned bit by bit to adjust to what is still at certain times of year, an alien place because this was where my children had grown up, where our home had been for so long. It was also the place where I had become a totally different person.

The individual I now was smouldered with anger towards the husband who was predictably creating so many reasons why the life of my former self could not be explored, investigated and recorded.

Flesh-Coloured Costumes

The idea was put to me in the first place by Stan, one of the DJs involved in the pirate radio station. It was after the office in Dean Street had closed, the venture itself then well and truly over, the remaining staff regarding me with hostility as they lingered, some on the pretense of packing up personal belongings. I was seen as responsible for the demise of the station because of an unwise relationship with the technical director who was languishing in a Dutch prison, waiting for a trial date. Events had moved so swiftly in recent weeks that I hardly had time to collect my breath before I became to blame for a spike in the central London unemployment figures. Stan had kindly suggested buying me a cappuccino at Le Macabre and was telling me that he would have to get a job, as a welder he said. I wondered what a welder actually did.

'I really didn't know he was embezzling,' I said for the fourth or fifth time in an hour.

'I couldn't see what you saw in him in the first place,' Stan was shaking his head and looking at me intently. I stared back almost but not quite dotingly. He was tall and good looking and I loved his voice, tinged with the North American accent he had somehow picked up in a very short space of time on a trip to Canada. He had always been a far more attractive proposition than the technical director. Why did he have to be married? He was infinitely preferable to Luuk Nijhof in every way. I wasn't game to say any of this so I said nothing.

Only a week previously as the station tottered on the very edge of possibly being saved, he and Paul, another DJ who now had hopes of returning to Forces Network, had been taken to the Astor Club where the hostesses had impressed them. Now he returned to that topic.

'You could get a job in that place,' he said, looking me up and down in much the same way as my grandmother was wont to do in years past when assessing how many bags of beans, peas or potatoes I might be relied upon to fill in one afternoon of industry in the fields of North Kent.

'What does a hostess actually have to do?' I asked cautiously. He gave me a dismissive look as if he had only half heard the question and declined to answer for a second or two.

It was a totally serious question because I knew very little about night clubs and how they operated. My sole experience had been a single visit to the Embassy club as a teenager in the company of workmates from Francis, Day & Hunter where I diligently typed letters in the Copyright Department. I had not been aware of the presence of hostesses on that occasion.

'Same as in any other club,' he now said. 'Let's face it, London's full of clubs.'

'Is it?'

'Ever since nineteen hundred or so,' he said knowledgably. He told me that the very first nightclub had been opened in a basement behind Regent Street by a woman called Freda Strindberg and it was called The Cabaret Club. For a number of years she tried in vain to emulate night life in Vienna and had patrons like Jacob Epstein and Ernest Hemmingway but the police had closed the place down in the end.

'She went to New York,' he said, 'And did much better there.'

I was impressed that he knew so much and told him so.

Stan warmed to his theme and added that after the First World War dozens of clubs had sprung up including the Gargoyle in Meard Street which was still going strong.

'The Gargoyle had hostesses way back in the twenties,' he said. 'They used to give dancing lessons then at a guinea a time.'

'How do you know all this?'

He said he couldn't remember how.

Later I learned that almost immediately they sprang up the newfangled night clubs attracted not only the elite of English society but a fair proportion of the criminal element also. They rapidly became places where a gentleman would not take his wife.

Some of these establishments had innocuous sounding names like the Shaftesbury Social Club in Great Earl Street which was described by one vindictive ex-patron as being a haunt of thieves and vagabonds serving overpriced beverages that were more than likely doped, though he was unclear as to the general objective of the latter assertion. The Radio Club operated out of 55 Old Compton Street and did a roaring trade providing alcohol and a dance venue to hundreds of eager patrons. A few doors away a Spaniard called Canals ran the Black Cat Club with the help of his wife Grace. Throughout the twenties and early nineteen thirties similar late night drinking clubs came and went and hostesses became firmly established whether they gave dancing instruction or whether they didn't. In the end mostly they didn't.

'I'm not sure about being a hostess,' I told Stan uncertainly, 'Anyhow I can go to Brook Street Bureau and get a secretarial job.'

What dull enterprise might I be typing letters for in a week or two? Without any doubt it would not be a breathtakingly exciting commercial radio station in the North Sea. Equally unhappily this might be my last coffee date for a long time with Stan Douglas if he was now destined to take up welding, whatever that might entail.

He returned to the topic of hostesses and the Astor Club. 'Great working hours,' he said, 'You start at eleven and finish at three.'

'You do mean eleven at night?'

'Of course I mean eleven at night – it's a night club – and you collect hostess fees from the customers. Mostly all you do is dance and chat with them, eat dinner with them – that kind of thing.'

'Is that all?'

'Well if that's all you choose to do – yes.'

'Do I get to keep the fees?'

He said indeed I did.

'How much are these hostess fees?' I queried, though I had already abandoned the idea once I realized the job would involve dancing. As far as possible I had avoided any social activity that involved dancing throughout my teenage years. I was not immediately drawn to ballroom dancing because in my family women did not dance with partners – they danced alone. An odd feature of tradition that I was beginning to realize with some alarm was possibly connected to their Diddicai roots. Women danced and men sat and watched and made encouraging noises from the edges of the gatherings, only deigning the join the women once they'd 'had a skinful' as my mother would say. Even at family weddings women danced alone or, failing that, with each other. As a result my prowess as a dance partner was limited to the brief flirtation at The Embassy Club and instruction in a basic waltz by an older cousin when I was thirteen. I suspected that the Astor hostesses would be required to have a great deal more proficiency as dance partners than I was able to muster.

'You get five pounds from each customer – so if you get two customers each evening then you would earn ten pounds, tax free too.'

He added in a quieter voice, 'And never forget that if you've got your head screwed on properly you can earn more by going home with them afterwards.'

Once I realized with some shock exactly what he meant having asked him to elucidate, I again hastily banished the idea whilst still maintaining a look of sophisticated interest on my face. I did not want him to realize that I was quite so easily scandalized. If I was going to catch him perhaps between marriages then it was important that he should see me as a trendsetter, a socialite even. I allowed myself to gaze indulgently at his profile. Oh how very much more attractive in every way he was than the technical director and the resulting relationship that had ensured that I so recently became caught up in a web of deception.

'I didn't know he was embezzling,' I said again.

'Where the hell did you think the money was coming from?'

But I hadn't thought and that was the problem. Being totally unaccustomed to money in any volume more than a few pounds at any one time, usually in the form of a weekly wage, it had not occurred to me to consider the question. I had simply believed him to be rich.

'I thought he was well off.'

'Normal people don't splash out for meals at the bloody Caprice every night do they?' He looked exasperated. 'They don't stay in five star hotels at the drop of a hat – you must have realized that the money had to come from somewhere surely?'

I shook my head and tried hard not to spoil my studied sophistication by allowing myself to cry.

He then said quite kindly that perhaps it was different for me, coming from the kind of family where money was not a crucial consideration. When you grow up surrounded by material things as I had, he said, maybe you do see life a bit differently. I fervently wished I had not invented quite such an affluent family and I struggled momentarily to remember which mother I had created and where I had told him we were living. Thankfully I began to recall Debs and her various lovers, her dress design business and the neo Georgian house in Gravesend with the rather smart bathrooms. Didn't I also have a few interesting siblings too?

'I wouldn't exactly say money was no object,' I said truthfully reflecting for a brief moment upon Nellie and the terrace cottage with the outside lavatory and no way of accessing hot water unless you boiled a kettle.

'Well maybe not,' he said and ordered more coffee, which was heartening because it meant he was intending to sit with me longer. 'But you do have to admit that it won't matter for a month or two whether you get another job or not whereas I've got a family to support.'

'My mother doesn't exactly hand out spending money,' I said, relishing the fact that for once this informational titbit concerning my family was one hundred per cent true.

He said again that if I wanted to make good money with little effort then I should consider working at a nightclub. If only he was a female that's exactly what he would do, he maintained. Maximum profit out of minimum effort. It would make life a whole lot easier at times; times like now.

We sat and drank the coffee in companionable silence until he glanced at his watch and said he would have to go, back to South London; the mother-in-law was coming over to have a meal with them. My heart sank a little.

'When will I see you again?' I tried not to sound too anxious and failed. He said he would keep in touch and after he left I wondered how. I had no telephone number to give to him and he had not offered to give me his. I supposed that we might bump into each other in Denmark Street or its environs at some stage.

It was early March and a bitterly chill wind churned down Dean Street spinning with it newspapers and the smart new cardboard fish and chip cartons that had lately lain abandoned in Soho gutters.

I bought an Evening Standard from news-stand on the corner of Oxford Street where the one-legged paper seller was beginning to bellow abbreviated and incoherent headlines to the first trickle of home-going Londoners. It appeared that Pablo Picasso had married a thirty-year-old, there was another threat of a Cabinet Reshuffle and one Elsie Batton, a hitherto unknown shop assistant but wife of a well-known sculptor, had been found stabbed to death with an antique dagger in the curio shop where she worked.

I was briefly lured from the misery of being accountable for somehow master-minding the sudden demise of Britain's first commercial radio enterprise together with the ongoing unavailability of the current man of my dreams by the latter story. I was still interested weeks later when her killer, Edwin Bush, became the first British murderer to be caught by the use of the newfangled Identikit Facial Composite method of crime detection.

Lingering on the windswept corner I considered what to do next. When the wind grew even stronger, though as always still reluctant to leave the central city streets, I turned towards the tube station and boarded a Northern Line train towards Charing Cross.

It was still comparatively early for commuter home-going and the station concourse was oddly uncrowded. I even got a corner seat in the first carriage of the first fast train to Gravesend, first stop Woolwich Arsenal. It seemed extraordinary that a few short weeks ago I had been living in a smart West End apartment with Luuk the Dutch sound engineer who had turned out to be a heating engineer, making frequent trips to and from Amsterdam as his Personal Assistant, eating at The Ivy and Kettners and buying cashmere sweaters from Bond Street. Now I was on a train heading towards the much despised terrace cottage in York Road, Northfleet. Tomorrow I would buy The Standard when the first edition appeared on the streets at ten am. I would find a bed sitter and get a typing job somewhere. These thoughts were black indeed. What I wanted to do instead was sleep for five years and attempt to erase some of what had so recently happened. Whether I would have tried to rid myself of my own poor judgment was quite a different matter because the greater part of me realized with troublesome clarity that given the same circumstances again I would have cheerfully walked the same path, choosing excitement always over common sense. It was not even as if I found risks easy to take. Courage was most decidedly not a particularly prominent characteristic. Cowardly described me better but somehow or other I found myself quite unable to follow any route labeled practical or sensible. It was almost as if where level-headedness began I invariably halted. I now wondered, not for the first time, why it was I had to be so different from what my mother called 'nice, normal girls'.

'I dunno what gets into you,' she was inclined to say more and more helplessly. 'Why is it you can't just be like the other girls round here? All the girls you went to school with are married now – with babies. Lovely little families they've got. You don't see none of them gallivanting off to foreign places with married men do you now?'

And no, you didn't see them doing that, or any of the other things I had been by overwhelming desire for excitement compelled to do. As a daughter I was a disappointment, like a child who had been adopted or somehow swapped at birth. Once I had asked her, 'Am I adopted?' and she had looked at me incredulously.

'Adopted?'
'Yes, adopted!'
'Why would I adopt a kiddy? You only adopt if you can't have your own now don't you?'

Then she said as an afterthought, 'Or you take on your sister's baby or your cousin's for instance. I could have taken on Little Doris or even Little Violet with no trouble if I'd wanted to.'

With motherless cousins proliferating in the family around the time I was born I knew this was true and so I lapsed into silence and so did she except to add that The Authorities would never have let her adopt a child properly in any case. We both knew that this was a reference to the general 'unsuitability' of our large and shiftless family and their ongoing failure to find acceptability in any aspect of life.

We rarely discussed these things. There were no heart-to-hearts or mother and daughter chats such as those I, largely unsuccessfully, tried to initiate with my own daughter years later. From time to time Nellie made a covert reference to a matter close to her heart and generally I ignored her or treated what she had said with undisguised contempt. Consequently she had a habit of backtracking hastily and later, if necessary, claiming that she had never meant what I thought she had meant.

When I was a small child she had talked to me at length on matters that pre-occupied her, disregarding the fact that I was far too young to understand much of what she said. The monologues might even have come about simply because I was at three and four years of age, a perfectly safe audience, credulous and uncritical. She harboured a deep distrust of others, including her own family, yet she was eternally stuck to them.

Stuck like glue, as she would undoubtedly have said herself, in awe of the ever-dominating Old Nan, her mother, disliking most of her many sisters, disapproving of their numerous offspring, yet attached to them all in an inexplicable intimacy.

Commitment to family had completely subjugated her desire as a newly-wed to rid herself of them by moving from the environs of Crayford where they all now lived somewhat uneasily in post-World War One Council houses. On she went eight or nine miles deeper into industrial Kent, to Northfleet, a suburb of Gravesend on the banks of the Thames. Perhaps the distance between them was not great enough because after a while they simply accommodated it by visiting with less frequency whilst striving to have her allocated a house nearby and listing her with various arms of the Crayford council. According to several slightly differing departments she and her new family were living, in overcrowded and insanitary conditions with her mother and most of her sisters at one and the same time in various locations. And had there been any semblance of truth in these latter claims they would each have cheerfully accepted the status quo as they had accepted house living in the first place. Although they were quite content to spend the harsh North Kent winters living as others did inside their council accommodation, they might quite uncomplainingly move with tarpaulins and odd bits of fence post to a hurriedly erected shanty town on the fringe of field or and meadow as soon as the pea-picking season began in late May each year. And there, if necessary, they might even remain until it was time to get ready for the hop picking season three months later.

In general it was not their habit to engage in any paid work that did not involve as many of them as possible, including the family's youngest members and my mother, who had grown up knowing that all children are expected to contribute and earn their keep within the group, now desired for some inexplicable reason to discard the idea of unpaid child labour where her own offspring were concerned. In the same swing from tradition she would not allow my brother and I to go barefoot – ' D'you want people to think you're a gypo?'

She greatly desired that we should attend school regularly so we would learn to read and write – 'You'll be called a Pikey if you can't read.' School attendance had not been high on her own parents' list of priorities and in fact Old Nan herself was totally and increasingly aggressively, illiterate.

'I loved reading – me – when I was a kid,' Nellie said occasionally, 'And I loved it if me Mum let me go to school on a Friday because then we had silent reading. We had poetry too on Fridays – I loved poetry, me.'

Despite these disclosures her own literary horizons were less than wide, her reading matter as an adult being mostly confined to women's magazines and Mills & Boon romances with an occasional history book thrown inexplicably into the mix.

As a closet poetry fan myself, once I asked her what her favourite poems had been, quite convinced that she would be hard pressed to elaborate. To my surprise she said, 'Funnily enough I loved that one about Old Meg the Gypsy who lived upon the moors. And that one starting with Oh to be in England Now that April's there – that was a real favourite of mine. And that Lady of Shallot too. Sad that one was. Then there was the one about the poor chap who married a mermaid and was forsaken'

'Did Old Nan mind you liking those poems?' I queried cautiously, much astonished.

'Well I can't say as I ever told her about it because me Mum was dead set against education. Always was and always will be. But in the winter months she'd let me and Maggie and sometimes Maud and Martha too, go up to the school.'

After the initial trauma of the First Day Infants Class where we newcomers seem to have been abandoned with no explanation from our various mothers as was the custom at the time, I developed a cautious liking for school myself. Once I mastered the complicated process of learning to read, I became intoxicated by the only partially restricted access to books, row after row of them, lining the walls of the Big Children's classroom. By the time I was eight years old my dream was to become a Book Monitor like Shirley O'Keefe who was nine. Her dream, she told me, was to become a librarian and she told me that she had eleven books of her own at home, including a Children's Dictionary.

'We've got three books,' I told her honestly.

'*Peoples of the World in Pictures*', '*Home Doctor*' and '*The Wonders of Europe*' were the extent of our home library for a number of years.

My many cousins were each greatly surprised to learn that once I reached my seventh birthday I had been enrolled in the local library by my father and was soon in the habit of reading several books each week. Reading as a leisure activity did not appeal to any of them and this lack of interest even extended to the Enid Blyton books I, along with most of my classmates, enjoyed so much once we reached an appropriate age to appreciate them.

When I tried to explain to my cousin Patsy how exciting the Famous Five books were she looked at me with utter contempt. 'You'll go blind if you do much more of that reading.'

As for Old Nan, she found any pre-occupation with education quite unnatural and had for some years now considered me to be a lost cause as far as fitting in with family ideals and ethics was concerned. My adventures in Holland and what she called 'them foreign shenanigans' had shocked her deeply, primarily because within families like ours, married people did not openly stray from the sanctity of their partnerships as Luuk had done. Young women were supposed to remain chaste at least until they found the man who was to be their husband. Once that had been established then certain forms of intimacy could be allowed, although sexual intercourse itself was frowned upon until after the wedding ceremony.

Although by nineteen sixty with the advent of television in every home, and articles on contraception within the pages of every monthly magazine, the general acceptance of these restrictions was beginning to break down, the march of progress was slow to reach families like ours, situated as we were just below the bottom of the social strata. The conventions and practices that had held us together for decades were infinitely tougher than promises of a magic pill that ensured babies were only ever conceived at times most convenient to their parents. Even thoroughly modern girls of marriageable age like those of my cousins who had not yet become married women would not have considered abandoning the excitement of a wedding for a fling in a foreign capital.

We were programmed to be fixated on the state of matrimony. From a very early age the most popular girls' game had been 'Weddings' and from then on until the happy day itself, conversations between us revolved around what kind of dress might be worn and how many bridesmaids would be involved. You could say that we were one dimensional and although I had fought against these norms for as long as I could remember, there were times when I was drawn to the idea myself. Usually, however, I was able to shake off the momentary lapse by visualizing something more attractive like a weekend trip to Paris in the company of someone like Stan Douglas.

Sadly, the closest I had come to a trip anywhere with Stan, had been by placing myself as near to him as possible and entering into a relationship with the bogus sound engineer. This had merely resulted in him being toppled from his lofty perch as a disc jockey and hurtled towards the nether regions of welding. I still had not worked out what a welder actually did, and where and how he did it.

My mother was watching a quiz programme when I let myself into the house as quietly as possible and tried to escape to the floor above without her noticing which was of course impossible given the dimensions of the place.

She called after me with offers of cold corned beef and salad and because I had given her a heavily censored version of the demise of the radio station, asked how I was faring with the finding of another job.

I told her that one of the DJs was being taken on by another station and wanted to take me with him as his personal secretary and that the job would start in a week or two. She seemed satisfied to some degree and so I told her that I would also be moving out in a day or two because I had found a flat near Marble Arch. She had, at least, heard of Marble Arch.

I ate some of the corned beef and thought absently upon what her reaction would be if I told her about the job that Doug was urging me to consider, as a hostess at the Astor Night Club. Never having crossed the threshold of such a place in her life her first impression might have been one of complete amazement that such glamorous occupations existed at all.

'I might even take an interim job for a few weeks in a club,' I said.

She wanted to know what kind of club and I said it was a night club a bit like The Embassy Club.

'You mean you'll be on the telly?' she asked doubtfully.

Though my information on nightclubs was minimal I was reasonably sure that they didn't feature regularly in television programmes so I said no, a different kind of club where they had dance hostesses.

She lowered her voice. 'Not one of them London strip clubs?'

That had not occurred to me but I doubted that The Astor was a strip club and said so. I was surprised that she knew anything about such places and could only imagine her information was gleaned from The News of the World.

'They say them girls dance naked in the strip clubs,' she said confidently, 'But of course that's completely wrong. Nobody in their right mind dances naked – no, they just look as if they're naked – they wear flesh coloured costumes.'

'Really? I didn't ask how she had manufactured this snippet of information. I most certainly would not be going anywhere near The Astor if it turned out to be a strip club. Even the idea of a flesh coloured costume would not induce me to do so.

Chasing the Sound Engineer

It had been my last night living at home. The very next day I left 28 York Road for ever, feeling less than hopeful and with four pounds to my name. I was only to return on odd occasions over the next few years on brief visits. Eventually the area became destined for re-development necessitating the whole row of houses on our side of the street to be completely demolished before the end of the decade. Although the other side remains to this day, after some years it was as if our row had never existed at all, lingering only as patchy memories in old black and white photographs. But long before that took place a lot happened, including my venture into the shadowy world of nightclubs.

The first job I took during that cold and windy March, however, was as a temporary shorthand typist in an engineering company called Mitchells in Bloomsbury where I was sent by Brook Street Bureau within the next day or two. I had already organized to share a double bedsitting room in Onslow Gardens, South Kensington with a girl called Jennifer Swann whom I met via the accommodation columns in The Evening Standard. Jennifer was eighteen and had recently arrived from Canada to spend a few months recuperating from the traumatic birth of a baby daughter and her parents' insistence on the child's immediate adoption. She had an older sister who lived in Knightsbridge with a racing car driver and knew people like Donald Campbell and Sterling Moss. I did not know much about racing cars or their drivers but I was impressed all the same because I had actually heard of some of them. Almost immediately Jennifer took me to parties at her sister's flat where I was introduced to arrogant young men with names like Bradley and Scott who were involved in stocks and shares and drove fast cars. Although they had some of the attributes I had in the past ascribed to imaginary boyfriends in that they at times wore sheepskin jackets and drank at The Punch Tavern, none of them impressed me sufficiently to make any attempt to pursue even the briefest of relationships. However, I was at least able to study their upper class accents at close range and make a better job of copying the vowel sounds.

The work at Mitchells was mind-numbingly dull and within a few weeks so, I decided, was Jennifer Swann. The only oasis of excitement was when Sterling Moss turned up occasionally to drink instant coffee with us and try to persuade Jennifer to allow him to take her out. She was now so terrified of men, however, that she always declined and although I stood by hopefully he never actually asked me to go anywhere with him.

Generally speaking life in South Kensington was turning out to be rather less exciting than I had anticipated and Jennifer Swann a far from stimulating companion. She still mourned the loss of her infant daughter whom she had named Penny. She told me she would be a tiny bit happier if she could have news of her from time to time, but her mother had insisted that was impossible. It would not be good for Penny at all and Penny's welfare had to come first.

'What happened to the baby's father?' I asked.

She hesitated and gave several sighs before saying, 'You know in Canada it's not like here – you don't just have BBC radio, you have local radio. We had local radio in our town and Penny's father was one of the DJs – I met him first of all on a school trip to learn how radio worked.'

I told her about Stan Douglas because I thought he had briefly worked at a Canadian radio station. I fervently hoped it wasn't the same one but Jennifer said her DJ was called Sal short for Salvador and when he found out she was pregnant he had disappeared to Montreal. She hadn't heard from him since. I felt sorry for her but that did not help to make her less boring.

I made friends with Shelagh and Maggie from the floor below, who immediately promised to be more interesting as both had worked in Paris as au pairs and been taken on holidays with their employers to places like Cannes and Nice. Maggie had a boyfriend who took up most of her attention but at weekends Shelagh and I took to hitchhiking out of London and visiting those towns where our lifts finally deposited us; Cardiff, Leeds, Shrewsbury, Ross-on-Wye and Hastings. One Bank Holiday weekend found us as far away as Glasgow. Gradually Shelagh and I began to grow closer and confided in each other completely. She told me that her greatest desire was to get pregnant and hopefully have a daughter. So far, despite trying hard, she had not been successful and was beginning to think that she might be barren. I told her about my recent love affair with the sound engineer and my desire to become at least as well acquainted with his disc jockey colleague now turned welder. I also told her about the damage to and ultimate ruin of Radio Veronica and the fact that everyone involved seemed to be blaming me for something I had no knowledge of. She listened sympathetically and said that one day the truth would undoubtedly come out. I would be able to clear my name eventually she thought. I was grateful for her support and said that unquestionably one day she would get pregnant.

Before very long life became humdrum once more and I began to wonder if Luuk the sound engineer had actually been sent to prison for his crimes and what kind of sentence he might have been given. I decided to apply for a job as a shorthand typist with a company situated in Voorburg, in The Hague where I knew he had lived with his wife. This was of course a remarkably mindless decision.

The seed was sown one evening after a working day at Mitchells. I made a detour to the tube station via nearby Denmark Street, something I did frequently, always hoping to stumble across the would be pop stars and musicians I half knew in order to greet them effusively, one and all in the hope that I might be invited for a cup of tea in Julie's Café or better still, a vodka and lemonade in The Dog & Duck on the Bateman Street, Frith Street corner. On one momentous occasion Johnny Kidd, whom I barely knew at all, fresh from a meeting where he heard that 'Shaking All Over' was doing brilliantly in the charts, escorted me into the Snug at the rear of the pub where we downed a great deal of alcohol. Denmark Street was deserted on this evening, however, and I was just turning the corner into Charing Cross Road when I almost walked into Stan Douglas.

I was thrilled and tried to sound casual, almost indifferent as I said, 'Oh hi – fancy meeting you.'

He stopped and we had a few minutes of desultory conversation before I asked, 'Have you got time for a drink?'

He looked at his watch and then nodded letting me lead the way along Bateman Street. I was pleased to find the Snug completely empty.

He drank a pint of something dark brown and masculine and I drank vodka. I asked him what, if anything, he had heard about the fate of Luuk Nijhof.

'Well as a matter of fact I was told a few days ago that he only got six months,' he said. 'His wife paid back a lot of the money he owed so he was lucky really – luck seems to follow him around – no wonder he's known as Lucky Luuk! He should be out any time now.'

And so the germ of the unwise idea of was sown and in the days that followed began to niggle away at me.

'How have things been for you? How's the welding?' He said he was still working some night shifts but he had a number of projects in the pipeline. In fact he was hopeful of work with Radio Luxemburg. I gazed at him lost in admiration and because I knew that Jennifer was spending the night with her sister, invited him back to Onslow Gardens. He hesitated, glanced at his watch again and then said he would have to go and make a telephone call.

When he returned he said, 'OK – but first let's go and get something to eat – definitely *not* The Caprice. How about a burger?'

I said I would love a burger. I didn't mind what I ate just as long as I could have him with me for the evening and, fingers crossed, perhaps through the night. We ate burgers and chips in South Kensington and once back at Onslow Gardens I made instant coffee, changed into my dressing gown and imagined that I looked very sexy. By the time he left to return to his long-suffering wife early the following morning my devotion to him had increased greatly.

I felt no guilt about attempting to pursue the relationship with him and I was able to put his family out of my mind most of the time. Neither did it occur to me to put myself in his wife's position and consider how I would feel if I was her. It was as if neither she nor their children existed as real people at all.

He began to call on me from time to time, at times meeting Jennifer when they talked about Canada and local radio stations. One weekend he dropped by with one of his children, a little boy of about four whom he was supposedly taking to the museum for the afternoon. I made copious cups of coffee and we sat talking while the child played co-operatively with an uninteresting collection of china animals belonging to Jennifer. From time to time he looked up and asked his father if this place was the museum.

It was close to museum closing time when they finally left and headed towards Cromwell Road. These odd visits went on over weeks with the result that I grew ever more attracted to the idea of a relationship with him. Nevertheless the niggling desire to find out what happened to Luuk did not go away and I still went for the job interview in The Hague on a night flight paid for by Ndola, the company that manufactured hair dyes. No matter how attractive I found Stan, I was also unable to resist the lure of excitement, the opportunity to do something different. It transpired that what Ndola wanted was someone who was able to write advertising material for products sold in English speaking parts of the world and of course I could do that.

Ever since my first trip to Holland in the latter part of the previous year, when I had quite suddenly been introduced to the idea of foreign travel by Luuk, I had grown increasing drawn to visit the air terminal in South Kensington late at night to pretend I was a bona fide traveler. Sometimes I even took the transfer bus to the airport and I can only imagine now that passenger checks must have been lax in those days because I don't remember being asked for travel documents at any stage and I certainly never paid a fare. This time, however, I was a proper traveler even though my flight was an unpopular one, leaving as I recall at about three in the morning, arriving in Amsterdam just an hour later.

It was extraordinarily exciting to be back in the city. I now no longer remember how I found my way from the airport to the central station or how difficult it was to discover which train to take to The Hague but I must have done so without incident and I imagine that at The Hague I would have been met by one of the Ndola staff. The office was situated quite close to where I had already discovered Luuk had lived with his wife and I assumed, rightly as it turned out, that she still lived there.

What I remember clearly is being given a typing and a spelling and grammar test by an elderly Dutchman whose English was better than my own, then being offered the job, and taken out for dinner to an Indonesian restaurant in the Hague before being deposited at the station once more to wait for the train back to Amsterdam. Before I could turn around, or so it seemed, I was on my way back to London having promised to start work with them in ten days' time.

When I next saw Stan I was able to bring him up to date. He looked disbelieving and told me that he thought I had made a very poor choice and it wasn't ever going to be a good thing to be working so close to where Luuk and his wife lived.

I said that the affair was over and as I would not know Luuk's wife if I tripped over her in the street I couldn't see what the problem was. He said well as long as I kept out of her way he supposed it might be all right. However, I had already half made the decision not to keep out of her way because I had become more and more curious about her and why she went on supporting a man who had let her down so badly. But first of all I would settle into the job, write English advertising copy and enjoy the experience of working quite legitimately in a foreign country. It was with some regret that I put my not quite possible relationship with Stan on the back burner for a while.

'I might be with Luxemburg by the time you return,' he said hopefully. As I walked away I half considered changing my mind about the job but of course I did not do so.

Mr Josef Singer, my boss, told me that I would be able to work for a few months before I would need to apply for a work permit and that the process would be organized for me so I did not need to worry about it. As it had never crossed my mind to concern myself with the business of work permits, I had not given the matter a moment's thought.

I found the work very easy but learning to speak Dutch was not. As most of my colleagues, and in fact most people in the country under the age of forty, all spoke English to some degree, some of them very well, most were anxious to practice on me. I was invited to lunches, dinners and parties, and it became very difficult to persuade anyone that I really did need to learn the language. A bed sitting room had been found for me with a young couple who lived nearby. Both of them spoke good English, were pleasant to be with but it soon became apparent one weekend when the wife went to visit her mother that her husband was keen to extend his relationship with me in areas where I did not really want to go. I moved in with Elisabeth who typed in the same office. She had just bought her own apartment in a block not far away and had a three-year-old son who was placed in what she called 'a children's home' from Monday to Friday with other children of unmarried working mothers. She collected him on Friday evenings and took him back there on Sundays. I believe now that it was his room I occupied while I lived with her. His name was Martin and very quickly he learned to converse with me in English, calling me his 'English Aunt'.

Sometimes at weekends I went to Amsterdam to visit The Five Flies Restaurant where Luuk and I had frequently had meals. We had got to know Wim the bartender extremely well during our time in the city and he had quickly become aware of Luuk's cavalier attitude and misuse of other people's money and the consequences involved.

'A real conman that Luuk,' he said, polishing glasses and gazing at them approvingly as he did so, 'But a lucky fella you know – he could have gone in prison for a whole lot longer.'

I nodded and sipped my free gin that tasted like jet fuel. I was keeping an eye on the other people in the bar because I soon learned that a smile in the direction of a lone male customer could often result in an invitation to have dinner with him. Eating at The Five Flies was something I was very keen to do, even if at the end of the evening I invariably had to fight off the advances of my host who had misinterpreted my willingness to join him.

'Well it's not much fun to go to prison at all,' I said truthfully. Although I had been astounded and unbelieving when first told of Luuk's major transgressions by the Amsterdam Police, there was a part of me that was still fond of him, and a smaller part that felt there might after all be a perfectly logical explanation for his behaviour. Perhaps, in spite of everything, he would be able to explain what happened. Maybe he was not the criminal I had recently been led to believe he was. It could have been just a giant misunderstanding.

I ventured to share one or two of these thoughts with Wim, who looked at me in disbelief and said very firmly, 'Oh no indeed young lady – I think you will find that is not so. Anyhow apparently he's coming out next month so you'll be able to ask him yourself!'

And that is how I learned that Luuk, having served part of his sentence, and being a model prisoner, was being released early and even the date of his release.

I then made the most imprudent decision to cultivate the acquaintance of his wife, Lotte by pretending simply to have rung the wrong doorbell in the wrong street . My name, I said was Susan Wiltshire and I was looking for a girl I had met whilst hitchhiking in England a few months previously. I have since forgotten the mythical girl's name and why she was staying in Voorburg but what I do recall is that she had invited me to come and visit if I was ever in the area – and now I was! What could be more simple and believable?

She was a good looking woman, tall and heavy boned with clear grey eyes and hair tidily piled on top of her head. The apartment was minimalist and strikingly clean and tidy like all Dutch homes. There were a few photographs on a side table. One was of her as a child with a pony. Another was of Luuk looking younger than I remembered him. I asked if it was her son and she paused and looked at me hard before saying no, it was her husband who was away on business. Perhaps it was at that moment that she had the first doubt about me. She began to ask me a lot of questions about myself and my family. I talked happily about Debs my make believe mother and her dress design business. I had not replaced Debs with someone more suitable in more than a year, and because of the excitement of recent months but I was beginning to tire of her a bit. If she was going to stay in my life then she definitely needed to move house or go into a new business venture.

Lotte made coffee and put a pretty little plate of biscuits on the table between us. She even offered me a bed for the night but I said it wasn't necessary because I had another friend in the area who was expecting me. That was true at least because Elisabeth was expecting me back for dinner. We said our goodbyes and before I left she gave me her telephone number and invited me to call on her again before I went back to England which I had told her might be within the next day or two.

Ten days later I stood watch over the apartment block on Luuk's release date. Fortuitously it was a Saturday and I was able to monitor the place from the cafe opposite. I was there when it opened at seven thirty in the morning, sitting among the early morning coffee drinkers and cigar smokers, all of them elderly men and all glancing at me curiously from time to time. I saw Lotte leave and get into her little Citroen car at about nine but it was almost midday before she returned, parking carefully outside once more. He emerged from the car first, still wearing the long Burberry raincoat he bought with my help and advice in The Haymarket months previously. He was carrying an untidy parcel under his arm and a small case in the other hand. She retrieved a hessian shopping bag from inside the car and followed him towards the apartment building. Then they disappeared inside together and I was left, among the cigar smokers, trying to control my fast beating heart. It was several days before I could bring myself to dial the telephone number she had given me in the hope that it would be Luuk who answered but although I tried on a number of occasions he never did and I always hurriedly replaced the receiver when I heard her voice.

Despite my foolhardy behaviour it came as a surprise when some weeks later I was told by Mr. Singer than my application for a work permit had been declined. When I asked why he shifted from one foot to the other and looked very uncomfortable.

'Some time ago it seems you were found in a hotel in Amsterdam with a married man,' he said, 'And that man was sent to prison for fraud...'

'But it was him committing the fraud – not me,' I argued, feeling I had Right on my side.

He nodded, 'Yes, it was him – and I certainly understand that it was a love affair but nevertheless it seems you have recently tried to renew your acquaintance with the man – and he is still married.'

For some reason it now seemed imperative that I should be allowed to stay in Holland and somehow speak with Luuk. However it became ever clearer that with the firm support of Lotte, he was not going to make that objective easy to achieve. In the end there was little I could do except remain outraged and accept the inevitable. I was to return to London without too much delay. Before I did so I spent more time in front of his apartment and once I thought I saw him staring down at me from behind a twitching curtain. When I waved, the curtain stopped twitching. I was never to see him again.

A Showgirl at Last

It was disheartening to have to return to London when I was not quite ready to do so. In my absence Maggie and Shelagh had moved from South Kensington to a large house in Leinster Square, Bayswater where Maggie's older sister Ellen was housekeeper and where as a result they had first choice of the best rooms when they became available. They rapidly organized a room for me on the second floor, room twenty two.

'Cheer up,' Shelagh advised when I related the long and obviously rather tedious story of the work permit that had not been granted, 'Now you're back we'll have all kinds of capers and larks.'

We had developed a speech idiom that incorporated a great many outmoded words and phrases and this greatly amused us so I dutifully added that there might even be merry japes though I felt far from optimistic.

Maggie's sister lived uneasily in the basement with Warren her Australian husband and Carol her infant daughter. Most of the rooms at number thirty two and the houses on either side, which Ellen also managed, were let to Australians and as a last resort, to New Zealanders probably as a result of Warren's frequently discussed home sickness for the antipodes. They were very noisy, drank heavily and partied late into the night at weekends. Most were men with names like Bryce and Garth. The three or four women were all called Jan. Maggie, clearly much under her sister's influence, was very accepting of them as a group but Shelagh and I kept as much distance between them and us as was possible. It wasn't always possible because they were an affable and gregarious group and more than keen to include us in all their social activities.

In those first few weeks I was able to see Stan only intermittently and it became more and more difficult for him to spend long periods of time away from his family. Clearly he and his wife were going through one of their many crises or alternatively while I had been away he had found someone more desirable than me to have an occasional fling with. Shelagh said I should leave him well alone as she thought it most unlikely that his wife would ever totally relinquish him and in case they had two little boys who needed their father. Her conscience in such matters was infinitely more developed than my own and I continued not to pay too much heed to the consequences of the children finding themselves apart from their father. In truth I had scarcely given the matter much thought at all and at first found her considerations quite surprising.

'They're not at all happy together,' I said.

'But she's still his wife and you're not,' she snapped, 'Maybe they're trying to make it work – if that's the case he won't want to be wasting time on you will he?'

I didn't really see why not but decided not to pursue the topic.

London itself seemed to have changed in the few months I had been away decidedly odd though that was. There was a new vitality in the city as though it had suddenly become a happier place and that the great metropolis itself was aware that the Sixties, decade of ultimate decadence, was about to begin. Although people like me, completely absorbed in their own small worlds, were largely unaware of it, Britain was well into what was later described as a 'period of post war boom'. Towns outside the capital were in the throes of an enormous period of industry with factories on their outskirts busily turning out all manner of British-made goods. Newly-weds found they had more disposable income than their predecessors and could out of the blue afford to buy all manner of extravagant household items such as refrigerators and vacuum cleaners, even washing machines that had until then been seen as luxury items. The subsequent cultural changes were now beginning to be noticeable. The older generation was still pre-occupied with ridding itself of the effects of war and deprivation but the young were more and more disinclined to pay heed to the warnings regarding frugality given by their parents and threw themselves headlong into a frenzy of spending. Until the start of the sixties youngsters from working class suburban backgrounds had two categories of clothing – that for every-day and for working, and that for 'best'. With the advent of cheap, colourful chain store clothing lines, the categories became blurred. Young women no longer owned best dresses and shoes, kept at the back of the wardrobe for outings with boyfriends or going to parties, because fashions were changing fast and best of all, prices were dropping with equal rapidity. Visits to the hairdresser were becoming common as were purchases such as hand cream and perfume.

During my absence The Twist had arrived and even ten-year-olds in playgrounds were spending their playtimes in furious practice. I noted this with a mixture of horror and delight; it was at last possible that the dreaded quickstep was on the way out. Shelagh and I practiced twisting at weekends from within the safety of her basement room.

Until the nineteen sixties even central suburbs such as Kensington and Bayswater were relatively traffic free and children played on the streets without undue incident. This was to briskly change as more and more young people on their way up abandoned buses and mopeds and opted for Hillmans and Minis. Traffic congestion quickly spread into side streets and exhaust fumes began to pollute the previously reasonably fresh air in parks and squares. The children of the early sixties were soon to be banished into playgrounds to occupy themselves safely. Local community groups began to set up the first adventure playgrounds in an attempt to entice them from the remaining bomb sites, now designated as potentially dangerous.

Television was beginning to overtake radio as the most popular form of home entertainment and even young women like us soon became familiar with the subsequent eruption of advertising from our brief glimpses of Ellen's twelve inch black and white set in the basement of number thirty two. *A Double Diamond works wonders....All because the lady loves Milk Tray.....Esso Blue Paraffin* - the jingles memorable half a century later.

As times changed even Soho, one of my most beloved areas of the city, had without warning been propelled past its golden age. The Colony Room in Dean Street had been distinctly a part of the fifties and although the décor and atmosphere had not altered much by the beginning of the next decade, the drunks who regularly propped up the bar such as Daniel Farson and Francis Bacon had aged significantly enough to be less amusing. In previous years the well-known faces of the area still started their day with coffee at Torino's on the corner of Dean and Old Compton Streets and I had been assured at the time that the café was a favourite haunt of all manner of artists and writers. Torino's had now disappeared and its patrons hurriedly turned their attention to Bar Italia just around the corner. It had first opened for business in Frith Street in the late nineteen forties and had been run by the same Italian family ever since.

So many changes took place in less than a decade that in an area less resilient than Soho the ambiance might have collapsed. Even minor commercial developments carried a certain transformation into the streets. The advent of large and affordable freezers meant that the huge blocks of ice hitherto mysteriously delivered in the depths of the night to cafes and restaurants, suddenly vanished overnight. And so went the early morning aroma of slowly melting ice forming little rivers into the gutters to meet discarded apple cores and ice cream wrappers, then to be churned up by the first of the street sweepers on their daily rounds.

The fifties and the world where Dylan Thomas still drank daily at The French House on Dean Street seem a long way away. Never daring to enter that hallowed place alone I had to wait to be taken, on a couple of occasions inexplicably by a husband of one of my cousins, described as 'flash' and somehow or other making a lot of money by dubious means that were never quite explained. He seemed to know Gaston, the legendary landlord extremely well and so, at the age of sixteen or seventeen I was impressed to be told that the pub had been the meeting place of the French Resistance during the war. Gaston claimed to have been born in a room at the top of the building at the outbreak of World War One which may or may not have been true. What was evident was his limited patience when it came to dealing with drunks. It seemed that Bacon, Farson and Thomas had all been ejected from the premises on a number of occasions and Farson even banned for extended periods. Gaston was fond of telling the tale of how Dylan Thomas managed to leave his sole manuscript of 'Under Milk Wood' under his bar stool following a night of extreme drunkenness, appearing several days later to gratefully retrieve it.

The well-known Soho eateries were all still thankfully present and intact with the advent of the sixties but although I had made it my business to patronize most of them during the frenetic spending spree with Luuk Nijhof, they were beyond my limited means when I returned to London after the Dutch work experience.

Shelagh and I on one occasion tried to persuade an elderly accountant who had given us a lift back into London on one of our hitchhiking adventures to take us to Quo Vadis on Dean Street. We even managed to get him to linger outside for a few minutes to observe that plenty of tables appeared to be available inside. I tried to generate some interest by telling him that on the second floor of the building Karl Marx had written 'Das Kapital' but he was unmoved and we progressed to The Corner House in Coventry Street.

We had better luck a week or two later with two burly Americans who wanted to be shown Soho after driving us from the Salisbury Plain into central London. Having read somewhere that The Gay Hussar in Greek Street was the possible haunt of spies, emissaries and undercover agents, they were determined to go there and we were very happy to accompany them. I had been there only once and loved the romantic European atmosphere and the menu which seemed to solely consist of Goulash and red cabbage variations.

This was the London that now hovered on the threshold of the new and significant decade, and although we did not know it the birth of what was later known as The Swinging Sixties had already taken place. The popular music scene was developing at a startling rate. In Wardour Street the Marquee Club, featuring jazz, skiffle and blues, had been open since nineteen fifty eight though Rolling Stones had yet to feature in their first gig there. Further down the street La Discotheque was about to be born, London's original disco and destined to become immensely popular. Nearby El Condor, owned by Peter Rachman was already being managed efficiently by Raymond Nash of the infamous criminal Nash Brothers and The Bag O Nails in Kingly Street had been doing a roaring trade for several years.

A vast array of unregistered drinking clubs had sprung up, very possibly as a result of the nineteen fifty nine Street Offences Act that had speedily and efficiently cleared the streets of prostitutes. They had now either morphed into club hostesses or were giving French lessons on the upper floors of the old buildings. The area continued to harbour all the necessary ingredients for the various elements of vice and was synonymous with sex and general depravity.

One of its most renowned night spots at the time was Murrays Cabaret Club situated in a Beak Street basement and operated by Percival Murray since the early nineteen thirties. Percy Murray, who liked his staff to call him Pops, was a strange man who never failed to remind me of a department store Santa Claus. The club was famous for its lavish floor shows where dozens of showgirls paraded the small stage in costumes that were both glamorous and exotic. On my frequent ramblings of the area I always stopped to examine the posters and photographs outside, safely in daylight hours allowing myself to be envious of the girls who worked there.

One day I noticed a small handwritten sign. 'Showgirls Wanted – No Experience Needed.'

Surely that couldn't be correct. A showgirl unquestionably had to know what she was doing. She would have to know how to dance for one thing. The hated Quickstep flashed in front of me. I shuddered. But then it did say in the most unambiguous terms that no experience was necessary. I walked firmly on towards Piccadilly Circus because I was a shorthand typist and not a showgirl. My pace was brisk and I stopped only to buy a cup of coffee at the Coventry Street Corner House, and then I walked back to Beak Street to re- examine the sign.

Showgirls Wanted. No Experience Needed. No room for argument within those few words. I tentatively tried the doors which were firmly closed before turning back towards the tube station.

When I later discussed the idea with Shelagh she suggested that I should go back at a later time of day, perhaps at about six o'clock when she thought night clubs might begin to come to life. She thought I might have to pass a job interview of some kind. We both wondered what form it might take and she thought I would have to demonstrate, possibly in my underwear, that I was capable of a Showgirl-like dance routine, maybe even the Twist. She advised investing in a matching black or red frilly underwear set and more attention to Twisting. We practiced more diligently that evening and the next afternoon I bought a very expensive low cut bra and matching satin briefs from the lingerie department at Whiteleys. At five thirty I set off for the West End wearing the satin underclothes and a great deal of make-up.

'Mr Murray is auditioning this Friday,' a short sighted woman at the reception desk said, looking at me with complete uninterest. 'Come back then – three pm.'

Home again with the new underwear removed and folded, I discoursed on the possibilities endlessly with Shelagh. I said more than once that if it didn't work out I could always go back to typing and she more than once agreed and tried not to sound too bored. I had already suggested that she too have a go at becoming a Showgirl Without Experience but she had viewed the idea with genuine horror.

On Friday just before three I joined half a dozen other hopefuls in the lobby of the club and we were directed one by one into Mr. Murray's office where he sat behind his vast desk looking more than ever like an affable Father Christmas. He leaned towards me and was able to awkwardly shake my hand as he asked me my name which I changed on the spot to Jane.

'Well nice to meet you, Jane. Ever done any work like this before dear?'

'No – not at all,' I told him brightly and as confidently as possible, as an afterthought adding a dazzling smile.

He first of all wanted to ascertain how I could 'move to music' telling me that there was nothing to dancing, it was all a question of whether you had a feel for rhythm or not. I swayed about the room to a tune I no longer remember and then he asked me to remove my sweater and skirt so he could have a look at my body. Holding my stomach in as resolutely as was possible, I did so and he said more to himself than to me, ' Very good legs....very good legs'.

And a couple of minutes later I was hired.

'You get nine pounds a week dear,' he said as he made notes on a piece of paper in front of him.

One of the head showgirls whose name is now forgotten was detailed to show me and the two other girls who had been hired that afternoons, the ropes.

We had to turn up to rehearsals, we had to keep the costumes we were allocated in good repair and we were not allowed to fraternize too closely with the clientele.

'What do you actually mean?' asked a girl called Marie.

'No case jobs,' the head showgirl said.

Marie nodded and I soon found the term meant we were not allowed to sleep with clients for money. I was extremely relieved because I had no intention of doing so and in fact the thought had never crossed my mind. I was there to be a glamorous showgirl, not a prostitute of any kind. Once I had the various dance routines under my belt I firmly intended to move away from Murrays and on to traditional theatre and variety via dance troupes such as The Bluebells or The Tillers. I pictured a very direct route to the top with very possibly my name in lights outside at least one West End theatre before too long.

I had absolutely no problem with turning up for rehearsals because becoming someone who trod the streets of Soho, vanity case in hand, heading for a genuine rehearsal was something I had yearned to do since the age of sixteen. Emerging from the tube station and catching glimpses of myself in Regent Street windows I was reassured that at last I looked the part. Although the other girls grumbled when rehearsals went over time, I was simply delighted to be part of the production and happy to stay hour after hour executing dance steps.

Fortunately for me the form of dancing required by a showgirl came almost naturally and I learned all that was required more than easily. Two weeks from the first rehearsal I was thrust with little ceremony into the middle of the back row of dancers at the Cabaret Club floor show. A week later I was appointed understudy/standby dancer to Geraldine, a front row girl with a much more prominent position. I was almost delirious with delight and rapidly all thoughts of shorthand and typing evaporated.

There were two cabarets each evening and between shows we were expected to sit out with the customers and could earn five pound hostess fees each time. The girls who were married or engaged could opt out of the hostess obligations but Pops tried not to employ too many who fell into that category. I quickly found that he had a habit of developing short-lived crushes on some of his employees and I tried hard not to do anything that caused him to notice me too much. This proved more and more difficult as the weeks passed because Pops was most decidedly a 'legs man'.

The clientele all appeared to me to be completely ancient with the exception of groups of wealthy young Arabs who were supposed to be studying at the London School of Economics. Our hostess duties gave us the choice of ordering Fruit Cups at eighteen shillings each or champagne at seven pounds a bottle. I learned that the

Fruit Cups were the best bet if I was to perform the second floor show with any degree of precision.

The club customers were by no means all male although that was generally the case from Monday to Thursday. Fridays and Saturdays were called 'Family Nights' by Pops who staunchly claimed that he ran a family oriented business despite our near nakedness. The Monday to Thursday regulars rarely brought in their wives and mothers but that was most definitely not the case later in the week. The weekend floor shows featured comedians and vocalists and from time to time other dance acts. Our duties were rostered so that if we regularly sat out with customers, we only had to work every second Saturday. This arrangement caused dissent from time to time between those showgirls who did not do hostess duties and those who did.

Although Murrays Cabaret Club has earned a somewhat notorious reputation in the years since it closed, it actually was for the most part a well thought of establishment and its regular customers featured people like Princess Margaret and King Hussein as well as various Peers of the Realm and the great and the good amongst the business fraternity.

One night Marie and I sat with a club regular, Stephen, who had brought with him a man called Guy whom he clearly wanted to impress. Stephen was only in his late forties but to me at the time he seemed like an old man. However, he was easily spared the senior citizen category by his extraordinary charm and charisma.

'You were sensational in the cabaret,' he told me and went on to demand that I tell him all about myself. With Stephen such a request was never simply out of politeness because he genuinely wanted to know all about everyone he met. He listened attentively as I launched into my latest fabricated family, his eyes always on my face, urging me to tell him more.

I told him about Gail, my mother who had started life as a teenage showgirl and about Mark, my father who had been prevented from marrying her by his aristocratic family. He asked far too many questions about Mark's side of the family and so I had to quite brutally refuse to give him any further details. I had been brought up in a series of down-market theatre boarding-house lodgings I told him. Just me and my mother, who had now developed quite severe arthritis and was no longer able to work. I regularly sent money to her, I told him, and if I did not she would be quite unable to survive.

'We can't have that,' he said kindly, handing me two five pound notes. When he asked for my telephone number I gave it to him at once.

The band was playing 'That's Why The Lady Is A Tramp' which was our signal to leave the tables and get ready for the second performance of the evening. I would have rejoined him afterwards but both he and Guy seemed to have disappeared.

Stephen had left an impression on me and I asked one of the other girls if she knew anything about him because I had seen him in the club from time to time, often quite alone.

'He doesn't usually pay to go case,' she said, 'But he's quite generous with hostess fees and sometimes will pay you to go to a party with him – if he can't persuade you to do so for nothing that is.'

That is precisely what did happen. Within a short space of time he asked me to accompany him to a special dinner party to be given by friends of his who had a house in Hyde Park Square, offering me money when I seemed less than keen.

'You may find them slightly eccentric darling,' he told me when we met for coffee in Crawford Street a day or two before. 'Hod is an antique dealer and his wife is Czech – she comes from Prague. She's terribly sexy.'

I must have looked uneasy because he then went on to enthusiastically talk about the food that might be served. 'They provide the most fabulous food, really exotic dishes. At the really big parties there has been roast peacock.'

I marveled at what a peacock might taste like and decided it would have a definite gamey tang to it.

Stephen was continuing to talk, very fast, clutching his second coffee refill. 'They always have fascinating guests – all kinds of people – government officials – surgeons – lawyers, even a bishop once.'

I knew he wanted me to make a good impression on these important people when he took me shopping to buy a suitable dress from Harrods, pale blue silk with three quarter length sleeves, understated and designed to make me look every inch a high class tart struggling to become an acceptable society lady.

I was dubious about the invitation and wondered what my hosts would really be like, torn with indecision about accepting it. Stephen simply increased the promised payment.

I later grew to know Horace Dibben and Mariella Novotny well. Mariella was as economical with the truth about her background as I was about my own. It would appear that she had in fact been born in the East End of London in 1940 and that her father came from Czechoslovakia. Her real name was said to be Stella Capes and I could only admire her for changing it to Mariella Novotny which definitely had a more exotic ring to it. She claimed to be the niece of the former President of Czechoslovakia which may or may not have been true. After leaving home in her teens she became a striptease dancer and part time prostitute and was of most striking looks so she did well and advanced in both these areas.

In nineteen fifty nine she met Horace Dibben, an antique dealer thirty-five years her senior and within a few months she married him saying she would never find anyone who loved and cared for her more than he did. And presumably she was correct because as a wedding gift he gave her a sixteenth century manor house in Sussex.

She is said to have worked in Washington and become involved in relationships with leading politicians including both Jack and Bobbie Kennedy but whether this is true or simply evidence of her over-active imagination I have no idea. She also claimed to have been lured to the United States by a television producer, Harry Alan Towers and said that she only went because she had wanted to become famous and do something to make her widowed mother proud of her. The trip resulted in both she and Towers being charged with violation of the White Slave Trafficking Act according to Novotny. She returned to Britain in mid nineteen sixty one and turned her hand to running sex parties in London for the amusement and edification of her husband and his friends. And now I was about to meet her for the first time.

Stephen was annoyed to find we were the very first guests to arrive but it gave me an opportunity to chat with Mariella and attempt to make judgements about her. She was, rather surprisingly I thought at the time, very charming and chatted very naturally about all kinds of topics. Both she and Horace greeted Stephen with what seemed like genuine affection.

I found the house both impressive and imposing though I could not help noticing that the furnishings in many ways followed the trend I had by now become accustomed to in night clubs. Huge gilt edged mirrors, dark red patterned carpets, dim lamps with vellum shades on side tables with spindly legs and huge chandeliers above. Two very tiny dogs of indeterminate breed shivered beneath the chair where Mariella sat. She was dressed in black velvet and wore a diamond choker with matching ear-rings. I had no doubt at all that they were real.

We drank champagne as we talked and she asked me about the clubs where I had worked and listened attentively to my answers, turning every now and again to make a comment to Stephen and Hod. As the level in my glass decreased I began to relax and halfway through the second glass, when several other guests had arrived I became a little giggly.

Twelve of us finally sat down to a dinner of roast venison with red cabbage preceded by a caviar selection and followed by a stilton cheese. We drank what Stephen later said were excellent wines and I watched fascinated as the table centre piece, a huge penis sculpted from ice, slowly melted into a silver bowl of rose petals.

The guests began to leave the table to take coffee in the drawing room according to Mariella. Now Stephen whispered in my ear that as it was my first time I could simply watch what happened next and was not obliged to join in. In any event, he said, he had another three girls turning up soon who would be more than happy to do anything that might be asked of them. One by one the guests divested themselves of their clothing and went on chatting with small cups of coffee in their hands. Then Mariella appeared with a whip in her hand, now stripped of the bottom half of her black velvet dress, looking very shapely with six inch heeled black patent shoes. One of the men then knelt in front of her and begged her to whip him which she most obligingly did. Several others waited their turn patiently but Mariella said that first she would like to have a woman to whip. I felt most uneasy and struggled to appear relaxed and unconcerned.

Stephen looked encouragingly in my direction and I shook my head, hoping desperately that I did not look too inexperienced and said maybe next time – tonight I was going to be a voyeur. At that moment the doorbell rang and Stephen rushed to open it probably because he knew that the 'after dinner girls' had arrived. Two were colleagues from Murrays and the third I had not met before. They were offered drinks and briskly got out of their clothes, one of them offering herself as the evening's 'slave' to Mariella and the others taking care of the rapidly emerging sexual needs of several of the male guests. After another hour or so the sexual energy of the dinner party attendees had diminished considerably and we all sat around in the huge drawing room, drinking more coffee, the men discussing stock prices, the women talking of baby sitters, and school fees and looking as if they were now anxious to leave.

'Well what did you think?' Stephen asked eagerly when we left. 'They both liked you very much – I could tell that.'

'I don't know,' I said and added that I would have to give the question some thought. I was not prepared to tell him what I really thought. That to me these pillars of society looked more than a little ridiculous, lining up to be whipped by an ex striptease dancer; that more than a small part of me was shocked by the behaviour; that I was concerned that I might have to become involved if I attended for a second time. I knew that Stephen had of course paid the three after dinner girls who had arrived like mini whirlwinds, dressed in their best and anxious to perform their duties as diligently as possible. I also knew that he was unquestionably grooming me to become fully involved at some future stage. I was being manipulated but there was something about Stephen that I could not help myself liking.

As the weeks went by I got to know the later much-reviled Stephen Ward a great deal better, was introduced to a number of his close friends and consequently was taken to an array of parties where I was introduced to sexual practices that in my naiveté I had not known existed. Friends in high places meant a great deal to him and he went to any lengths to please them.

Somehow for all his obvious sophistication he had never quite grown up. He was a successful osteopath with rooms near Harley Street where seemingly he treated only the rich and the famous, or at least they were the only ones he talked about. He was also an artist, constantly making drawings of his patients if they would allow him to. He thoroughly enjoyed his work and from what his patients said, he was also very good at it.

At the same time he was relentlessly enthralled by his own success and that it had allowed him to build relationships with those he saw as of great consequence. He was an incorrigible name dropper, talking constantly of the Ministers of Government, members of the Royal Family and stars of screen and radio whom he had treated and sketches of whom adorned the walls of both his flat and his office. His father had been a vicar in the Anglican Church and had eventually become Prebend of Exeter Cathedral. In his late teens Stephen had spent some years in France and Germany and it seemed to be that is where he first became fascinated by the world of deviant sex, night clubs and those who staffed them. Later, in a possible attempt to put a stop to these unacceptable interests, he was packed off to America where he trained as an osteopath.

These bits of information were offered in fits and starts because although Stephen talked a great deal, it was mostly about others, only rarely about his own life. He had a true curiosity about the lives and ambitions of everyone he came into contact with, including the many and various young dancers, models, showgirls and prostitutes he made it his business to become friendly with. He was uninterested in women of his own age and seemed to only feel secure with those much younger. As he got older the girls seemed to get ever more youthful.

Much of what has been written about him over the years is wildly incorrect. Stephen Ward's sexual demands upon each protégé who appeared at his side were minimal and generally speaking quite straight-forward. When he was alive none of his friends would have described him as a pimp because everyone who had ever come into contact with him knew that he was unfailingly generous. Although many young women took advantage of the various offers he made to them to come and share whichever flat he currently occupied, he rarely made serious attempts to recover rent from them or demand they cough up their portion of the quite substantial telephone bills. On the contrary he applauded their attempts at housekeeping if they happened to order a Fortnum and Mason hamper at his expense because at least they had realized there was nothing in the cupboards. Stephen was a charming and unstinting host, providing the friends who later deserted him in droves, with liberal quantities of both loyalty and hospitality. And therefore he was certainly taken great advantage of, a fact he was quite aware of yet lacked the fortitude to make changes in case he hurt someone's feelings. Consequently he was always slightly in debt, always living somewhat beyond his means, matters he cared little about because maintaining links with friends meant far more to him than money in the bank.

It was through Stephen that I met Clive, a prominent city lawyer with a large and imposing home in Holland Park and ultimately through both of them I was over the next few years propelled into a world I was more than bewildered to find existed at all.

A Force to Be Reckoned With

Although I was initially enthralled by the glamour of working as a showgirl the allure wore off remarkably quickly and I began to get more and more irritated by the surfeit of petty seeming rules imposed upon us by Pops. Every now and again he would issue a directive for a shoe inspection and if our shoes, which we had to provide ourselves, did not blend with our costumes to his satisfaction then he imposed fines left, right and centre. Similarly, out of the blue he would inspect our hair to ensure it was styled correctly and if not then the same fines came firing from his office. It seemed to depend entirely upon his mood. One of the girls said she had previously worked at The Jack of Clubs in Brewer Street and the regime had been a great deal easier. She told me she now wished she had never left.

A week or two later I walked through Brewer Street and inspected the club from the outside, decided it looked pleasant enough and applied for a job. I was interviewed by Mr. Norman Isow, the owner's son. They never employed more than four hostesses he told me, and we did not have to double as showgirls. He seemed to see this as an advantage for prospective employees but I only felt regret that my show business career was to end so abruptly before I had found fame and fortune. Their cabaret generally consisted of comedy acts and they also employed a resident vocalist, Miss Jo Mahoney who sang to the accompaniment of the jazz pianist, Art Fairbank or the Ted Taylor Trio. We hostesses were not required to start work until eleven each evening and we finished at three the following morning. We did not work at weekends and the club paid us a basic rate of five pounds a week on top of which we were allowed to ask for three pound hostess fees from everyone we sat with.

He added, 'We maintain a low hostess fee – and what arrangements you enter into with the customers over and above that is entirely up to you.'

I smiled briefly and tried to look as stylish and worldly as possible because at that stage I had not yet entered into any extra-curricular activity with a customer and in fact had quite decided never to do so. What on earth did this man think I was?

The club was situated beneath Isow's restaurant. It was named after the owner, Jack Isow, who seemed to show little interest in it but was prominently visible in the restaurant. Broadly speaking Isows was a Kosher restaurant also serving a great many other dishes. It had always been a popular meeting place for the entertainment industry and regulars had their names in gold letters on the backs of their chairs. The names included such luminaries as Judy Garland, Bette Davis, Frank Sinatra, Rod Steiger and Danny Kaye

Jack Isow owned a number of adjacent premises including that which had housed the old Doric Ballroom that had for years straddled above Walker's Court, an alley running between Brewer and Berwick Streets. In the late nineteen fifties he had rented The Ballroom for five thousand pounds per year for a period of twenty one years to Paul Raymond for his inspired Reviewbar, an upmarket strip club that outlived all similar establishments in the neighbourhood. This venture had been good for both of them, particularly Raymond who eventually became richer than the Duke of Westminster.

My first night at The Jack of Clubs was memorable. I arrived feeling very uneasy and was instructed to sit with the two other resident hostesses at a table close to the dance floor. Joanne was a tall slim Welsh girl with vivid blue eyes and an abundance of black hair. Shona was a redhead from South London and I warmed to her immediately. Later I found that prior to the nineteen fifty nine Street Offences Act they had both worked the streets of Soho and were operated by Maltese pimps; facts which if I had known sooner might have caused me food for thought coupled with some horror. Until meeting Joanne and Shona I, like most people, had seen prostitutes, and street workers in particular as a species apart and seriously contaminated. They were both so ordinary and conventional they hovered on the edge of being boring. Shona's conversation mostly concerned her three-year-old son Vincent whom she loved to distraction and whose father was 'Sonny the Malt' a formidable pimp of whom I had never heard.

They had been working for the Isows for at least a year and before that in a number of drinking clubs, those opening mid-afternoon and closing before midnight of which there were many they told me. I was still on a learning curve with regard to London's nightlife and largely unaware of most of the pertinent facts. I tried to ask the kind of questions that would inform me without exposing my woeful ignorance which was not as easy as it might sound.

'A proper club like this one,' Joanne insisted, 'is a really good place to work – it's classy.'

'Are the drinking clubs not as classy then?'

Joanne looked as if she thought I might have asked in jest. 'We have to drink proper champagne here,' she said by way of explanation, 'And we don't get commission do we?'

I deliberated upon what she meant by commission and then Shona said, 'At Bella's Bar we got five bob for every champagne cocktail we drank – but it wasn't real champagne of course so you could drink a dozen of them with no problem.'

It might then have crossed her mind that I lacked the requisite job experience because she asked me where I had worked previously and when I told her about Murrays Cabaret Club she was at once impressed.

The champagne at the Jack of Clubs was indeed the real thing and drinking a whole bottle when seated with a customer steadfastly staying on gin and tonics was to become challenging for me although my new colleagues seemed to cope quite well. They both said that it was the second bottle that was the problem and had perfected various techniques for disposing of it which involved liberally dousing the carpet and adjacent pot plants. Oddly the club's exotic houseplants did not just do well but unquestionably thrived on their nightly soakings with Pol Roger. Even so there were times when I went home with my head unpleasantly swimming.

That first night the three of us were 'booked out' quite early on in the evening by a group of Swedish business men who spoke no English whatsoever but were intent upon enjoying themselves to the maximum.

'We have to order the champagne right away,' Shona said. 'At least four bottles as there are three of us at the table – and get them to buy us a meal too. We'll try to get our hostess fees before Jasmine comes round with the nighties.'

I was confused to find that we were expected to prevail upon our customers to make purchases of teddy bears and nightdresses if at all possible, as well as ensuring that the woman in the cloakroom, as well as the waiter serving our table got substantial tips.

The club had begun to fill up nicely and at a nearby table a dozen or so good looking men in their thirties and forties sat down together and conversed in low voices. I noticed them particularly because of their silk shirts and costly looking dark suits.

'Look at those Darts – it's a good thing we're already booked out,' Shona observed. Joanne nodded and shuddered theatrically. I idly thought that odd.

The Swedes were co-operative and happily provided champagne and dinner, followed by the hostess fees in cash. They were, as far as I was concerned, much too keen on dancing and the dreaded Quickstep reared its ugly head quite quickly. However, after several glasses of Pol Roger I was not lacking in confidence and simply asked the bandleader, Ted Taylor, to play The Twist instead. When he co-operatively did so both Joanne and Shona looked horrified but the weeks of practice with Shelagh meant that this ultramodern dance step rang no alarm bells for me and I twisted away happily with my Swede obediently following my lead. I began to actually enjoy myself.

I became so engrossed in twisting that although I was aware of a bottle hurtling through the air close to my right ear it did not occur to me to stop dancing even when it crashed against the opposite wall. The band was still playing, though more hesitantly than a moment or two before and so I continued to dance on, oblivious to the fact that my partner had already beaten a retreat along with most of the other customers. It was only when the music finally stopped that I looked around me at the ugly devastation of what had once been The Jack of Clubs.

Several tables had been upturned, screams came from female customers cowering beneath the few that remained upright and it appeared that most of the well-dressed table of men in well-cut suits were in physical combat with the staff. The club manager, Mr. Pinot was bleeding copiously from a cheek wound and there was now blood all over the dance floor which I slipped on as I made my way drunkenly towards the cloakroom. Joanne and Shona were nowhere to be seen.

When I tried to get into the cloakroom I found the door had been locked from within and I had to batter on it requesting entry before the elderly Italian attendant finally opened it an inch or two. The other girls had locked themselves in one of the cubicles. I did the same and hissed at them from under the dividing panel.

'What on earth's going on?' I tried to sound casual because for all I knew this might be a normal occurrence at the club. I was beginning to feel rather more sober.

'Darts...' Shona hissed back. 'We're very lucky we were already booked out otherwise we'd have to have sat with them.'

I decided not to ask for a definition of darts. It was over an hour before Police and Ambulance had both been and gone and the girls deemed it safe enough for us to leave the premises.

Mr. Isow Junior was still talking to one of the officers but he called out, 'Give it a day or two – see you on Monday girls,' as we made our way up into Brewer Street. He sounded resigned.

We shared a taxi back to Bayswater because Shona and Joanne both lived in the next square to me each in a bed-sitter similar to my own.

'Why did you carry on dancing?' Shona asked curiously.

'Well I thought it better to just carry on – I was trying to ignore it.'

They looked at each other and then Joanne said, 'We thought you were crazy.'

Weeks later when I got to know her better she elaborated and told me they had both decided that I must be 'as tough as old boots' to have so brazenly ignored the violence around me and Shona had even said that it wouldn't be wise to cross me at any stage as I was clearly a force to be reckoned with.

On the way home that morning I continued to justify my behaviour because I did not want to admit I had been too drunk to notice what was going on, 'Oh well that group looked quite respectable when they came in....'

'Respectable?' Joanne sounded amazed, 'They were Darts – and the Kray twins were with them. That Ronnie Kray is mad – surely you know that.'

I did not know that so I said, 'I imagine there are worse people in London than the Kray twins.'

They both lapsed into a respectful silence which I recognized and was confused by.

I had of course heard something of the Kray brothers from the girls at the Cabaret Club but during my time there they had not appeared as far as I had been aware. Later I learned that 'Darts' was a specific nightclub idiom that referred to those recently emerged from or even those about to enter Dartmoor Prison. Although theoretically most clubs were happier when these groups did not pop up among the clientele, they were at the same time reluctant to exclude them. In some cases businesses were already paying protection money to the very groups expecting to be hosted and so it was unwise to refuse them entry.

As far as the twins were concerned, they had begun to move their attention to the West End of London in the mid nineteen fifties when they acquired an interest in a drinking club called 'Stragglers' near Cambridge Circus. By that time they were already providing protection for the notorious Jack Spot who felt generally threatened by the proliferation of Italians on his patch. By nineteen fifty eight they had business interests in drinking clubs and billiard saloons in suburbs like Stoke Newington, Whitechapel and Aldgate and were very anxious to progress further West. Reggie was a great admirer of Billy Hill whom he endeavoured to emulate. Ronnie on the other hand didn't think much of Hill. As for Hill himself, it is said that by the time he was due to retire he was absolutely petrified of both of them.

The Stragglers had been owned and run by an ex-docker called Bill Jones and before the involvement of the Krays was a place where violence was prone to break out, which of course reduced profits. When the twins became aware of this and dropped by one evening to offer their mentorship they were at once offered a share in the place and thenceforth it began to run smoothly and profitably. I never found out whether the fight at The Jack of Clubs on my very first night was choreographed by the Krays in order to demonstrate to the Isow family just how much damage could be done in a very short space of time, or whether it was just a tiff between mates. Either way the damage did not prevent the Isows from opening a few days later when the only remaining evidence of the fracas was the broken mirrors in the bar and a startling line of stitches across Mr Pinot's face. Regardless of what really happened and although I had seen little of the notorious brothers at Murrays, they began to frequent The Jack of Clubs on a regular basis.

Although I had previously been oblivious to either their reputation or their presence in Percival Murray's establishment there was now no avoiding them and I rapidly became completely informed regarding the exploits of the Kray twins and their elder brother Charlie. Their criminal encroachment into the West End of London had well and truly begun and they were soon taking money from a number of Soho clubs including The New Life in Frith Street, The New Mill in Macclesfield Street, now very possibly The Jack of Clubs itself and they certainly had a part share in protection money gathered by other gangs from places like The Astor, The Bagatelle and The Starlight. As Reggie said to me himself one Tuesday evening when I was unfortunate enough to be sitting with him, 'I've always worked hard you know Jane, and as my old Dad always said, hard work pays off – but you've got to be prepared to put in the effort.'

I found myself enthusiastically agreeing with him and even felt lucky on that particular evening because although the twins were hard to tell apart on a slight acquaintance, and we all tried to keep our acquaintance with them as slight as possible, it was a relief to find I had been partnered with Reggie rather than Ronnie. Ronnie was at times psychotic and the only advantage in being his dancing partner for the evening was the fact that although he claimed to be bisexual his preference appeared to definitely lean towards young, good looking men and therefore he was most unlikely to request what Mr. Pinot the manager delicately termed, 'greener pastures.'

Reggie on the other hand was aggressively heterosexual but I soon discovered that he had a well-developed sentimental side that revolved for the greater part around his mother whom he told all and sundry was 'a saint'.

'There ain't nobody in the world like my Mum,' he was wont to pronounce after a few glasses of Pol Roger, and his eyes might even glisten with a tear or two. 'She's a saint – the way she looked after me and me brothers all them years. There ain't nothing I wouldn't do for her....'

I asked him question after question about his mother, Violet, waiting at home in Vallance Road, Whitechapel ready to make her boys their late night cups of milky cocoa and warming their pyjamas in front of the fire. Strange though it seems the twins still retained their shared room in their childhood home and seemed to live half the week with Violet and the remainder in their upmarket apartment which at that time was in Knightsbridge, close to Harrods Department Store. Reggie spoke non-stop and Violet's virtues were relayed to me in no uncertain terms. She had always fought 'tooth and nail' for her boys, it seemed, and when they were only six or seven years old and had already got into a variety of different scrapes at school, she was always prepared to 'go down there and take on that bastard of a headmaster'. I nodded admiringly and when I thought the time was right, told him about my own poor old Mum, living in Gravesend and now almost crippled with arthritis which meant that although I would have much preferred to live in the city, I felt forced to go home to her every night after work, a journey of twenty miles and by mini-cab a considerable expense.

'You've got to look after your Mum Jane,' he agreed, 'Always remember that when you was a kid she looked after you. You've only got one Mum haven't you? You always have to remember that.'

And although it was most unwise to ask the twins for hostess fees because their attitude was generally that the girls who sat with them for an evening of champagne and twisting, were privileged to do so, that evening Reggie handed me ten pounds and told me to buy something nice for my Mum. I thanked him profusely.

'I was gonna ask you back to my new place for another coupla drinks,' he said, 'But I know you want to get home so another time perhaps.'

Ronnie, surprised by his twin's sudden munificence, also brought out his wallet and handed a similar amount to Shona before they paid the not inconsiderable bill and even left a tip.

Shona and I said our farewells and beat a hasty retreat into the cloakroom.

'How did that happen?' She asked.

'Just keep talking about their Mum,' I suggested and she looked at me uncomprehendingly.

'Their Mum?'

'Just try it,' I advised, 'It worked a treat with Reg – and Ron just didn't want to be left behind that's all.'

We waited until they had left the premises before re-appearing.

Mr. Isow junior stood at the top of the stairs, 'Well done girls.'

As the months went by and business improved for the twins they could at times be even more generous.

In the early sixties, the brothers were still flexing their muscles in the area to some extent and appeared to reserve their more imprudent and psychotic behaviour for those areas east of Soho. Their worst transgression as far as the Isows were concerned being when Ronnie turned up early one evening to shoot dead Frankie Fraser. Frankie had a table booked in the restaurant but failed to appear and later the disagreement between them, whatever it was, was sorted out more amicably. When he heard about the gun incident the doorman at the time, a huge man said to be a retired heavyweight boxer fresh from the provinces, grew visibly pale. Apparently a week or so previously he had successfully barred the twins from entering the restaurant because neither were wearing ties. At the time they apparently, freshly oiled with copious cocktails from Raymond's Reviewbar upstairs, accepted it very well. However, the doorman took great care when walking the nearby streets for the following month or two and was said to have told people he never felt easy in the job or the area again. He wished someone had taken the time and trouble to warn him about them.

I appreciated his sentiments because after my success with Reggie, diverting his attention to discussion about his mother, I fear it went to my head and one evening a little worse the wear for champagne I unwisely agreed to go with him and his brother to look at a warehouse in Whitechapel they were thinking of renting. It was while we were looking around the premises that an elderly associate known only as Fitch arrived, dapper in a silk mohair coat and carrying a holdall from which he produced a number of guns. Ronnie began to examine them with enthusiasm.

At some stage I stupidly asked if the weapons were in fact real. Ronnie demonstrated by firing three shots into the darkness of the warehouse and I have never forgotten my shock and amazement and the abject terror that followed. My heart raced and my whole body pounded to match the rapid beats. It was difficult to breathe and a pain in my chest was so acute I began to fear that one of the shots had somehow or other penetrated me.

'Yeah – they're all real darling,' he said nonchalantly. As we left the place I made a pledge to myself that I would take great care never again to get into such a vulnerable position with them or those like them. I would certainly never question the authenticity of weaponry in the future.

In spite of the obvious dangers of associating with London's criminal element, because I was still relatively new to the heady world of nightclubs and gangland Soho I tried to take all these developments in my stride. Although I missed the glamour of being a showgirl at Murrays, in some ways I rather preferred the straight hostessing job in Brewer Street where I felt my natural talents were best deployed. The work was essentially glamorous enough and the financial remuneration was generally speaking better than typing for a living. I enjoyed meeting new people, talking to them, ensuring that they liked me and I enjoyed being wined and dined. However the pressure to become involved in 'greener pastures' was building up and I knew it was only going to be a matter of time before I had to make a decision in this regard. I had told Joanne and Shona that I had recently had an operation and that explained my general reluctance for a while, but it couldn't go on forever.

One night I was sitting with a man who first said his name was Derek van Heerden and that he was a publisher and later in the evening claimed he was the playwright, John Whiting. Quite possibly he was the worse the wear on champagne when he made the latter remark but either way he seemed to know more than I did about John Whiting's plays and so I was impressed. When he asked me to go back to his hotel room with him I heard myself agree and it was only when we actually got there that I began to have doubts.

He had sobered up a little when he said, 'How much do you charge?'

I thought it best to be honest and said, 'I don't know – what do you usually pay?'

Then I added, 'I haven't actually done this before.'

He looked at me as if he did not believe me and then said, 'I will only pay you ten pounds and I want you to stay the night – is that OK with you?'

I thought for only a moment. I had been earning only ten pounds a week as a typist and at Murrays Cabaret club slightly less so I thought it was fair enough. At least he hadn't asked me to stay for a week. Had he done so I might even have agreed.

'And I don't allow condoms,' he said firmly.

'That's OK,' I said and later was to fervently wish I had not acquiesced.

I stayed with him until daybreak by which time he was sprawled across the hotel room bed, deeply asleep.

As I left the place I imagined the reception staff stared at me curiously but in reality they were completely ignoring me.

I now felt totally different and I imagined that everyone I passed on the street allowed more pavement space between themselves and me because I was now defiled. It was as if I had a placard across my forehead that announced sex for sale. Home again I lay for an hour in the bath hoping to wash away the overwhelming feeling of contamination.

Shelagh's attitude was pragmatic and she told me she didn't understand why I was 'going on and on about it.'

'I feel so different…..' I told her and began to cry.

'Oh for heaven's sake,' she sounded totally exasperated, 'You certainly didn't stress out about charging for dancing The Twist...or for eating dinner…or drinking champagne. It's just one more step in a new career. Look at it like that and you'll feel a lot better.'

I attempted to look at it like that and failed.

'It's all very well for you to give advice but you have absolutely no idea how it feels to make that career step.'

She and Maggie were preoccupied with their planning of another trip to France and shortly I was to be left mostly friendless. I wished I was going with them

'Maybe you should be doing it yourself,' I suggested, 'Think of the money you could earn that would go towards your trip.

'I didn't say I would never do it did I?' Shelagh's voice grew sharper. 'Maybe one day I will. Who knows? Anyhow as far as you're concerned you're still the same person as you were this time last week – you've just had a new experience that's all. Think how good the money is.'

I thought how good the money was and after a few more days managed to adjust to the fact that I was now a prostitute. There was no other word for it because the term sex workers had not yet been introduced. I would compromise by not doing it again unless it was absolutely necessary. During the weeks of that neophyte period I had reason to bitterly regret the whole experience. The first indication that something was not quite as it had been, was acute nausea when walking past the coffee houses of Berwick and Dean Streets which took me completely by surprise. I was, after all, a coffee devotee. This was followed not by morning sickness which I might have been able to cope with but evening sickness which was much harder to accommodate. I began to wish I had never met and been tempted by the man who had claimed to be John Whiting.

The problems of early pregnancy were compounded because each time we hostesses were booked out with customers we were required to order a meal, come what may, the food coming down from the restaurant kitchen above and therefore, somewhat surprisingly for nightclub food, very palatable.

Suddenly the Gefilte Fish, Cholent and Chopped Liver was disgusting and indigestible and the Matzah Ball Soup nauseating. I took to ordering mixed salads with no dressing and was reprimanded by both Mr. Pinot and Mr. Norman Isow.

'This diet of yours simply won't do,' Mr. Pinot told me, 'We cannot have girls on the staff who are ordering dressing-less salads.'

I apologized, feeling like a chastised schoolgirl. I would try to do better.

When they realized I was pregnant both Joanne and Shona were helpful and sympathetic but their contacts for pregnancy termination were out of date and in fact Shona claimed that she had felt quite diffident about abortion since the birth of her three-year-old son.

She asked me if there was any chance of me keeping it to which I answered firmly in the negative. Although I was generally anti-abortion I knew that this particular pregnancy had to end.

One evening the man whom I now felt was totally responsible for the position I found myself in, appeared in the club again and sat alone sipping from a whiskey glass. I foolishly approached him and rather tearfully told him that due to his 'no condoms' rule I was now pregnant. I'm not quite sure what reaction I expected.

He looked up briefly from his glass and said calmly and clearly in diction audible to all in the general vicinity, 'I really don't care if you're pregnant dearest; have twins if you like, but please do be *quietly* pregnant and with dignity...'

Mortified, I ran crying to the cloakroom, followed by a sympathetic Shona who said, 'What on earth did you do that for? That just wasn't sensible.'

I tried to be quietly pregnant. Without the support of Shelagh and Maggie now somewhere deep in France, I felt very much alone and so feeling powerless to deal with the problem, I wept a great deal.

I rang Stephen whom I had been avoiding since I left Murrays, primarily because he had appeared to be indignant that I had made the decision without consulting him. But he was also in France and not due to return for three weeks. A couple of my colleagues from Murrays were staying in the Wimpole Mews flat, availing themselves of his hospitality. When I told them my problem they were unable to help either. So the pregnancy continued and by the time I met Michelle it was into its thirteenth week.

Michelle was the new hostess, taken on because young Mr. Isow said that business had picked up and we were doing nicely for the time of year. I was now instructed to leave the table by the dance floor hitherto shared in companionable gossip with Joanne and Shona. From now on I had to sit on the other side of the room, close to the entrance stairway with Michelle.

Michelle was twenty-six years old, she told me, and had worked in clubs since leaving home at fifteen. She had started with fruit cups in a number of drinking clubs. She came from Hendon and had planned a career as a ballet dancer but when her mother died suddenly of cancer when she was fourteen her father had put a stop to what he called all that nonsense and enrolled her in a typing course after school. That's why she ran away and she had not seen him or any other member of her family since. The sudden and enforced termination of the ballet lessons had meant that all the muscle that had built up in her upper legs over years had turned to fat almost overnight she said and she would never be able to forgive her father for that.

She had a flat in the Edgware Road close to the Praed Street corner where she lived with a Siamese cat called Bamboo. She had her cocktail dresses made by a dressmaker in Finchley, usually ordering six just before

Christmas each year, her favourite music was modern jazz and she had just bought a red Triumph Herald car which was parked not far away. Each year she went for a month to Spain or Italy, quite alone, for what she called 'a working holiday' where she met wealthy men and made a great deal of money. It was quite possible to have a really enjoyable holiday at the same time she told me.

I learned all this about her within the first hour of meeting her and I was impressed. When she asked me about myself I told her about the mother I had conjured up for the Kray twins, the one with serious health problems who lived in Gravesend. I also told her I was pregnant.

To my great joy and surprise Michelle immediately said that if I wanted a termination she had a friend who might very well be persuaded to do it for me. She would ask him. A day or two later she said he was prepared to do so only if I had already given birth to a child. My heart sank and I asked her why. She said he felt the whole business was too distressing for someone who had never been pregnant before. He was anxious not to take chances.

I hastily acquainted her with my mythical daughter Sarah, whose father I had decided was to be Stan Douglas. I hadn't seen him for a while but thought he wouldn't mind because after all this was an emergency. I made her four years old and safely living in Kent living with my cousin Margaret. Michelle said she would convey all this to her abortionist friend. She did so because two or three days later I met Vidar Gebhard-L'Estrange.

On A White Charger

He turned up at my room in Leinster Square precisely at the time agreed, a slim man in his mid thirties with a mop of dark curly hair and compassionate eyes the colour of autumn chestnuts. He announced that he had come to 'help' with my problem. The charge would be twenty-five pounds in cash and I was more than anxious to hand it over. He was only a part time abortionist and although he told me the story of how he came to be in that position, I now no longer remember the details. What I do remember is how kind he was to me during that Easter period of nineteen sixty two.

I felt almost abandoned at the time with both Shelagh and Maggie now travelling somewhere in France or Spain or Italy. The house in Bayswater had become lonely without them. Most of the Australians and New Zealanders had moved on also for further travel in Europe and had been replaced by earnest school teachers and accountancy students. I had nothing in common with them and began to feel my room on the first floor, overlooking the leafy square to be an island of misery and neglect. It was into this well of loneliness that Vidar appeared on that sunny afternoon one week before Easter nineteen sixty two almost as a latter day Lancelot or Bedevere, on a white charger.

I was quite unprepared for the gentleness and consideration he showed me. He stayed with me throughout the three days that it took to dislodge the child within me, first of all with injections of glycerin into the uterus and when that did not seem to be working, with soapy water. The concern he showed to me was very seductive. No-one in my life to that point had ever been as kind as he was.

The fetus appeared early on the morning of Easter Sunday and I was exhilarated to suddenly be free of it. As most women who have been through such an experience know well, there is nothing more invasive than an unwelcome pregnancy and the emotional relief of being rid of it is charged with adrenaline. I felt pitifully indebted to him and raised no objection when he stayed on to comfort me for another day or two. He went out to shop for food that might appeal to me, made me copious cups of coffee, ran baths, wrapped me in blankets and talked to me about his life. By the Wednesday that followed that particular Easter I was quite captivated and listening to him in fascination. It did not take very long for me to begin to fall in love with him.

He was just thirty-four years old, he said, and had been born in Germany of German parents. His mother was forty when he was born and his father in his early seventies. He had a brother six years older called Rollo. His brother was a famous yachtsman and lived in Garmisch-Partenkirchen, a mountain resort in Bavaria. His mother was a von Carolowitz, from an aristocratic family. She and her siblings had been brought up in a castle called Kuckuckstein in Liebbstadt a village in Saxony. I had only haziest of ideas as to where both Bavaria and Saxony were but I preferred to let him believe I was rather more knowledgeable than that so I asked no questions but merely nodded attentively.

His father had spent a great deal of time in America as a young man. His family owned silk mills and had been very wealthy. Vidar's parents had met during the First World War when his mother was a nurse. He did not elaborate on the circumstances of their meeting and I did not ask.

He enjoyed talking, and so he talked on, sometimes for hours at a time, telling me stories mostly concerning himself and his family that under normal circumstances I would have found intensely boring but for some reason now both intrigued and entertained me.

He told me how he came to be living in London, that he had been sent to Ireland after the war to study physics at Trinity College, Dublin. There were long and convoluted reasons why he switched from physics to medicine and in fact completed the first four years of the course and equally complex and elaborate reasons why he then was forced to drop out and why he then studied music instead – piano to be precise. One of his greatest loves, he told me, was music. He was a talented pianist and loved to play Chopin. I looked at him in total admiration and realized with some regret that my significant passion for Stan Douglas, recently revived via our imaginary daughter, Sarah, was dwindling fast.

He explained that he only rarely carried out abortions, when he was very short of money, like now. His business, he told me, had come up against problems. Well it was really to do with his last girlfriend, Irena. He had in recent years made his living as a sound engineer and had, whilst living with her, been half working from home which happened to be her flat in Knightsbridge. She had a rich father who paid for the flat but he became upset when on a sudden visit from Brazil he found Vidar living there and to add insult to injury, carrying on a business there. So to cut a long story short, all the recording equipment had to be hastily put into storage and was now costing him quite a lot with ongoing bills on a monthly basis. Another ex girl-friend, Christine, had kindly taken him in and he was now living with her in Ladbroke Grove where she had the top two floors of a house. It wasn't ideal living with Christine of course because she still had an emotional attachment to him although it was not reciprocated. He would like to leave as soon as possible but that meant finding a place he could afford and arranging to get his equipment out of storage so he could set up in business again. It was not going to be easy.

But perhaps not so hard either because I was delighted to hear that he was a sound engineer. That was something I fancied that I knew a little about although my knowledge was limited if I was to be entirely honest. However, it was something I was at least familiar with and able to converse upon with some degree of confidence. I told him about my experiences in music publishing and with Radio Veronica, heavily editing some of the less desirable details. I knew a lot of people in popular music I assured him, once it was up and running, with me by his side his business could only go from strength to strength. He nodded and with delight I could see that he was thinking through the various computations of a possible relationship.

'I wonder if we would get on all right if we actually lived together,' he said more to himself than to me. I hastily assured him that I thought we would because although by that time we had known each other less than two weeks, I was already half convinced that he was the person I wanted to spend the rest of my life with. I could not believe my good fortune to have at last met a man who not only treated me like a special human being, but was possessed of an enormous intellect, came from an extraordinarily interesting family and was better educated than anyone I had so far met in my entire life.

I realized with a little regret that he would of course want me to give up my night club job which by its very nature would now be totally unsuitable. Vidar would not want me to continue to be involved in that kind of work, of that I was certain. I was more than a little surprised to find that in that respect I was totally wrong.

'It really is a very good thing that you have an evening job,' he said one afternoon as we sat companionably drinking coffee together in Christopher Dean's, the 'in place' of the day in Queensway opposite Whiteleys, a place where you could not only drink coffee but buy records, both EPs and LPs. I was sitting close at his side rather than opposite, hoping that the other coffee drinkers would realise that we were very nearly a couple.

'Why is that?' I asked, trying not to drain my cup before he drained his own.

He paused, half smiling in a manner that made his mouth crinkle delightfully, 'Because it means that if and when we live together and I resurrect my business you will be able to help me in the day time – yet you will be earning money at night. '

He finished the last of the coffee and hunched his shoulders, his manner suddenly becoming much more serious. 'For a while you know, you will be the only breadwinner – you do understand that?'

Of course I understood it and was desperate to be so. I nodded. He smiled again and his hand touched mine and gave it a little squeeze. 'For the first few months of course you will be supporting us both.'

I had only the most fleeting second of small hesitation that bordered on uncertainty because those were the days when men still supported women. Women were as yet unaccustomed to even paying for a cup of coffee in places like Christopher Dean's when in male company and so the idea of a man being supported financially by a woman, especially one so new in his life, was an unexpected one. A vestige of common sense within me knew and fully understood this and urged me to stop and think but I firmly ejected it.

Instead I nodded with enthusiasm. He squeezed my hand a little more firmly and told me how very grateful he was for my understanding of the position he found himself in.

Even so I was still more than doubtful about continuing to work as a night club hostess with all it entailed whilst living with the man of my dreams, as he was fast becoming.

'I could get a job as a telephonist in a mini-cab company,' I suggested. We had left the coffee shop and were crossing the road, heading back to my room in Leinster Square. He stopped in amazement in the middle of the road, causing a taxi to swerve around him and yell a minor obscenity in his direction.

'What on earth for?'

'Well it would be working at night – but not as a hostess...'

Why did I need to explain something that was so glaringly obvious? If we were going to live together as a real couple then I did not want to continue in a job that revolved around selling sex. I was anxious to give myself one hundred per cent to him; I wanted him to be the only man in my life.

'And not nearly as well paid,' he responded and looked at me the way one does when admonishing a small child for some misdemeanour slightly more than minor.

'Why on earth work all evening for the low hourly rates these people in mini-cab companies get paid when you can earn so much more as a hostess? It seems remarkably foolish.'

We had now turned into the square where newly emerging spring flowers sprouted bravely from the borders of the central garden and even the branches of the plane trees burgeoned with new growth.

I felt slightly foolish as I began to explain to him that I wanted to be totally faithful to him and that I had imagined he would find that situation desirable. As I have said before, this was the early nineteen sixties and thoughts of 'open' relationships and free love although very possibly more than on the periphery of the lives of the more avant-garde, I was definitely not one of them. Although I had worked in a night club long enough to feel comfortable as a part of London's night life, I was still easily shocked and the pregnancy had made me vulnerable. Later Vidar was to tell me this was on account of my working class roots and background of Catholicism but now we were still in the first stages of our relationship at a time when he was inclined to appear to pamper, even cherish my self-esteem.

Back in my room he explained to me that my feelings were laudable but a little outdated and more especially so since I would soon be supporting two people rather than one. Not only that; we would be living in a flat rather than a room with all the additional expenses that running a flat entailed, and of course we would need some form of transport, even if it was only a modest little van. He thought he might be able to get hold of a mini-van quite cheaply. Was I quite sure I was ready for the responsibility, he was keen to know.

Of course I was ready. I reassured him immediately and he kissed me chastely on my forehead and told me I was quite the sweetest girl he had met in a long time. At once I was suffused with blissful happiness because at last here was a man who might come to love me as much as I would almost certainly love him. We became totally immersed in lovemaking and I was exhilarated with the ecstasy of being one with him.

Later I sat on the edge of the bed half draped in a Marks & Spencer's night gown, contentedly watching his clumsy attempts to make instant coffee on the gas ring, my whole being still sizzling with the joy of our physical rapport.

'You know,' he said as he handed me one of the blue and white striped Denby mugs I had only the day before bought in Whiteleys at his suggestion, because they were quite the best mugs of their kind he had ever encountered, 'There is no need at all for you to feel so ambivalent about your work – about selling your body for money I mean – no need at all.'

I heaved a small sigh of relief which I thought he expected and asked him why not because most men would be terribly jealous. I did not add that my genuine opinion, the opinion that was tucked away somewhere in a corner, was that some form of sexual possessiveness would be the most normal reaction under the circumstances. I knew I would be inconsolable if he, perish the thought, was to be unfaithful to me for some reason. But that would not happen because I would ensure that we built the most solid base on which to stand our union. Nothing would come between us.

'I did think that I would find it very odd to have a girlfriend who became involved in selling her body to others,' he was saying, 'But you know having given it a lot more thought recently, since we met, I find the idea rather exciting. Thinking of you giving yourself to another man is very sexy you know. I'm sure that if you thought about me in bed with another woman you would feel the same. It would arouse you – don't you agree?'

'NO!' I screamed to myself, 'NO…you do not agree at all. You find the idea quite, quite unacceptable.'

My heart was beating faster than usual; I could feel it. I said, 'I don't find that idea at all sexy.'

'Why not?' He looked deep into my eyes and stroked my cheek. 'When I think about you with another man there is a part of me that knows you are doing it for me – for us – that's a very powerful idea you know, an idea that at the same time excites me sexually. Is that so wrong do you think?'

'Yes you do think that is wrong,' said the innermost remnant of personal integrity, 'Tell him so at once.'

'No – it isn't exactly wrong,' I ventured after a pause, 'It's simply that I haven't given it enough thought I suppose.'

He nodded approvingly, crumpling the empty Astoria packet, a cigarette brand like many others, long disappeared from supermarket shelves. It lay softly deflated between our Denby mugs on the plastic topped table and the brand aroma, destined to be forever associated with him, hovered about us as nicotine residue was apt to do in those days. He said he would go out to buy more cigarettes and asked if I wanted him to buy some Peter Stuyvesant cork tipped for me. I was pleased that he remembered the brand I smoked myself even though I was trying hard to cut down and because he then found he was out of money, gave him a pound note with which to buy them. He said he would also buy more milk so we would be able to drink more coffee that evening and kissed me once more. I should think about what we had been discussing while he was gone, he suggested. So I gingerly began to examine the idea and still found it not only distasteful but vaguely improper and could not imagine myself reaching even a small degree of acceptance of it. Prostitution seemed minor in comparison and I now wondered how I could have found that particular decision so difficult to come to terms with because there was a basic honesty about the financial transaction involved in prostitution. It did not come anywhere close to the disruptive emotions that are involved when one human being develops a love attachment to another.

I should tell him what I really felt. I knew that. Of course I knew that, but I was already fearful that exposing my feelings on the matter of the exclusivity of our sex life would push him away from me. I did not want him to begin to feel that possibly I might not, after all, be the woman he could share the future with. After all sex was merely one aspect of our relationship and his thoughts might be simply his way of assuring me that my current work in the field of hostessing and prostitution must not be allowed to come between us. We had to be bigger than that and we would be. Nevertheless I thought it would be some time before I could fully appreciate the full breadth of his ideas about fidelity and as it happened I was right.

When he came back bearing Peter Stuyvesant, Astoria and two cartons of milk I said I had explored my own feelings and realized that I was allowing common convention to stand in the way of the possibility of exploring a new way of looking at not just sex but life itself. He was overjoyed he told me because for a moment he had feared we two were making a dreadful mistake. But if I was prepared to listen and to learn, then he was prepared to walk alongside me and help me on my journey.

What a relief!

He told me that I should work hard over the next few months and save as much money as possible so that we would have a deposit, if it should be necessary, to put down on a furnished flat, somewhere central if at all possible. Until one could be found, he would continue living in Ladbroke Grove in Christine's spare room. He had explained that Christine was very much an ex-girlfriend, the one before Irena in fact as he had explained. Well to be perfectly frank, he said, she had in the first place shared him with her best friend, Joy. He had lived with them both in a flat they rented in Barons Court. And yes, he had certainly had sex with them both because neither of them were concerned with petty jealousies. Each had been very fond of him and he rotated between their beds on a week by week basis so that it would be fair. There was an understanding between them that if another of their boyfriends came to call Vidar would be required to get out of that particular bed for the evening. In fact, thinking about it now made him realise that was when he first began to develop his sexual philosophy. He was indebted to them both because they had enabled him to reject carnal resentment in relationships. Joy had returned to Ireland eventually and Christine had moved on to Ladbroke Grove and had come to his aid recently at a time when he most needed friends, when his business had failed.

Because I had not yet learned how to reject resentment of any kind in relationships I began to harbour a great deal of it towards Christine and longed to be able to pluck him away from her and her infuriatingly efficient care and attention. She worked as a secretary in a small publisher's office near Piccadilly Circus and earned only ten or eleven pounds a week with which she provided very well for Vidar. He had a hot meal every evening and sometimes she left porridge for his breakfast before leaving to catch the bus to the office though he only rarely ate it because he usually slept until midday and cold porridge is not pleasant. She also washed and ironed his shirts and underclothing and generally made sure that he was able to leave the house looking reasonably well groomed. He had a lot to thank her for and I began to loathe her with an intensity that quite surprised me and which was hard to hide from him. The sooner we found a flat to move into together, the happier I would be, there was no doubt of that.

At that time most young Londoners lived in furnished bed-sitting rooms or small flatlets, rented on a weekly basis. Unfurnished flats were very hard to find because they involved a security of tenure that the majority of landlords wished to avoid. In order to rent an unfurnished flat a considerable deposit representing several months' rent might be involved and there was no guarantee that it would be returned at any stage. To complicate matters, we would need to get permission from the landlord to convert one of the rooms into a recording studio which might be difficult because as Vidar explained to me, there was a perception from most people that where recording studios were concerned, an excess of noise existed, which of course was not the case. I was dubious when he said this, but I decided not to argue on that point.

When I returned to work at The Jack of Clubs after Easter, now firmly in a relationship with Vidar L'Estrange, I excitedly explained all these things to Michelle who listened attentively and then told me that she thought I was making a mistake.

'The problem with Vidar,' she said, 'Is that he can't just meet a girl and have a fling with her – he has to make a bloody meal of it. It always ends badly.'

She shook her head, took a large gulp of the gin and tonic she had ordered and paid for herself, because if we were not booked out with customers we had to pay for our own drinks.

'What do you mean?' I asked aggressively.

'Look,' she said quite kindly, 'He's got a really good side but quite honestly he won't turn out to be the man you think he is. He starts off well but honestly, my advice is to break it now while you can.'

She lit a cigarette while I looked at her furiously and explained all over again how caring he had been towards me.

'Of course he's caring – he overdoes kindness, and there's a part of him that really means it but all his relationships end in disaster. And he's very bloody kinky. Believe me, I know what I'm talking about. I've known him since I was fifteen.'

He had been one of the first people she had met when she ran away from home, ending up that first night in an all night café in Covent Garden. Vidar had been there in the café, on a trip over from Dublin where he was studying at Trinity College. They had become friends and kept in close touch over the years though she swore she had never ended up in his bed, because she was always too wary of him. Women fell in love with him easily and she couldn't understand why. Poor pathetic Christine had been in love with him and then that awful fat South American girl, Irena. She had known both of them. And now me! She looked at me in amazement and said, 'I know that nothing I say is going to have the slightest impression upon you.'

I agreed with her that it would not.

At that moment Mr. Pinot came towards us saying, 'Come along girls, we have two gentlemen from Manchester who are anxious for dancing partners....' And as we got to our feet, he bent forward and lowered his voice saying 'I think you will also find that they are wishing for greener pastures later....'

I gave my gentleman a dazzling smile as I sat down. 'How lovely to meet you – My name is Jane and this is my friend Michelle. What's your name?'

'Call me Tom,' he said with an equally genial smile. 'Now will you girls have a bottle of champagne?'

Of course we would.

Tom and Bob, in the machine tool trade, provided two bottles in fact, ordered dinner and cigarettes which were only sold in packets of fifty, balked merely for a moment before buying us a nightie each and got permission for us to leave before the second floor show, spiriting us to a nearby hotel for greener pastures for which we were adequately rewarded.

It was still only three thirty am when we walked to Michelle's car which was parked in Dean Street. She said she would give me a ride home.

'How do you feel about going case now you and Vidar are planning to live together?' she asked as the car turned towards Oxford Circus, 'Have you discussed it with him?'

It seemed an innocuous question although later I realized that she asked only out of a curiosity to know how naive I might be. At that time I still had not quite processed the fact that most of the young and attractive women I had worked with so far, had steady boyfriends, some of whom were waiters and bar staff and well acquainted with the facts of night club life. Invariably in these relationships immunity had built around the topic of paid-for intimacy, nicely numbing any emotional hurts that might be involved.

' He doesn't mind at all,' I told her, only too keen to resume the conversation about him. 'In fact when I suggested getting a job as a night shift telephonist he said it would be silly because I can earn so much more in a club – and anyhow we need the money if we are to afford a suitable flat.'

Then because she had already told me she had a jazz musician boyfriend I asked her how he felt about the subject. She half shook her head disinterestedly and said they rarely discussed it and anyhow there were enough problems already because he was married with three children and she distrusted him when he said he was going to leave his wife.

Thinking back to my experiences with Luuk Nijhof and Stan Douglas I gave some thought as to whether either of them would have seriously considered abandoning the matrimonial home for love of me and quickly decided it was most unlikely.

'In my experience they never do,' I told her, wanting her to believe I was more proficient in the art of managing relationships with married men than I actually was. But she seemed to have suddenly lost interest in the subject and began to tell me about her newly established aquarium of tropical fish and that she would love me to come to her place some time to see them.

'The biggest problem I have with them is persuading the cat they are not his playthings,' she said, 'He's already murdered half a dozen guppies.'

By the time she dropped me in Leinster Square we had already agreed to meet on the following Sunday, to view the fish and then go on for a meal at an Indian restaurant, together with Vidar. She said he was very fond of Indian food.

Signs of dawn were already appearing in the sky and the first street cleaning trucks could be heard in

Westbourne Grove as I turned my key in the lock of number thirty two. I felt extraordinarily happy and could have burst into song. Heaven must be like this.

A Lark Arising

My supreme happiness continued during those first few months of our relationship despite the fact that Vidar seemed to be in no hurry to move from the security of Christine's all too comfortable maternal influence. My contentment was principally because I was now very nearly part of a couple and no longer felt alone. It was a feeling new to me, one that was both heartening and uplifting. Each day when I woke I felt so gratified to be part of his life that I could have soared skywards like a lark at daybreak. I never tired of simply walking the streets and parks of West London in his company and I was even happier when we scanned the columns of the first edition of the evening papers and went to look at flats together. Sometimes those showing the properties to us thought we were married and addressed me as Mrs. L'Estrange and I glowed with delight, especially when he didn't immediately correct them. He would have corrected them immediately had we been living through a different age, flat-searching fifteen or twenty years into the future perhaps. However, this was the early nineteen sixties and although the permissive society was about to explode, the general populace still frowned upon the idea of a man and a woman living together in a sinful unmarried state. It was a time when women in particular examined the hands of acquaintances for the reassuring sign of wedding rings. I soon took to wearing one, though in chunky silver rather than gold in order to further confuse. These minor elements of those early summer days were unnoticed by Vidar who was wont to ignore a great deal of what he would have termed trivia and I began to realise that he inhabited a different place in everyday life, placing himself there deliberately with the air of one anticipating a certain amount of respect from ordinary mortals.

This was not immediately apparent because he was on first acquaintance one of the most gentlemanly of males, not only holding doors open for both men and women but leaping to his feet whenever a woman entered the room, and being the first to offer assistance, no matter what it might entail, to those who looked as if they might need it. This attitude was seductive, especially to me, emerging from a different kind of background, one where men showed a great deal less concern for the feelings of females and might even be abusive.

He told me a great deal more about his family, some of the details being extraordinary and had I been less trusting I might have chosen to doubt their authenticity. But he had already talked to me at length about how deviating from the truth is never wise and those who dealt in lies were likely to come to grief. He avoided lies at all costs, he said, and that is why he especially resented questions that were too intrusive. He would rather not give a reply at all than respond with a lie. In general, he said, he followed the precepts of Eastern mysticism though he would not have described himself as a Buddhist. So when he talked to me about his family I listened with growing attention and what he said, allowing for hearsay, subjective interpretation and slight exaggeration here and there, turned out to be true.

Marie-Josephe von Carlowitz, his mother, was now in her seventies and lived in a tiny apartment in Munich. Her first marriage to a wealthy distant cousin of the Hapsburgs had ended in tragedy when the groom died whilst in Egypt on their honeymoon. In those days, Vidar explained, it was not uncommon for aristocratic young couples to go on one or even two year honeymoons in order to get to know each other. The idea was to forge a strong and close union without the distraction of outside influences. After the sad death, Marie-Josephe returned to the bosom of her family and did not expect to marry again.

Arthur Gebhard-L'Estrange had been in his sixties when they met and began the affair that led to their marriage once she had become pregnant with their older son. The couple began a nomadic life, never acquiring a proper home of their own, but living instead in a series of the grand hotels of Europe. Rollo had been born in nineteen twenty one and because of difficulties with the birth they were advised against having further children. The second pregnancy seven years later came as a shock to them and they travelled to Switzerland to consult the most eminent gynaecologist of the day who agreed to terminate it, one of the reasons being Marie-Josephe's age.

It is at this stage that the story became more complicated. Vidar said that because of the previous difficult pregnancy, there were scars and folds in his mother's uterus in which his fetal self was comfortably reclined, not anticipating the assault that was about to take place. He also managed to give the impression that protective spiritual forces were working hard on his behalf. Whether any of this is correct or not, for some reason the procedure did not work and so the pregnancy proceeded. Although Marie-Josephe in a number of frantic telephone calls to her consultant was insistent that she still felt pregnant and had experienced none of the usual signs that she was not, she was advised that it often took the body months to recover from a termination procedure, and she was not to worry because it was now quite impossible for her to be pregnant. By the time his parents realized that the celebrated gynaecologist was decidedly wrong it was too late to rectify matters and so in February nineteen twenty eight, Vidar Arthur Ewald Gebhard-L'Estrange was born.

It was a Sunday afternoon in July when he told me this story and although we were in the midst of an English summer, rain hurled itself in almost tropical fashion on the windows of Bayswater, shattering the odd silence in my first floor room. He was staring out at the downpour looking as if his thoughts were a long way away.

'All quite a shock for your parents,' I said hesitantly, not really knowing what to say.

He did not respond for a while and then said, 'Perhaps not such a shock to my mother because she told me often as I was growing up about the strange spiritual experiences she had around the time of my birth. It was quite apparent to her that my birth could not be prevented. It was mean to be.'

'For a specific purpose perhaps?' I was almost embarrassed to say such a thing, half expecting ridicule but he said in a soft voice that he was not really sure.

'Though what I do know,' he added, 'is that I stand on the shoulders of giants.'

Again I was at a loss to know how to respond. Who were the giants he referred to? It was probably not safe to ask as he clearly expected me capable of understanding the reference so I said instead, 'Not an easy position to be in.'

That appeared to be a safe response because he nodded and told me he appreciated my support.

Later, after we had returned through the rain from a spaghetti and meatballs meal in what had become our favourite casual eating place in a side street off Queensway, he returned to the story and told me that his had not been an easy childhood. Unique human beings, he explained, often have troubled childhoods. He now understood that he had not been an easy child to raise and it appeared that one of the reasons his father had abandoned the family was because he felt himself too old to cope with a difficult pre-schooler. Fifty years later, a child psychiatrist might have been consulted and a diagnosis of ADHD made followed by a daily dose of Ritalin. The marriage might very well have been saved or at the very least the boys might have been able to preserve a relationship with their father.

Vidar said that his difficulties continued when he started school and although his mother had enrolled him in the very best schools available, he was unfortunately expelled from at least three of them, well not exactly thrown out in disgrace he supposed, but it was suggested to his mother that he would do much better elsewhere. Only one headmaster had been really rude about him.

'I have never encountered such a self-willed, stubborn and aggressive eight-year-old in more than forty years of teaching,' that particular fool of a man had said. 'I do not wish to have him in my school for a day longer.'

At that point Vidar had told him what he could do with his bloody school which had embarrassed his mother and made the headmaster go purple with rage.

'A good beating would do him a world of good,' the man had advised but Marie-Josephe did not approve of beatings and they left the school immediately. He could not remember which one he was enrolled in next but apparently it was a more progressive place where he became very bored because he had to do a lot of drawing and painting and making clay models which he had no aptitude for. His mother then began to despair that he would ever learn to read and write and tried to teach him herself which was not a success. He asserted that he did not need to learn to read but she said that he most certainly did otherwise he would never be able to read books. Surely he wanted to be able to read books for himself?

He argued that there was always going to be someone to read them to him.

'Ah,' she said, 'now that you are a child that will work but what about when you are older and someone sends you a letter and you find yourself unable to read it – what then?'

Vidar told her that he would employ a secretary to read it to him.

'But what if that secretary deceives you – and reads you nonsense instead of what is really on the page?'

He told her he thought that scenario was most unlikely and indeed in that event he would have the person sacked from his employ.

As he related these events to me during those July days, I was full of admiration for the child he had once been, so sure of himself, so confident, so unafraid of the adults around him. I compared his eight-year-old self with me at the same age and shuddered. I had always been too ready to obey teachers because after all, they surely knew best. They seemed to me to be lofty individuals, from a different stratum of society, and were entitled to my deference. All those years ago, I had seen them rather in the same light as I now saw him.

He told me that his problems regarding school came to an abrupt end because he fractured his skull at the age of ten when he rode downhill on his tricycle head-first into a tree. His mother was then told that in order to recover properly he must not be subjected to any kind of stress that might make him become angry. As he was at the age of ten, still prone to frequent hysterical tantrums more reminiscent of a two-year-old, Marie-Josephe thought that the best way to proceed with his education was to hire a private tutor and once he had recovered sufficiently to concentrate, she did so. Strangely, or perhaps predictably, Vidar did much better educationally under the supervision and guidance of private tutors and for the next few years there were several of them, none abandoning him in disgust so he must have behaved acceptably. By the time he was twelve he could read and write acceptably well and do complicated mathematics very well indeed. He was also found to be musical, was taught piano and had lessons with the very best teachers of the day including the great Dinu Lipatti.

He had retained his love of music over the years and liked nothing better than to discuss his favourite performers with me and dissect their performances. Toscanini, he argued, was one of the greatest conductors the world had produced but he also greatly admired Herbert von Karajan. Guido Cantelli would have perhaps been as great as Toscanini if only he had lived and although he knew many people would disagree with him he found himself quite unmoved by Furtwangler. I had come from a world where only privileged children had piano lessons and the only classical music I had so far been exposed to was that occasionally played on Sunday afternoon radio programmes and so I simply listened to him and decided to adopt his views and preferences as my own. This meant that even years later when my musical tastes had become more developed, I was still reluctant to abandon Toscanini in favour of Furtwangler despite the fact that I now greatly admired the latter.

He told me that I should buy a record player so that we could explore music together and so of course I did. Then we went together to a shop on High Holborn to buy the kind of recordings he thought I should be listening to, Rubenstein playing Chopin and Liszt, together with Heifitz and the early recordings of Menuhin. He told me that Luisa Tetrazinni sang like an angel and so did Amelia Galli-Curci but that he did not think a lot of that Australian, Nellie Melba and so I obediently dismissed her. Thirty years on I was sorry to have deprived myself of her for so long.

I was more than anxious to make his views my own and because he felt that reading fiction, with certain exceptions, was a waste of time and effort, I largely gave it up and tried hard to read the kind of books that he read.

These concerned a woman called Alexandra David-Neel who explored Tibet and studied the religious views of the Tibetans. I found them rather dull but fortunately he was happy to explain to me everything I needed to know about the books, the writer and more importantly, Enlightenment and how to achieve it. He confided that although he himself was not yet a Fully Enlightened Being he was well on the way to becoming one. It required a great deal of meditation and contemplation and it was possible I might never achieve it myself but it would not hurt to try and he was happy to help me. And while he spoke on these matters, because I understood very little of what he told me, I daydreamed whilst trying to keep a focused and interested look on my face.

It became ever clearer that Mysticism in all its configurations loomed large in his life and featured frequently in the family stories he told me. His great-grandmother on his father's side, who came from Ireland had apparently studied magic under a famous French magician called Eliphas Levi with whom, reading between the lines, she seemed to have been having an affair. Her husband at times attempted to restrain her from her frequent visits to Paris and it caused problems between them. The Theosophical Society was, he claimed, founded at his mother's home, Castle Kuckuckstein, and Madame Blavatsky was a family friend, visiting the castle in Saxony on a regular basis. Having never heard of Eliphas Levi, and only dimly aware of Madame Blavatsky I was not as impressed as he had clearly hoped I would be.

He looked disapproving for only a moment before saying, 'Madame Blavatsky had considerable supernormal powers although I have to say that a lot of her work has been discredited – those absurd letters she was always finding that she said came from the Masters, for instance. The letters themselves were undoubtedly forgeries and not very good ones. It was she who invented the Masters in the first place of course. However much more important than that is the fact that to create or give birth to gods is in itself miraculous....'

I listened with half of my attention and he went on to explain in elaborate detail that Blavatsky was both genuine and a trickster and that most people, like his own mother for example, find themselves quite unable to understand this dichotomy. I at once tried to become more obviously observant, most unwilling to be put into the category of those unable to understand.

'My mother often discussed this apparent contradiction with my father. He would assure her that Blavatsky was not a trickster – the woman was undoubtedly genuine. She achieved the creation of the Masters as part of an important spiritual operation. Bit by bit she blew life into them.'

He stubbed out an Astoria that was in danger of burning his fingertips then immediately lit another.

'And largely she achieved what she set out to achieve,' he said. 'You know in 1890 Mathers claimed to have met one of the Masters who materialized in front of him in a London coffee house and told him the secrets on which The Golden Dawn was based.'

I had never heard of Mathers or The Golden Dawn.

He went on talking about how delighted he knew his father and Blavatsky would have been when they heard this because it meant that a host of dangerous demons would ultimately be defeated. I listened without processing anything at all. I now recall this lecture only because years later I began to have some glimmering of understanding of the attacks on Christianity that he was talking about, one of which was about to develop in the form of the hippy movement when thousands went to India in search of wisdom.

He concluded, 'Blavatsky understood only too well how Christianity makes men miserable sinners and although great thinkers like Copernicus have attacked the

Church on the basis of physics and astronomy, Blavatsky was the first to strike on a spiritual level and to this day the Church is not aware of the power of what she achieved.'

Three distinct elements appeared to dominate Vidar's life at that time and they were sex, music and philosophy and he was equally willing to talk about each in great depth and so consequently it was some time before he told me more about his brother who for the first few months he did not really speak of to any extent. However, by the end of the summer I had heard that Rollo was very famous in Europe. He had been a well-known actor but in recent years had achieved greater celebrity as a yachtsman, circumnavigating the world alone in small craft and consequently much feted. When Rollo was not on one of the world's oceans or appearing on German television shows he operated a music shop in a very pleasant lakeside town called Garmisch-Partenkirchen. Sometimes he sent money for Vidar to go and visit him which was quite pleasant but to be honest there were times when his brother bored him because he was so consumed with his own importance since he achieved notoriety. It was easy to be completely aware of the thread of resentment that ran through everything he told me about Rollo.

When he began to talk about sex I stopped half listening and began to pay more attention. I have to say that Vidar was a skillful, well-practiced lover, infinitely more proficient than most if not all of my previous boyfriends and that included the ones I had been more than a little in love with. Considering this, one might have imagined that as far as the sexual side of our relationship was concerned, there should be no problems whatsoever. However, unfortunately, that was not so because early on in the relationship he began not only to tell me that I was not as exciting sexually as he had hoped I would be, but also that he felt we should spend more time experimenting and he did not just mean with each other. He was very keen that we should take others into bed with us from time to time, both men and women and he was not terribly concerned which it should be. In fact, I could choose! When I greeted the idea with some horror he told me that my reaction was concerning and clear evidence of my sexual immaturity. If I became more sexually mature, he pronounced, I would undoubtedly become more interesting to him. If I was unprepared to work at this he thought it did not bode well for our future, especially if we were going to live together.

So I re-examined the idea in more depth and after a while I found I was prepared to try. He said he was proud of me because I had proved to him that I was open-minded and that meant that I was able to take new ideas on board. My heart sank a little.

'Where do we find these people to invite into our bed?' I asked nervously one Saturday evening when he told me that he felt the time was right to make a start on developing my sexual maturity.

He said he knew just the place and we went to a bar in Knightsbridge that he seemed very familiar with and later I realized that it was frequently primarily by gay men. This was long before homosexual law reform but places like this where men could meet in a convivial atmosphere were generally left alone by the police. It was here that we met Rene, a dress designer in his forties who Vidar told me excitedly would be exactly right because he was very keen for a sexual adventure.

He may well have been keen but it became abundantly clear that he had very little interest in me although he did the best he could. I found the whole episode rather embarrassing and it was hard to believe him when he told me he had been married at the age of seventeen to a beauty queen to whom he made love more than a dozen times on their wedding night. He insisted it had been a very romantic wedding and I tried hard to look convinced. Later Vidar told me he had been proud of me and I had demonstrated that I was more than capable of absorbing new ideas.

The good thing about the Rene experiment was that for several weeks he was sufficiently titillated by it to be quite satisfied by what was happening between the two of us as far as sex was concerned and I began to think that perhaps he had abandoned further experimentation. This, however, was not so and before long he suggested that as I had enjoyed our threesome with Rene so much perhaps we should try again, this time with a girl. And before I could ask where we were going to find a suitable girl he had whisked me into a nearby 'girls' club' in Bayswater where a series of short-haired, masculine-attired women with names like Steve and Tom danced with me and asked me why I had brought a boyfriend along with me. I was totally out of my depth because my knowledge of girls' clubs and lesbian activity was minimal and in fact on the odd occasion when I had actually come across women who wore men's clothes and adopted masculine names, I assumed that they were simply adult versions of Enid Blyton's George from the Famous Five series of books and explored the idea no further. Indeed that may have been the case but on this occasion I was required by the male they considered surplus-to-requirements to ensure that one of them went home with us. Fortunately before the end of the evening I was able to make friends with a young girl called Rabbit who said her real name was Veronica and she was more than keen to experiment. Again the situation did not work out exactly as Vidar had planned because not totally unexpectedly, Rabbit was attracted by me and not by him. However, she was basically a nice girl, surprised by her own sexuality and desperately anxious to cultivate a real girlfriend of her own. She must have had a number of setbacks to decide that I might be suitable, hindered as I was by the presence of a man very definitely in my life. For several weeks after the encounter she left flowers and gifts on the doorstep for me and invited me to go shopping for clothes with her, maintaining she wanted to develop a more feminine side.

Vidar began to exert ever more pressure and told me he wanted me to find a black lover because he would find that enormously exciting.

'I don't know any black men,' I said lamely thinking back to various boyfriends from the past and wondering where they were now.

He suggested that I could easily find somebody suitable on the street. I should approach them with confidence, telling them I had an enormous sexual appetite and would like to be with them for ten minutes or so. He said it was most unlikely I would be turned down. But there he was wrong because when I put this particular technique into operation the men concerned looked at me with horror, one even making the sign of the cross and saying he would pray for me. Later I decided he must have been a priest. Another was a rather tall schoolboy on his way home from football practice who threatened to tell his mum if I didn't leave him alone.

When Vidar would not let the subject drop I hit upon the idea of simply inventing a black lover whom I named Percy. Strangely it did not seem to occur to him that I might be lying and he told me that my sexual side was improving so much that at times he very nearly loved me. Then of course, my heart nearly burst with joy.

But the joy was short lived because it was only a day or two later that he told me that while I had been at work the previous evening he had renewed acquaintance with an ex-girlfriend called Lucy and they had ended up in bed together. He knew that with my newly acquired sexual maturity I would be very excited to think of him penetrating her. I burst into tears which surprised him and he took pains to reassure me that Lucy was nothing to him. His heart lay with me most of the time but just occasionally he needed to be revived sexually by another woman. He likened it to craving a fish-paste sandwich whilst acknowledging that his favourite sandwich filling was smoked salmon. I was smoked salmon, he said, and Lucy was simply fish paste. He was alarmed. Surely I could see that? Was I going backwards again heaven forbid?

I hastily assured him that was not the case. It was just such a surprise to find that he would want to eat fish-paste sandwiches while I was working. He looked at me doubtfully and as I wiped away the tears said that I was overly sensitive and needed counselling. Was there something in my past that made me like this, he queried. I pondered upon what I might invent to account for my odd sensitivities.

'If only you were more truly adventurous we could be absolutely right for each other.' He clutched his third strong coffee of the morning as he said this. 'But as I have said before, I really cannot cope with childish jealousies. My ideal woman is like a goddess, all accepting and acquiescent. I want you to be that woman and I know you could be her so easily. You merely need to make that leap…and in some aspects of course it is a leap of faith.'

He gently and patiently explained, not for the first time, how he could not live with envy in a relationship. A real woman is above such things and in fact aspires to be like to a deity.

I needed to work much harder at matching all those attitudes he required of me and during that period of nineteen sixty two, he partook of fish-paste at least once a week and usually told me so, and I pretended hard not to mind whilst minding very much. At the time I chose to believe that his honesty regarding this disclosure was commendable. It was years before I began to see the involved indications of sadism. Vidar at times delighted in observing the emotional pain and conflict he caused in others, particularly those who loved him most.

Happily, he had at last begun to realise that the threesomes he initially had in mind were not going to be a roaring success and one Sunday morning he told me that he thought we ought to start attending 'real orgies' now if I was agreeable. Of course I was agreeable although my heart was heavy.

'We must try to find out how we can locate these activities,' he told me. 'Surely you must meet the kind of people who would know.' Passing the responsibility onto me for finding that which would amuse him had recently become part of his mode of operation.

'Some of your customers must be interested in orgies,' he persisted. 'You won't find out unless you ask them of course.'

He did not understand how very normal and run of the mill most customers were, the glaring exception being Stephen Ward whom I had not seen for several months. I now considered whether it would be wise to introduce them. I knew they would get on like a house on fire. Stephen would be able to ensure admittance to as many group sex activities as Vidar could handle and at the same time guarantee that he met the kind of people he could have meaningful conversations with as well as name drop and boast about later if he so wished.

Nevertheless it was with some reluctance that I arranged for the three of us to have dinner together.

Troubling Deaf Heaven

Stephen was delighted to renew our friendship, and thrilled to make the acquaintance of Vidar. As I had suspected, they had a lot in common, including a preoccupation with the various features, facets and characteristics of aberrant sexual behaviour. They got along famously at once which was odd as far as Vidar was concerned because I was later to realise that generally he made it his business to dislike most of my male friends and endeavour to persuade me to dislike them also. Not so with Stephen, however and that was probably because he saw immediately that with all his connections he could provide access to the world of debauched orgiastic delights he so craved. And all this would be within a social group he was more than anxious to be accepted by. In many ways they were very similar except that Stephen leaned always towards wild exaggeration in any situation.

We met for what Stephen called a 'slumming it dinner' at Schmidt's in Charlotte Street where the waiters were known to be notoriously rude. The place had been opened by an immigrant butcher early in the twentieth century and gained in popularity over the years because although the food was cheap, it was reliably good as was the wine list. When we arrived it was, as usual on a Saturday evening, noisy and crowded but Stephen, there before us, had found a corner table away from the general hubbub and already had glasses of wine poured.

He kissed me enthusiastically on both cheeks saying, 'You naughty, naughty girl – you left Murrays without telling me where you were going. I thought I'd never see you again. I was devastated!'

We talked of trivial matters and both were pleased to find that they had some acquaintances in common, quickly getting on to the topic of what was then called, inexplicably, 'swinging'. Stephen said that since he last saw me he had made a number of new contacts in the swinging world and he would love to introduce us both to Clive, a barrister who lived in a hugely expensive house in Holland Park.

'He's got a place in the South of France too,' he told us, 'as well as an enormous estate in Scotland. His marriage broke up years ago. She was a dancer with the Royal Ballet Company and much younger than him. He gives the most astonishing parties and there are always very pretty girls there. You'll love him darlings...'

When we met Clive a week later I found that he was well acquainted with Horace Dibben and Mariella Novotny and that they and he seemed to be involved in some kind of contest with regard to who could hold the most talked-of and impressive Saturday night orgies.

Over the next few months we attended regularly in both Hyde Park Square and Holland Park, generally speaking meeting the same group of people, mostly married couples, lawyers, doctors, mathematicians and civil servants. Into these groups of outwardly staid and ordinary couples, both Clive and Stephen injected a succession of well-paid and pretty young girls selected from Murrays Cabaret Club by Stephen, or the more mysterious 'Connie's place' by Clive.

The evenings always began with drinks, in Holland Park served by Clive's manservant, together with genteel conversation following which we all sat down to dinner. One of Clive's hobbies was shooting and so his dinners featured grouse, pheasant and jugged hare served with very good wines which delighted Stephen. After dinner we immediately got down to the main business of the evening which was generally sado-masochistic sex beginning with what were called 'scenes'.

'I've got a simply sensational girl for us all tonight,' Clive said after the first of his dinners we attended. 'She is going to make a magnificent slave!'

'Oh goody,' exclaimed Stephen, clapping his hands like a small child at a birthday party.

The girl was African, thrilling Vidar who fantasised constantly about sexual encounters with black girls and was always asking me to find him one.

Her name was Lulu and she entered the room with her hands chained together, head bowed submissively.

Everyone waited to see what would happen next. I was particularly curious.

'You know what you are here for don't you?' Clive said to her.

'Yes Master, I'm to be whipped,' replied the girl.

'You are to thank me for each stroke you receive,' he instructed.

'Yes Master,' she said.

There followed a scenario that was to become very familiar to me, the girl being stripped naked and whipped across the buttocks and thanking Clive for each stroke as they got heavier and heavier. She seemed largely unconcerned, flinching only a little and later Mariella told me that she charged a hundred pounds an evening but that anyone who wished to do so could whip her.

Some of the guests did wish to do so and some, like Vidar, did not, but were anxious to engage in more orthodox activities with her. No-one was disappointed. I felt ambivalent about it all, especially Vidar's interaction with the girl but because none of the other women appeared to be similarly concerned, ultimately decided that I should follow suit and affect nonchalance. It was after all, much the same as me working in night clubs.

There was no need to be jealous. The girl had merely been hired for the evening.

Why then was I so plagued with doubts?

When, on the way home, Vidar told me that he had been thrilled with the evening, I had reason to be thankful for Lulu's presence at the party. He added reprovingly that he could not understand why I had kept my friendship with Stephen a secret for so long when I must have known they would like each other and have so many things in common. We had definitely moved forward because now that we were on the permanent swinging list, the pressure was relieved in other areas and I was no longer instructed to try to provide sexual dalliances on a regular basis with which to titillate him which was a relief. He even told me that he was pleased with the manner in which I was progressing in my sexual growth. Some of this approval had to do with the fact that when Clive invited me to become 'slave of the evening' for the next event, planned for a week or two later I agreed, although a little cautiously.

In the days preceding the event I even prayed for guidance, first in a traditional manner but God did not respond as far as I could ascertain. Then I prayed to the Virgin Mary but she too seemed to ignore me. Those in Heaven seemed to be having hearing problems and so in final desperation I sent out a general prayer to any deity that might be paying attention. None were.

The main duties of a slave were to be manacled without complaint, to be submissive principally to the men in the group, to thank he who wielded the whip and to be sure to address him as 'Master', to be able to withstand a reasonable amount of pain and to readily agree to intercourse with anyone who requested it. I was most unsure about the pain at first but it turned out to be predictable and physical pain is generally speaking a lot easier to bear than emotional pain. The initiation ceremony went without incident and Vidar was elated and told me I was coming along very well indeed. Subsequently I entered into the role of slave any time it was suggested and over the months that followed developed a reasonable immunity to the physical hurt involved. I had experienced a Rite of Passage in the dark world of sexual aberration.

That summer Michelle and I decided to leave the Jack of Clubs and take jobs at The L'Hirondelle in Swallow Street which meandered from the bottom of Regent Street through to Piccadilly. The club was owned by Turks who also ran a restaurant in the City of London and it was a very lively place. One of the reasons for the change was to try to escape the attentions of the Kray twins who had now made the Jack of Clubs one of their night spots of choice and the psychotic Ronnie's problems were not showing any signs waning.

The job move coincided with Vidar at last finding us a flat to move into which was exhilarating as far as I was concerned. Friends of his, Jessica and David Mycroft, had just bought a house in Northampton Square, Clerkenwell and were willing to rent us the top two floors. Vidar would be able to run his recording studio on the top floor and we would live on the floor below. I was hopeful that with his attention diverted towards re-establishing his business, we could spend less time at the swinging parties and perhaps even become an ordinary couple, living a more mundane life together. The day we moved was tremendously exciting and I was thrilled that at last he had moved away from Christine, whom I had still never met, but nevertheless heartily disliked. At least now I would have him mostly to myself and I was confident that our life together would improve because I was determined to become the most supportive would-be wife London had produced in a long time. I knew without doubt that the relationship was dangerously inequitable and ultimately destined to fail but I could not visualize a life without him and so, no matter how unwholesome it might become, I determined to devote myself to building a domestic base that he would value and not want to leave.

A mere week or two after the move, he began to compare me unfavourably with Christine and complain bitterly. It concerned the way I dealt with the laundry.

'My shirts are not being washed and ironed properly,' he pointed out. He was probably right. I had been using the launderette and ironing them in a rather half-hearted fashion once they had dried sufficiently.

'How should they be done?' I tried to sound genuinely disturbed though I was resentful.

'They should definitely not be sent to the launderette,' he told me decisively. 'It's so much better for the fabric if they are hand-washed and ironed whilst still damp. That's the way Christine did them for me. They are, after all, Sea Island cotton.'

It was clear that I was already failing in the area of wifely duties. I said I would try to do better.

'I was much better kept when I lived with Christine,' he added making himself sound like her pet project.

It seemed that not everything was going to immediately work out the way I had planned and quite quickly he became increasingly tyrannical.

I had commented on the beauty of some of his mother's silver, heavy knives, spoons and forks that came from Kuckuckstein and he had very self-importantly told me I was allowed to use as long as I remembered to clean them on a weekly basis. He decided I was not cleaning them well enough and forbade any further use of them which was a relief.

He became irritated if he discovered me reading a library book, or any book not on his approved reading list. I was now prohibited from doing so.

'Why?' I asked.

'Because it annoys me when I enter a room and find you simply sitting reading,' he said.

I was no longer allowed to talk on the phone if he was in the house because my 'endless chattering' also irritated him.

One of my regular customers, knowing I had recently moved and thinking I was living alone, gave me the gift of a poodle puppy, telling me it would be company for me. I was delighted because who wouldn't be thrilled with a puppy? I knew Vidar would also love him because he had often told me about the dogs he had in his life as a small boy and how attached he had become to them. In this case though he decided that if the animal was allowed to stay it had to be his dog rather than mine and also changed its name from Pepe to Puddles. Wanting the dog to remain I readily agreed and very soon Puddles realized that there was a definite pecking order and I languished somewhere around the bottom. He frequently reminded me of my place in the household with growls and little nips if he believed I had infringed his rights. After a while when we travelled in the car, the dog would not accept me being on the front seat; that was his place and Vidar supported his view.

During that first winter we lived together he told me more about his relationship with his mother who had, he said, behaved treacherously towards him.

'Nothing is as corrupt as a treacherous woman,' he said sadly, 'and my mother was capable of enormous duplicity.'

His descriptions of her sounded terrifying as he described how she had tried to control him all his life and he had the most enormous difficulty breaking free from her. The problems had begun as he had previously described, when he had tried to change courses at Trinity College in Dublin and give up medicine in favour of music. His mother felt that no matter what the difficulties, and there were a number because he had gone to Ireland speaking only poor English, he should stick to medicine and that playing the piano must be a hobby. But he was enormously drawn to music. He had appealed to an aunt in America, who was the guardian of a great deal of his father's money but she sided with his mother and refused to send him money. A further example of a treacherous woman.

His father had died in the mid nineteen fifties. He had been living in England, in a house in Devon, after many years in America where he had been in business with Aunt Eva's now dead husband. Vidar and his brother had expected to inherit the house or its proceeds but strangely his father had left everything he owned in England to the woman who had been his housekeeper for the last years of his life, Miss Mackay. She was a feckless and stupid woman and alcoholic to boot he claimed. The money from the sale of the house soon disappeared and she ended up living in a caravan on Dartmoor. Once he had visited her with Christine in an effort to get information about what had really happened in the last weeks of his father's life but she had tried to work magic upon him by gathering some of the hair from his head with a filthy plastic comb that she kept saying had belonged to his father.

'Are you sure about the magic?' I thought the idea fanciful but he said of course he was sure.

'I knew immediately why she wanted to comb my hair,' he replied darkly.

'Why was it do you think?'

He looked at me as though I was a moron. 'It's obvious. If a witch wants to work an effective spell against you she will first try to get some hair from your head, or nail clippings – they are incorporated into the hex and are very powerful. But I knew what she was up to.'

When I explored the basics of magic in some detail several years later, I found this was indeed supposed to be the case. I was in two minds about the idea until decades later the concept seemed to develop more of a reality with the advent of DNA profiling.

Now that we had a proper flat to live in, he was keen for us to entertain from time to time and give dinner parties that, if we invited the right people, might turn into orgies once the food had been consumed. I was doubtful because the facilities we had were far inferior to those sported by Hod and Mariella or Clive or Stephen or indeed any of the other people we had met in recent months. We now had a number of smart new friends such as Philip, who was a plastic surgeon and lived in a Mayfair mews house, and Stanley who was a film producer and had a large Park West apartment on Edgware Road, and Herbert a psychiatrist who was interested in magic and whose wife Lucy was a grief counsellor.

In order not to disappoint as a cook I took an intensive Cordon Bleu cookery course which I enjoyed very much and even excelled at, producing Coquilles St Jacques and Filet D'Agneau en Croute for our first dinner party. The guest of honour that evening was Clive and his girlfriend of the moment, Crystal whom I had known briefly at Murrays Cabaret Club. Happily for us all, after the meal that Clive could not stop extolling the virtues of, the evening descended into a slaves and masters game with Crystal and I sharing position of Slave of the Evening. When things went as planned Vidar was joyous of mood for more than a day or two, whistling around the place as he worked, bouncing along rather than walking, thanking me for the endless cups of instant coffee I made for him. Then I was ecstatic and imagined that his good mood would last forever and perhaps after all there was a possibility that we could become a normal couple.

The mood lasted a while when I was able to help him re-establish the business by persuading the people I was still in some kind of contact with like Stan Douglas, to provide work, to use his services rather than another's.

We were also able to arrange a great deal of work making demonstration discs for Salvation Army groups and Indian cultural groups. He was also, with my help, able to establish contacts within a number of night clubs and become responsible for the technical maintenance of their sound systems. These included Murrays Cabaret Club, The Ad Lib and Ronnie Scott's. So luckily the recording studio was bit by bit crawling back into operation again and Vidar was beginning to make a little money. This did not mean, however, that he was willing to contribute to the monthly expenses of running the flat and although the lease agreement was in his name, I was expected to pay the rent, the electricity, gas and telephone bills. I also in those first few months, paid for the mini station wagon he decided should replace his red second or third hand mini-van with. I could have refused to do so, naturally, but that would have incurred his displeasure and as I have clearly established, I was so much happier when he was content.

Even though we now had the kind of transport Vidar had wished for, he only rarely gave me lifts into the city to work and even in the winter months I still walked to the bus stop no matter what the weather was like, in the kind of heels destined to generate broken ankles. Somehow or other, I decided that was perfectly acceptable and so I did not complain. It was clear that more than a little of the masochistic expectations played out as Slave of the Evening, had rubbed off and become part of what I was becoming.

There was still a part of my persona that resented what was happening and rebelled against it fiercely and perhaps it was this he fleetingly came up against because from time to time he would tell me that I was quite impossible, that I did not want to change no matter how much I protested that I did, that instead I practiced a vicious form of passive resistance that rejected any kind of change for the better.

'You work against me always,' he maintained. 'I cannot quite put my finger on it – but your resistance to making the kind of changes that would make me happy is destructive.'

And although I tried to work out exactly what it was he meant, I was never quite able to do so because it seemed to me that he deliberately spoke in riddles when discussing how we related to each other, never allowing me to quite comprehend. Even fifty years later I can recall much of the bewilderment I felt when struggling to follow his reasoning as I tried to reach his expectations. Later the attempts to understand became ever more frantic and stained with panic as I contemplated how I would survive and face the endless years ahead without him. I was one hundred percent convinced at the age of twenty-three that I would never find a life partner who could compare with him. That at least was correct for it would be difficult to come across anyone who would match him in his egocentricity, overwhelming narcissism and desire to control those around him.

It is so effortless from where I stand at the moment, to see the many reasons why I fell precipitously in love with someone like Vidar L'Estrange. It was as if I had been searching for him or someone very like him, and so, after one or two false starts with men who were already married and basically decent, like Stan, or already married and basically criminal, like Luuk, I stumbled upon he who undoubtedly was to have the most profound influence upon my life. And he, who probably had daydreams about those as naïve and emotionally needy as I was, must have clapped his hands with glee to happen upon me via an unfortunate night club pregnancy.

Not only did I clearly see the danger signs yet studiously ignored them, those around me noted the dangers of the path I was treading.

Michelle, well versed in the emotional risks posed by associating with men who would take money from women, warned me again and again.

'He makes a good friend but it's not wise to become too emotionally involved with him. He has a nasty habit of initially putting a woman on a pedestal, then when she is safely up there, beginning to tear her down. I've seen it more than once.'

But of course I ignored her and when he suspected that she was trying to influence me he became angry and said that she could be manipulative, that I should not have too much to do with her if at all possible.

Stan, when meeting me for coffee and to hand over tapes that he wanted copied onto disc, queried the situation.

'I can't understand why you're so besotted with the guy – he's a great technician but he seems to have you totally under his thumb. You're no longer the girl I knew way back during the Veronica days. What's happened to you?'

I laughed and said he was imagining things and thought that perhaps at long last he had seen the error of his ways in ignoring my devotion to him over the years. Well, it was way too late because I was now in love with Vidar L'Estrange.

Stephen showed me his new flat and took me out for lunch at his favourite Italian restaurant in Crawford Street insisting that I let him choose what I should eat while at the same time telling me he felt that Vidar, though a lovely chap, was perhaps too dictatorial for me.

'You let him make all the decisions darling – that's not good – don't get me wrong because I really do like the fellow – he's awfully manipulative though and seems to want his own way all the time. Is he right for you do you think?'

Those comments, coming from Stephen Ward, who was an arch manipulator and in most situations quite determined that his way was the only way, were absurd but of course I did not say so but obediently ate the veal and pasta dish he had chosen for me and listened to the latest gossip about Pops Murray and his girls and how Crystal might come and stay in the new flat and that she seemed to have found herself a most unpleasant Jamaican boyfriend who was mentally unstable.

Even Jessica Mycroft, our landlady in Northampton Square, expressed concern.

'Are you sure you're happy living with Vidar?' she queried, meeting me on the stairs one afternoon when he was safely away from the area and very possibly partaking of the delights of fish-paste. 'He isn't the easiest man in the world to get along with – though he's very interesting and intelligent of course. He is also enormously kind too....'

I reassured her that I was blissfully happy and tried to avoid staircase meetings in the future though it was not easy.

Naturally enough the various comments were of concern to me, but only momentarily and what is of more concern now from the benefit of distance, is how rapidly I was able to file each conversation away into the dusty archives of consciousness. Those who tried so hard to advise me would no doubt be startled now by the clarity of my recall because I have no doubt that at the time they believed that I was only barely attentive to what was said. And so I was at the most immediate level but there was a part of my perception that was acutely aware of the fact that my attention was being drawn to a perilous situation I would be most unwise to ignore.

Work at the L'Hirondelle proved more lucrative than the Jack of Clubs although it took some time to realise that the manager, an unpleasant man who called himself Jude, expected substantial tips from the hostesses, not merely from their hostess fees but also from after club activities. Michelle said it was a nuisance but if we didn't pay him, we would be unlikely to be booked out with any regularity and of course she was correct. The floor show was on a more lavish style than that provided by the Isow family with more showgirls and no comedians. The star of the show was Josephine Blake, a tall good-looking blonde with the kind of talent that got her immediate attention. We hostesses were not required to appear in the cabaret and were merely expected to watch and loudly applaud with particular emphasis for the belly dancer who nightly snaked her way through the tables causing some embarrassment to the more conventional males.

One night a hostess called Rita who was reputed to live with a lesbian lover called Mikey, was stabbed by the customer she was sitting with. The attack took place just as Josephine Blake launched into her first number of the evening, Noel Coward's *'Senorita Nina from Argentina'*. Later she told us that it happened because the man, who ran a sheet metal business in Coventry, fell in love with her. When she told him that her heart had already been given to another, he came back the next evening to vent his frustration at the news. She was taken to the hospital and the police arrived and took the perpetrator away. Jude the manager was furious because the bill had not been paid.

It was at the L'Hirondelle that I met the most terrifying customer of my career, a good looking thirty-year-old who told me that his name was John. At first acquaintance he seemed to be as innocuous as his name. It turned out to be another of those situations where I should have heeded the advice of others.

'That man you're sitting with is a real bastard,' Carol told me as we stood side by side in the red and gold adorned toilet block, repairing our make-up. She was a small Jewish girl from Hampstead Garden Suburb who did not look as if she should be working in a night club; in fact her parents thought she worked as a night nurse in a convent. Michelle said the family were refugees from

Hitler's Germany and inclined to believe anything as long as it was sugar coated and in any case how could their well brought up daughter, happily engaged to a jeweler from Golders Green, possibly have a life they knew little of?

Now Carol repeated, 'That John is a real bastard.'

'Why on earth do you say that?' I looked at Carol curiously, patting the bouffant of my current hair-style and glaring at her through the mirror.

She paused, eye liner halfway to her face,.'Well don't listen if you don't want to,' she said.

'I am listening,' I assured her.

'Just be careful of him.' She gave a final glance in the mirror and walked back into the club.

On my way back to the table where John sat patiently, sipping from the second bottle of champagne I had managed to persuade him to buy, Sunita, a beautiful half Indian girl from Birmingham tugged at my arm and whispered, 'At the last club I worked in the girls were all frightened of that guy you're sitting with.'

I should have heeded these warnings because night club workers generally care about each other, but I decided not to because John had already given me a ten pound hostess fee, double the customary payment, and had invited me to go to Paris with him for the weekend. He would pay me one hundred pounds in cash if I agreed. I suppose I was more than eager to make the trip because I had never been to Paris and the appeal of the possible adventure was too hard to resist.

Vidar was doubtful and thought I should not have agreed to go but the thought of a weekend absence from the by now interminable Saturday night orgies was far too tempting. I told him that I might be sacked from the club if I did not go. What if John complained to the management about me?

He looked doubtful and asked, 'How much is he going to pay you for this trip?'

I lied and told him fifty pounds. Christmas was approaching and I longed to have money of my own to spend as I wished because it seemed that everything I earned was grasped somehow or other by Vidar and disappeared into his endless desires and needs.

He agreed with me that we could certainly do with an extra fifty pounds and so in some excitement I took a taxi on Saturday morning to meet John at the airport. He was charming and attentive and took me to his favourite places in the city after booking into the Ritz hotel where he said he always stayed.

'Did you know that the Ritz was one of the first hotels in the world to provide en suite services in every room?' he asked, ordering a bottle of champagne which he said we would drink before dinner. I did not know because I knew very little about the history of such places.

'And during the war the place was taken over by the Nazis – they used it as a kind of headquarters,' he added knowledgably.

He said we should have dinner sent up to our room but I was very anxious to expand the parameters of the adventure by going down to one of the restaurants and after some argument we did, where we dined on consomme and quail. It was almost like being back with Luuk once more and I reflected that life with Vidar, although emotionally rewarding, sadly did not ever include first class meals in first class restaurants.

It was not until after dinner that I began to think back to the warnings about John when he started to tell me a long and very involved story about being a kind of James Bond figure, paid by various governments to travel the world breaking up gangs of international criminals. He had consumed very little alcohol so I could not in all reality blame his change of demeanour on that. His stories concerning his own exploits became more and more wild as the night progressed and before long I realized that he had somehow or other managed to remove my passport from my bag and by three am I was being held hostage. He told me that he was unable to let me go because we were both now under surveillance from a very dangerous group of villains and that if I got up to any tricks and tried to leave he would be forced to kill me himself in order to preserve his own life. Nothing remotely like this had ever happened to me before so needless to tell, I was quite terrified. Looking back I suppose there were all kinds of things I should have done, like screaming for help, by attempting to gain authority over the telephone, etc., but I did not do so because I was by that time too frightened of him, particularly when I realized that he had left instructions for us to be left alone and so no-one came from housekeeping to perform any of the usual minor tasks that keep a hotel ticking over normally. My terror mounted as the hours went by and it was not until he fell asleep the following evening that I was able to discover where he had hidden my passport, locate the return ticket to London and make my escape. Even then I did not inform anyone at the hotel but simply left the place as quickly and quietly as possible and flagged down a taxi.

Back in London, minus the hundred pounds he had promised me because we had not got to that stage of the transaction before his deterioration of manner, I wondered what I could have done better to extricate myself. I realized that John would be far from pleased when he woke to find me gone so perhaps it would have been prudent to at least have left a note. It was Sunday evening and Vidar had gone out somewhere so at least I did not have to provide an explanation of what had happened. Instead I somehow or other found Carol's home telephone number and rang her tearfully.

'Carolotta darling there's a friend of yours who sounds upset,' her mother called out in a heavy Eastern

European accent. So this convent night nurse was Carlotta in her real life.

I urgently asked her what she knew about John and she asked me how on earth I came to find her home number. She then whispered into the phone that apparently he had a thing about locking girls up, not letting them go for hours, and telling them that he was some kind of Batman saviour of the world. Much of this was what had happened to me in Paris and so I very much regretted ignoring her first warning.

'He'll no doubt come back into the club next week and apologise to you,' she added, 'and you'll be tempted to actually believe him because he probably hasn't paid you what he promised.'

I could only agree that she was quite correct and when John did turn up a few days later, armed with flowers and having booked the best table, by the dance floor, I could not refuse to sit with him for fear of being sacked. He apologized profusely for his behaviour and gave me an envelope in which he had placed ten crisp ten-pound notes; then he begged me to give him another chance and go to Venice with him. I am ashamed to say that I was momentarily sorely tempted but wisely refused and then he grew very angry, flouncing from the building and telling the manager that I should be sacked immediately and that if I was not he would never return. Strangely, however, Jude did not react except to ensure that he had paid his bill. Later I realized that John was following Michelle's car as we drove towards the top of Regent Street where she was recently in the habit of dropping me so I could hail a cab. Instead of getting out of the car we both went on to her flat in Edgware Road where she invited me to stay the night. John's car was still parked outside several hours later when I woke early and peeped down into St Michael's Street, the narrow thoroughfare by the side of the building.

He stalked me for months, sometimes leaving flowers on the steps of the house in Northampton Square, sometimes ringing and telling me I was on his enemy's death list, and once gaining admittance to the house via Jessica and leaving a box of chocolates on the hall table. I became so anxious I left the L'Hirondelle and took a job in The Latin Quarter nightclub close to Leicester Square and later Michelle followed me saying that he had started stalking her simply because he knew she was a friend of mine. It did not occur to either of us to make a complaint about this behaviour to the police because we were only too aware that our career choice would have simply resulted in a great deal of merriment and very little action on our behalf. We put up with it and simply hoped that he would stop and after some months he did.

The Latin Quarter was at the time owned by the five Tolaini Brothers who had put in the wily Peter Benava, said to be of Greek origin, as their manager. The place was a great deal larger than the previous places I had worked in, and the twice-nightly cabaret was on at least as lavish a scale as Murrays. We were not required as showgirls unless someone was sick, in which case those of us deemed to fit the costumes and have the best legs were called upon to perform and expected, what's more, to somehow know the dance routines because we had watched them regularly twice each evening from Monday to Friday. Sometimes this worked and sometimes it didn't but as the stand-ins were placed at the back of the regular performers not too much harm was done. The regular dancers who considered themselves a cut above the hostesses were very unfriendly and unhelpful under these circumstances but Michelle believed that if we threatened them a little with the idea of retribution if they did not drop the nonsense and become more co-operative, it generally helped. I tried it once and she was correct. I realized that they were easily intimidated and like many people thought of hostesses or any woman involved in the sex for sale business, as somehow differing from normal human beings and therefore capable of any act of infamy.

As new girls to the club we were at once popular and although part of me hankered after the attention being a showgirl brought, there was more money to be made as a hostess and by Christmas I had made enough to finance Vidar's upgrade of some of his basic equipment which made him very happy. The more negative aspect of the place was that it had become a firm Friday evening favourite of various criminal elements such as the Krays, still trying to extend their business interests, and the Richardsons, a notorious South London gangland family whose commercial ideas at that time seemed to mirror those of the Krays and who resorted to organized torture when thwarted. This at times made for a certain amount of unease in the place because although the normal run of the mill customers were blissfully unaware of the undercurrents, hostesses, waiters and bartenders were only too conscious of it as were the Tolaini brothers themselves, welcoming both groups effusively but seating them on opposite sides of the room.

It was to the Latin Quarter that Reggie Kray brought his bride-to-be Frances Shea on her birthday and when she appeared to be embarrassed rather than delighted as the band played Happy Birthday, grasped her by the shoulders ordering her to enjoy herself because that's what he had brought her there for.

'You miserable looking cow – enjoy yourself or I'll knock your bleeding teeth down your throat.'

And so Frances obediently put a look of bliss on her face and settled in to thoroughly enjoy the evening.

Despite the obvious warning signs that theirs was not going to be a marriage made in heaven, after a number of postponements she married him a year or so later and after some months committed suicide which neither of the twins could understand.

'What did she want to go and do that for?' Ronnie was deeply shocked as he helplessly observed his brother's grief. 'Frances had everything a woman could wish for. He treated her like a princess my brother did.'

No matter how we tried to avoid sitting with the twins or indeed the Richardsons, if we were not already booked out, when they descended the stairs into the place we were only too aware that protesting was not acceptable. We knew better than to actually ask them for money but on a number of occasions they were generous. Once seated with them it was prudent to be pragmatic and as charming as was humanly possible. The next tour de force was to avoid accompanying them anywhere once all the champagne had been consumed and the club began to close. It seemed that the Krays in particular always had a party to go to at which they required female company but the night of the gun demonstration in the warehouse was still fresh in my mind and I was emphatic in my anxiety to avoid a repeat performance.

My story was that although I now lived in London, my mother, in Gravesend, was still very unwell and therefore as often as possible I went down to see her after work, particularly on Fridays. And predictably Reggie, who liked my company, said that he understood entirely. The unfortunate consequence was that on several occasions he hired a taxi and paid the driver to take me the twenty-two miles to Gravesend. Once I ascertained that the drivers were not regulars for the twins, I extricated myself from the situation south of the river and we turned back towards Clerkenwell. Once, however, the pensioner Fitch was instructed to drive me personally and I found myself abandoned in New Road, Gravesend outside a suitable looking house with the added problem of him suggesting I make him a cup of coffee. Once he realized no coffee was forthcoming, and left, I walked around to the station and waited for the first train back to London. All this was inconvenient but infinitely preferable to ending up somewhere in East London with a Kray who might have a loaded gun in his pocket.

The approaching Christmas seemed significant for Vidar and for me because it would be the first together in our own home. I planned a tree and coloured lights and thought deeply on what to cook on Christmas Day. Vidar himself suggested that as Michelle would be alone we should ask her to share our festivities and so we did. The day before Christmas Eve, after work, she and I went to Smithfield Market to buy a goose and although it was tempting to buy a traditional bird, complete with head and feathers, to pluck and gut ourselves, we opted for an oven-ready version instead.

We exchanged presents on Christmas Eve in the German tradition and I still have the china pig moneybox, his sides emblazoned with 'Immoral Earnings' that Michelle gave me. I gave Vidar a new leather wallet and matching cigarette lighter because it was years before we all gave up smoking. He gave me an Indian book about how to become the perfect woman and also a tiny Steiff teddy bear because he knew how much I loved them. It is hard to describe the magnitude of my happiness that Christmas. It was as if all the gods had paid heed to my prayers and were smiling upon me in unison.

Once With Friends Possessed

It becomes difficult now to recall with any accuracy when we were first aware of what became known as The Profumo Affair. The fact that men in positions of power and authority, like John Profumo, had relationships from time to time with girls like Christine Keeler, was unremarkable. The fact that they had been brought together and their relationship orchestrated by Stephen Ward, was even more unremarkable because that's what Stephen did so very well. He delighted in the introduction of pretty girls to influential men and he gossiped endlessly about the results of such liaisons. It seemed a harmless pastime and it ensured his popularity. Stephen liked so very much to be popular.

As the drama unfolded frantic Chinese Whispers were exchanged between his associates and acquaintances that over the weeks became more and more embellished and exaggerated.

'Were you at the party Hod and Mariella gave where that awful girl's boyfriend arrived with a gun?'

'Have you heard that Stephen is going to be charged with treason?'

'Did you know that Stephen introduced Clive to Enoch Powell?'

Within a short space of time there was an uneasy hiatus in the general Saturday evening romps and revelries as some individuals were selected for police questioning regarding certain charges that might be brought against Stephen Ward, and consequently his former friends and their friends began to distance themselves both from him and from each other. Holidays were hastily arranged and the swingers of West London fled to New York, Paris or Rome for extended periods.

Vidar and I could not afford a sudden holiday and luckily we were not selected for investigation but we anxiously scanned the newspapers daily in an attempt to discover exactly what point the police probing had reached and whether the whole business was likely to blow over. It did not and eventually at a preliminary hearing at Marylebone Magistrates Court Stephen was charged with a range of improbable misdeeds which included living off immoral earnings, procuring, keeping a brothel and performing an abortion. Most of his wrongdoing was further described in such vague detail as 'introducing young women to men for the purpose of sexual intercourse.'

Try as they may, the investigators failed to make any of the girls under the age of sixteen and as sexual intercourse was not in itself against the law, it was hard to take any of this too seriously. As for the idea of him living off immoral earnings, we were all totally aware that the girls who took advantage of Stephen's unfailing hospitality, often lived on his benevolence for months. Even so, those who had for years availed themselves of what his friendship offered, now were reluctant to count him even among their most casual acquaintances.

Vidar decided that we too could no longer afford to be seen as supporters and we should wait to see what was looming at the Old Bailey case and furthermore, in the interim we should attend no more of the swinging parties. As no-one was hosting them this was quite easy to achieve. It was not long, however, until his craving for sexual titillation led us into what I saw as far more hostile situations.

He thought it might be fun to spend the occasional evening on Hampstead Heath, with me only partially clothed and attempting to attract voyeurs. Then when we had attracted them he and I should have sexual intercourse for their general entertainment and gratification. And so, clad only in a flimsy negligee I found myself trailing over the heath on a particularly windy and cold Saturday followed by a procession of shifty-looking men armed with cameras. It was not a successful interlude and even Vidar agreed that it might be better for it not to be repeated. He then suggested picking up hitchhikers on the motorway whilst I sat topless in the seat beside him. Their sexual curiosity would be aroused, he thought, and then the three or four or even more of us would be able to indulge in some kind of happening that would be very exciting all round. This idea was not destined to work out terribly well either because most of the hitchhikers were quite bewildered by what they had encountered and some positively terrified.

I began to yearn for the good old days of straightforward Saturday swinging where I was obliged only to turn up, make pleasant conversation, eat good food, be manacled, whipped or caned and make myself available for straightforward sex. Generally speaking the people involved were pleasant, the hosts more than generous and from time to time I had actually met people I became moderately friendly with like Kathy the TV cook and Wendy the wife of the producer of horror movies.

Vidar was invariably suspicious when I became too friendly with other women and questioned me closely about what we had got up to and talked about if we met for coffee or for lunch. He particularly distrusted Kathy the TV cook probably because she was astute and made it clear that she did not like him very much. However, he never actually prevented me from meeting them because he was always hoping that I would one day suddenly develop my lesbian side, whilst not losing my heterosexual side altogether. He desperately longed to possess a woman who would bring home others she was anxious to sleep with. And, though there seemed to be some dichotomy involved, these women would somehow or other become more than eager to welcome Vidar between the sheets for a glorious threesome.

He still regularly saw his own friends of both sexes and some of them I was never introduced to and not allowed to ask questions about. For the sake of day to day equilibrium I had learned not to upset him by showing too much curiosity. He rewarded my restraint by telling me that I was at last beginning to grow into a real woman but added that the transition was slow.

It was a summer filled with anxiety as everyone who had known Stephen waited for the outcome of the trial. From time to time there were telephone conversations between his former friends, always cached in obscure terms because there was more than one rumour afoot that phones were being tapped. Those of the main players who had avoided being called as witnesses wisely stayed away from England until the whole sorry business was over, occasionally making long distance calls to check upon progress.

Stephen Ward committed suicide on 30th July before the Judge had finished his summing up of the case. He realized that he was going to go to prison and he could not face it. The shock and astonishment echoed through West London on a thousand telephone lines.

'Bloody idiot,' said Clive, ringing in from somewhere near Cannes.

'No backbone at all,' observed the psychiatrist whose back had been manipulated by Stephen on a regular basis and for whom he had provided a monthly tonic in the form of an attractive underwear model from Milan.

'Nice to have the whole thing over and done with,' the horror film producer observed cautiously.

Slowly people began to drift back into London and meet just for drinks and cagey chats about what had happened.

Clive even gave a daring 'Remembering Stephen' party where a great deal of champagne was drunk followed by a moderate dinner after which each guest said a little about Stephen and their relationship with him. Wisely no manacled slave was hired for the event and it turned out to be quite a sombre affair.

Vicky, one of Clive's current favourites, had lived with Stephen when she first came to London from North Wales.

'I remember him as being one of the kindest men I ever knew,' she said, 'I mean, he really did care about people and want to help them.'

Then she burst into tears, followed by several of the other women present, including me.

'Perhaps we should have made more of an effort for him,' ventured someone which suggestion was ignored in the hasty kerfuffle involved in the pouring of more champagne.

Vidar did not seem to feel guilty about the way we had joined the herd and fallen away when Stephen was in most need of emotional support. I could not feel the same and wished I had shown more courage.

I was still in the throes of grief and misery about his death in early August when my new friend Rosalind and I came too close for comfort to the Great Train Robbery.

Rosalind had recently joined the hostess staff at the Latin Quarter and brought with her a number of her regular clients from previous workplaces so she immediately became popular with the manager, Peter Benava. On this particular evening we had been booked with a group of motor dealers from Buckinghamshire who insisted we accompanied them back to a late night party at an impressive house near Aylesbury. It seemed a long way from Gerrard Street, Soho but we were to be well paid and so we agreed and were finally able to leave the party after six in the morning to find the surrounding countryside teeming with police.

The robbery involved huge sums from a Royal Mail train heading from Glasgow to London at Bridego Railway Bridge near Mentmore. The fifteen-strong gang headed by Bruce Reynolds attacked the train after tampering with the line signals. We were half familiar with some of the robbers such as Gordon Goody, Buster Edwards, Charlie Wilson, and Ronnie Biggs because they were habitual club goers. It was said later that the gang got away with over two million pounds (almost fifty million today) and the greater bulk of the money was never recovered. Strangely enough no firearms were involved though Jack Mills, the train driver was beaten over the head with a metal bar, the injuries being severe enough to incapacitate him for life.

As we drove the country lanes we were stopped again and again by police.

'They must realise we're drunk,' Rosalind observed, drunkenly easing the car forward after the third time a posse of officers shone torches on us, opened the boot, asked our names, where we were going and where we had come from then signaled us on. Neither of us could understand why they abruptly became so uninterested in us. Later we learned that after the robbery the gang hid out at Leatherslade Farm which was just a hop, skip and a jump from where we meandered through the Buckinghamshire lanes. Their journey back to the farm took them along the same minor routes Rosalind and I navigated so drunkenly. They reached the farm about an hour after the robbery when the first reports of the crime were being made. Apparently they immediately counted the proceeds and divided it into shares and they listened to their police tuned radio, learning that the authorities realized they had gone to ground within a thirty mile radius of the crime scene.

Apparently they had taken the precaution of arranging for someone to come to the farm once they left to burn it to the ground but this did not happen and ultimately this failure was their undoing.

Rosalind said a day or two later that was a great pity and if we'd known we could have offered to do it for them. Someone had told her how much the failed arsonist had been paid. She was outraged on the gang's behalf.

'It wasn't as if we weren't in the area,' she said.

The newspapers had got the story very early and over the following weeks it became the talk of the West End, almost edging the Profumo Affair to the sidelines, glasses being raised in cocktail bars all over Soho and Mayfair in honour of the robbers. As the weeks passed and the train raiders seemed to have somehow slipped through the cracks of the frantic investigations, their names were spoken more reverently. Those who had barely passed them on a club staircase or stood beside them in the urinal, now claimed much closer acquaintance with a certain amount of pride.

'I knew old Brucie Reynolds when he was just a boy,' said an elderly would-be associate as he propped himself up on the bar of the Latin Quarter's upstairs cocktail lounge.

'A right tearaway he was then – but always a good side to him, you know. I used to see him of a Saturday morning taking the dog for a walk.'

'Buster and me went to school together,' confided someone else from the other end of the bar and as the weeks passed Ronnie Biggs gathered more and more close friends that his life had once briefly touched.

As the months progressed the Swingers of West London cautiously began to occasionally resume their previous activities which to me was almost a relief.

The absence of the regular gatherings had created weekend islands of monotony for Vidar and I watched anxiously as he began to turn his attention to experimenting with drugs. He was careful not to indulge too directly himself but liked to observe the reactions and behaviours of those to whom noxious substances had been given. Invariably I was always first to be selected.

It started innocently enough with marijuana, of which he had no fear and even smoked a little himself. However, he always wanted me to smoke a great deal, inhale deeply and became angry when I resisted.

I was not exactly afraid of marijuana but I did not like the effect it had on me and was anxious to avoid too much of it.

'This is just another example of you working against me,' he said. 'A further example of your passive resistance – it is quite pernicious.'

And when he said things like that I always hastily rethought the situation and in this case decided that there were far worse things than marijuana and so I obediently began to inhale deeply, wishing I had done so when he first produced it because by then it had become too late to reverse his irritation.

'You always, *always* have to be pushed before you will obey me,' he said, 'then by the time you do what I have asked of you all the joy in it is lost – why is it you do not seem to understand this. Do you actually enjoy spoiling any small pleasure I have?'

And then I would more than likely begin to cry and he would say I was making a scene and ensuring that his life was totally miserable and he wished he could get rid of me.

Contemplating life without him was too painful to consider for more than a moment or two. I fervently wished I could become more obedient.

However, when he produced some LSD a week later I was less than enthusiastic about trying it. This was at a time when the adventurous and liberated all over the city were experimenting with the drug and wild stories of what happened whilst they were under its effect terrified me.

'You will be totally protected,' he assured me, 'because I will take care of you and make sure nothing unpleasant happens.'

But I still did not want to try it. Not because I did not trust him to ensure my physical safety but because I was afraid of the disturbance of thinking that would inevitably take place. No-one could protect me from that.

Again he was angry and once more accused me of always undermining his plans and spoiling things for him. Yet again I cried and vowed to try to do better.

A few days later I found myself in the position of coming under the influence of the drug unintentionally when he delivered it on a sugar lump into a cup of coffee and of course I should have been suspicious in the first place when he offered to make the coffee. Making coffee was nowadays my job.

There followed thirty-six hours where I dwelt in a twilight place floating from one hallucination to another, some of them pleasant but most disturbing, even terrifying. At some stage he took me out and we drove around the city. When I got out of the car to walk a little I imagined that I could stop the buses as they hurtled by simply by touching them with one finger.

Years later I developed Temporal Lobe Epilepsy and some of the auras I experienced were similar in nature, at times pleasurable and amusing but more often distressingly chilling.

When he gave the matter of the LSD incident some thought he said that overall I had behaved well and that he was pleased with me but nevertheless he could not forgive me for forcing him into deception. It had not been his first choice to administer the drug surreptitiously.

'I do not enjoy engaging in dishonesty,' he said, 'but when you are so persistently obstinate you force me to do so.'

How did he come to that conclusion? I hesitantly sought an explanation.

'How is it that I force you?' I asked then added hastily, 'Because I really don't want to be the sort of person who forces you into behaviour you find uncomfortable – I want to be a different kind of person, really I do.'

He looked at me gloomily and gulped the coffee I had just made. I sipped mine, now safely sugarless.

'You say you want to change and I always half believe that you do. But although you understand perfectly what would make me happy you constantly work to destabilise my happiness. When you decide you are not going to try something like LSD for example, you leave me with no alternative but to administer it to you by deception, and that is something I really dislike doing I can assure you.'

I understood perfectly by that time.

'I'm sorry,' I said and we both sat in silence.

Of course I knew I was involved with a man whose thinking deviated substantially from that which could be considered normal but he had told me on innumerable occasions that he was not a normal human being. In any event, whether he was normal or abnormal, my passion for him had become an obsession and there was always the chance that at some stage in the future he might change and become more ordinary. I would be there to support him if and when that happened.

In that hiatus before the swingers resumed their partying, I encouraged him to tell me more about his spiritual beliefs and how he had moved towards them. He spoke of Occult Philosophy and Magic and reminded me that there had been a great deal of interest in these matters on both sides of his family. He talked about a book his father had written concerning the great truths that lie in fairy tales and legends. I asked if he had a copy of it but he said he did not and that in fact it would be very difficult to find a copy if indeed one still existed although decades later his son found two for sale via the internet and bought them both, reading them from cover to cover.

As we spoke further about magic I began to wonder if I could change him by using those forces we discussed but abandoned the idea when he emphasized how dangerous magic could be.

'All thoughts have a tendency to materialize,' he said seriously. 'That is why magic undoubtedly works but it is also destructive and can rebound and do enormous harm to the person performing it. Great care must be taken to put protective barriers in place.'

How did these barriers work and where could I find out more about them?

'The protection exercises are far from easy to understand,' he told me, 'let alone put into practice. I doubt very much if someone like you could develop the capacity to utilize them.'

I was suitably admonished. What made me think that someone like me would ever be able to rise to the lofty heights of someone like him?

'Magic is both powerful and magnificent,' he explained, 'but it can go wrong and do great harm.'

It was at this time he first began to claim to now be a Fully Enlightened Being and I had little idea of what that happy state entailed and when exactly he had finally achieved it. He talked about the last Buddha and how to reach a full understanding of knowledge and I came to grasp a little more, enough to realise that the state he spoke of would never be something I would personally have to grapple with. Life as a Fully Enlightened One was clearly not easy and demanded a great deal of innate ability to absorb and process unusual information. If human intelligence was what was needed then I was never going to make the grade. He explained more about the path along which he had struggled in order to achieve his present state of knowledge and said that although it had awarded him power so that he could recognize evil when he came across it, that had not made the journey much easier. He now leaned further and further towards Eastern Mysticism and as this had become more pronounced he had developed something akin to a permanent state of hatred for the Catholic Church, hurling abuse at Jesus Christ in particular but saving most of his odium for 'that harlot, Mary, Mother of God.'

As a lapsed Catholic who had at one time more than toyed with the idea of life as a nun, I found this rather shocking. Like most Catholics, I waited in trepidation for the thunderbolt of retribution that would imminently strike him and when it did not eventuate I was just a little surprised. One way and another he was instilling a great deal of fear into me.

I decided to leave the Latin Quarter and took a job at the newly opened Bal Tabarin in Hanover Square, the latest venture of Paul Raymond. Michelle and Rosalind joined me a week or two later. The club had opened in a blaze of publicity with waitresses dressed as Bunny Girls serving drinks and meals to customers. There was a great deal of confusion regarding the Bunnies initially because the customers viewed them in the same way as they viewed the hostesses and propositioned them for sexual services. For the duration of the life of the club there were ongoing misperceptions about their function and at the same time justifiable resentment from The Playboy Club in Park Lane where Bunny Girls reigned supreme and the clientele was less confused.

Another of Paul Raymond's innovations for the club was to hire some hostesses who had never worked in night clubs previously, presumably because he thought they brought with them a degree of inexperience and virtue that he liked the idea of. He was said to have been at one time a rather religious man.

Shirley and Alma were housewives from Harrow, neighbours in fact and how they came to apply for jobs at the place remained a mystery. They explained to the rest of us that both the manager and Mr. Raymond understood that they would not taint their marriage vows by sleeping with customers for money, but had been hired purely for hostess duties. If they happened to sit with a person who required extra services then they would pass him on to one of the rest of us. We undoubtedly resented them just a little as they sat at the prime table by the dance floor in their housewifely best, the radiance of righteousness hovering about them.

However, our resentment was short lived because within a few weeks they left the place without explanation.

'Well those two didn't last long,' observed Rosalind with satisfaction. We all nodded agreement.

When the club first opened it was very popular with full tables most evenings but as the months went on it waned in popularity and eventually one evening we arrived at work to find the place had burned down after closing on the previous evening. The fire had started in the kitchen apparently and what a few of us had noticed was that at closing time, Paul Raymond was strangely still in the place in earnest conversation with his manager whom we only knew as Johnnie.

I promptly applied for a job with Freddie Mills in his newly opened establishment and was amazed to be greeted and interviewed by Shirley the housewife, now hired by Mills as his Head Girl. Shirley had somehow or other in a very short space of time become adept at running the floor, booking out other hostesses, and quizzing them as to whether they were willing to do extra business after hours. She was still married, living in Harrow and nicely paying off her mortgage. Her friend, Alma, she told me, had found the job did not suit her. She could not fit it in around the demands of her two-year-old and the criticism from her husband.

Freddie Mills was a retired boxer, in fact he had been the British light heavyweight champion for a number of years. Upon his retirement he became an actor, appearing in a number of films and also television shows. He had a large number of contacts from the world of boxing and show business, and it turned out later, from the criminal underworld too, so perhaps it wasn't a great surprise when he turned his attention to running a club, The Freddie Mills Nite Spot, in the nineteen sixties. The premises had been a Chinese restaurant for some years previously and being at the top end of Charing Cross Road, was in a prime position.

The place was distinctly different from others I had worked in so far. The clientele was made up of men who clearly did not have expense accounts and who were much less inclined to buy champagne or pay hostess fees. However, it was busy and there was money to be made if we were prepared to drink brandy. I thought I might easily be able to manage brandy night after night but it did not take long for me to discover that it was impossible and I found myself becoming far too affected by it. At other places it had been relatively easy to dispose of superfluous champagne on the carpets or into the pot plants but it never seemed quite as easy to get rid of the brandy that way. There were no pot plants and possibly the clientele was more attentive.

I left the Nite Spot without a backward glance when I heard that the old Bal Tabarin premises in Hanover Square was shortly to be taken over by Danny La Rue and that he would be employing hostesses. I only gave Freddie Mills further thought when he was found dead in his car at the back of the premises a year or so later. Shortly afterwards I was told that the police were calling for all his former employees to come forward for questioning. I did not respond to the appeal.

A number of rumours began to circulate about him. Initially his death had been thought to be a suicide brought about because he was getting into financial difficulties businesswise. The club had still been busy most evenings when I left the place but later its popularity had waned.

Some began to say that he had been killed by a Triad who were determined to regain the prime site and turn it back into a Chinese restaurant. That seemed unlikely.

Others said that although he was married with several children, he was secretly homosexual and had been found accosting men in a public toilet and was about to be charged with indecency. I found that hard to believe also.

Lola, who had worked with me there, said that he had been in love with the singer Michael Holliday, and had killed himself on account of Michael's recent death. She then added that she had been reliably told that Freddie had also been having an affair with Ronnie Kray. The twins had at times been much in evidence at the club and the idea of someone choosing death over a close relationship with Ronnie Kray was at least easier to believe.

Lola knew a little about the inner workings of life as a criminal's consort having been closely associated with one of the notorious Nash brothers, overlords of North London, for a number of years. He finally allowed her to leave him when she gave birth to their now six-year-old daughter she told me, and then related a number of chilling stories about the child successfully threatening others at her Islington primary school by maintaining she would 'get her Dad to sort them out.'

Even allowing for exaggeration the idea of the one-time prize fighter being driven to despair over a tangled liaison with a criminal lover was compelling.

Then the police perhaps predictably decided that because of the angle of the bullet wound, Mills' death was definitely a murder rather than a suicide and both the

Triad and the Krays were prominent in discussion once again. Finally it was suggested that Mills might be the serial killer 'Jack the Stripper', responsible for the deaths of eight women whose bodies had been found on or near the banks of the Thames over the previous few years. That also seemed less than likely although someone had to be responsible and there has never been a believable explanation for the crimes. The women were all prostitutes and their deaths were to throw a shadow over all of us in the sex industry over the next year or so when shocked workmates claimed connection to one or two of them.

Hannah Tailford was thought to be the first victim, found early in February nineteen sixty four, near Hammersmith Bridge. She had been strangled and several of her teeth were missing, a feature of a number of the subsequent crimes.

Irene Lockwood was found a couple of months later, close by and it was then that police decided they might be looking for a serial killer.

Frances Brown from Edinburgh was discovered in an alleyway and had been with a friend when she was picked up by the man believed to be her killer. The friend, Kim Taylor, was able to give a detailed description of both him and his car.

Helen Barthelemy, from Blackpool was found just a week or two later in an alleyway in Brentford.

In July Mary Fleming from Scotland was discovered in a Chiswick street and not long afterwards Bridie O'Hara, in a storage shed on a nearby trading estate.

It was then that the crimes began to be linked to others from previous years. Elizabeth Figg had been found in Chiswick as long ago as June nineteen fifty nine and Gwynneth Rees more recently in November nineteen sixty three.

Chief Superintendent John Du Rose was put in charge of the case and interviewed thousands of suspects before holding a news conference making the statement that the suspects had been narrowed down to a mere twenty, later changing that to ten. After the news conference Freddie Mills was found dead and the crimes inexplicably stopped.

Girls we worked with claimed to have known Hannah Tailford and Frances Brown and both were connected in a peripheral way to the Profumo Affair. I could not recall either of them but was told that they had been involved in Stanley the film producer's side-line of pornographic movies. I was only half aware that he had a side-line and still question the validity of this statement because this was a time when a lot of things were said that turned out not to be entirely accurate.

The resemblance to the Ripper killings of the previous century was uncanny. The Stripper's reign of terror had ceased quite suddenly and there were few clues to keep the investigating team busy. Of course Du Rose had a favourite suspect, a Scottish security guard called Mungo Ireland. Ireland appeared to be a respectable married man in his forties but he had become a suspect shortly after Bridie O'Hara's murder when flecks of industrial paint were traced to the Heron Trading Estate where he was a security guard. Shortly afterwards he committed suicide but although he remained a strong suspect as far as Du Rose was concerned, it was later found that when O'Hara was killed he had actually been holidaying in Scotland and therefore could not have been involved.

TV's Crime and Investigation Channel in a programme called 'The Dinenage Murder Casebook' theorised that the killer could have been Harold Jones, a convicted murderer from Wales. He apparently killed two young girls in nineteen twenty one when he was only fifteen. He received a life sentence and was released twenty years later. He apparently turned up in West London many years later. It was true that all the Stripper murders had similar features to his earlier crimes but he was never considered as a possible suspect. Indeed, although he had killed as a teenager there was no evidence that he was a psychopath or that he led anything other than an exemplary life after being released from prison.

Although the finger of suspicion finally pointed towards Freddie Mills, there seems to be no hard evidence that would keep it there and in the final analysis it seems almost as unlikely as him being a closet homosexual.

There is no doubt that sudden violent death was closely linked to world I now worked within and when young women like those previously discussed, are brutally slaughtered, it of necessity clouds every after hours transaction and enforces an unpleasant climate of apprehension and mistrust. So we all waited with growing anxiety for the crimes to be solved and they never were.

Despite all the anxiety, however, during those years I was only truly familiar with one victim of murder. Hazel from Wolverhampton, who had worked in both the Bal Tabarin and the Latin Quarter, was found dead in her Paddington flat early in nineteen sixty four, strangled with her own bra. The killer was later discovered to be not a client as we had all suspected, but a visiting boyfriend who was later found not far away at Paddington Station, collapsed in tears and vowing his eternal love for her. All of us who had known her breathed a sigh of relief for it is as unnerving to come up close to murder as it is to rub shoulders with the compelling social forces that trapped and cornered poor Stephen Ward causing him to choose to die rather than go to prison.

It takes years to recover from such episodes.

An Audience With Madam Sandra

Moving into the employ of Danny La Rue at his newly opened club in Hanover Square proved to be a sound decision and Danny turned out to be an ideal employer. I could not honestly say that I liked the club manager very much. Bill Biem was German, an uncompromising man who did not like hostesses. When Danny took over the premises that had previously housed the Bal Tabarin until the sad fire, he brought Bill with him from Bruce Brace's Winston's Club in Mayfair where they had both worked for six or seven years.

Danny was born in Cork in 1927 and was the youngest of five siblings. The family moved to England when he was six or seven and he was brought up in Soho where his mother was a seamstress. During the blitz the building where they lived was destroyed and the family moved to a village in Devon, a quite different way of life. It was there that he apparently developed his first interest in dramatics. Later he said that because there were not enough girls in the village drama group he always got the pick of the roles, claiming that his Juliet was most convincing. Later he served in the Royal Navy, following his father's footsteps thereafter developing his skill as a female impersonator.

Among his celebrity impersonations were Elizabeth Taylor, Judy Garland, Marlene Dietrich and Zsa Zsa Gabor. We saw all of these and more in the nightly cabarets which were quite sensational and the most entertaining I had experienced to date. Twice-nightly floor shows that don't change for six months are often tedious to sit through night after night but Danny's never were. This probably had something to do with the fact that his back-up staff were as talented as himself with Ronnie Corbett and Barbara Windsor also permanent fixtures when I was there, together with some outstanding comedy writers.

As a female impersonator Danny was aware that the club could easily descend into a haunt for gay men and women and he worked hard to ensure that the reviews were special enough to attract a wide audience. He was immediately successful and the place rapidly became the most popular night club in London, filled to capacity night after night.

The clientele provided opportunity for good money to be made and it seemed that the people who visited the place were more than prepared to invest heavily in the experience, easily acquiescing to multiple bottles of champagne, meals, night-dresses, teddy bears, cigarettes and hostess fees. A great number of them were also keen to arrange after hours assignations also.

The many visitors included a range of celebrities such as Judy Garland and her daughter Liza Minelli, who on two or three visits readily consented to join the floor show and sing along with Danny. Another frequent attendee was Rudolf Nureyev, comparatively newly-defected, and so exquisitely handsome that our hearts fluttered as we willed him to ask for a female companion, which he never did.

When the cigarette girl was absent from duty, Danny decided that as I fitted the costume, I should sell cigarettes for the evening and unlike my previous experiences in the role, I found that at Danny's I received more than generous tips and gentle queries as to what I might be doing later from those with leg fetishes. Of course I took advantage of every opportunity.

One evening I sold cigarettes to Paul McCartney and his then girlfriend Jane Asher who were quietly sitting at a corner table together, unnoticed because it happened to be one of the evenings when Judy Garland was also present. Although he looked vaguely familiar it was only later that I realized who he was when several of the other girls told me how much they had envied me.

It was at Danny La Rue's that I met Dennis Crane, a businessman from Manchester, involved in machine tools, who fell in love with me and gave me a monthly allowance of two hundred pounds for the next several years as long as I was always available to be at his disposal when he made his monthly trips to London. As he only stayed two days on each occasion, I happily acquiesced. Of course I soon began to regard his visits as an intrusion into my life, which is always the way with such an arrangement although I was later to wish that I had treated him better when he transferred his affections to Michelle who had the good sense not to alienate him.

I still look back on my time at Danny's with enormous affection which is more than I can say for some of my other workplaces. This was in a small way also due to the fact that in other areas my life seemed to be improving. Vidar was no longer intent on feeding me hallucinogenic drugs every weekend, or insisting that we trawl the motorways in search of the sexually obsessed. The swinging parties had now resumed although it must be said in a rather more decorous manner than previously. Without Stephen's influence they were less frenetic and less interesting and Clive began to fill his place though effecting the job rather differently it must be said. Where Stephen had much of the time relied upon charm and persuasion to encourage girls to attend and so impress his friends though following up with money if all else failed, Clive more sensibly perhaps relied on straight business transactions.

It was probably more practical in the long run because there was no place for feelings to be hurt or misunderstandings to occur. The invited guests, particularly the males, were just as happy to turn up and just as dazzled by the charm and enthusiasm of the young women they were introduced to. More importantly as far as I was concerned, Vidar was happier than I had seen him for a long time, delighted by the array of beautiful women he was allowed to sexually interact with. Furthermore, at least I knew what he was doing and with whom.

Shelagh and Maggie had long since returned to London, the latter now married almost happily and living with her market trader husband in East London with three children, two-year-old Trinity and three-month-old twins Victor and Nicholas. Shelagh was fired with enthusiasm and at last about to become a mother herself though minus a husband. She meanwhile worked as a nanny in Knightsbridge and on her Sundays off sometimes came to visit me in Clerkenwell. She was hard not to like and so Vidar quite liked her for which I was thankful for friends he did not approve of were not exactly made welcome. He did not like me offering her glasses of Campari and soda whenever she visited, however, because although I always bought the alcohol he felt it belonged to him and said she only asked for it because it reminded her of being in Spain where she had become pregnant. She was not a true devotee of Campari, he told me. This made me nervous when he entered the room and noticed the giveaway colour of the liquid in her glass. Shelagh was apt to remind me that these small details pointed to the fact that a long term relationship with him was not going to be easy for me.

His general patience and tolerance became ever more marginal and on one chilly winter afternoon when he failed to find a suitable sweater from the little pile, newly washed and on the top shelf of his cupboard, he took a full bottle of sherry and dribbled it deliberately over all the clothes I owned including into shoes and handbags.

'But why?' I was aghast, then stupidly because surely nobody would deliberately do such a thing, 'Was it by accident?'

He glowered, empty bottle in hand, his shoulders twitching. 'No – it wasn't an accident. I was looking for a sweater and I couldn't find one but there were all your clothes so nicely in their place. It made me angry, very angry.'

I opened his cupboard and took a sweater from the pile I had recently so lovingly laundered and handed it to him. He pulled it over his head and when I began to cry told me I was making another bloody scene about nothing.

'I just don't understand sometimes why you do the things you do.' I had wanted to say 'sadistic things' but didn't dare. 'I find it incomprehensible sometimes.'

He looked disbelieving. 'Because you leave me no option, no option at all.'

On another occasion because he thought I had been rude to him whilst Shelagh was visiting he waited until she left some hours later and then suddenly, quite out of the blue, hit me over the head with a hammer, splitting my scalp open dramatically. The amount of blood frightened me and so I went to St. Bartholomew's Hospital to have it attended to and the story alarmed them. Somehow someone notified the police and they came and took a statement and drove me home which startled him. Vidar was afraid of the police and did not like to be forced to answer their questions. Luckily his answers and his demeanour convinced them that he was merely a risk to me and not to society in general and so he was warned and told he must not in future hit women with hammers because it was dangerous.

They advised me to reassess my relationship with him and I said I would do so.

If such an episode occurred now, he would undoubtedly be arrested and charged but in those days such incidents were termed 'domestics' and treated with a certain amount of disregard.

As his behaviour towards me deteriorated I grew more and more frantic for the relationship to improve. Then he told me that he did not want to live with me any longer because my basic attitudes were not acceptable.

'How are they not acceptable?' I felt a familiar knot of despair tighten within me.

'You absolutely refuse to do my bidding – you work against me always.'

'But I will change – I know I will change. Just give me time to make changes.'

My heart began its familiar thumping and my throat constricted as I tried to stop the tears flowing. How he hated it when I cried. I vowed to try much harder not to cry so much.

Finally, after much pleading, he agreed to give me a further chance to improve and of course I heaved another sigh of relief and told myself that this time I would make a concerted effort to become his dream woman. Try as I might, it was never quite clear how I could realistically achieve the goal. There was always an area where I failed and he was always there to point out my failures more and more triumphantly.

I nursed a longing to become part of the ordinary, everyday world, to merge into one of the young housewives I saw shopping in Chapel Market with their small children. I envied Jessica and David, now expecting their first baby and excitedly building on a nursery extension to the back of the house in Northampton Square.

Several years passed in this unhappy manner with Vidar reminding me how I could never be the real woman he sought and me begging to be allowed one more try. He needed my financial support because I now paid the rent and all the bills, so he agreed to allow me to try again and yet again but now added that all the affection he had once had for me had been lost.

'You and I are no longer a couple,' he said. 'I have sex with you, but it's not because you are my partner – it is because you are there.'

Yes, I told him, I understood perfectly.

Clive, now giving as many of what he described as 'straight' parties as swinging ones, invited us to most events and gave Vidar for his birthday an English translation of the French erotic novel, *'The Story of O'* by Anne Desclos. He was greatly excited by the gift and urged me to read it and to learn.

It was a tale of female submission in which a young girl known only as O is taught she must be constantly available for oral, vaginal or anal sex and offer herself to any male who belongs to the same secret club as her lover, Rene. He dictates that she is regularly stripped, blindfolded, chained and whipped. Her buttocks are branded, her labia pierced and she is not only given to all and sundry for their sexual gratification, but also ordered to lure females into the club. She generally does as she is bid and eventually in despair asks for permission of her Master to die, which permission is granted.

In nineteen fifty five the book won the French literature prize Prix des Deux Magots although at the same time obscenity charges were brought against the publishers and a publicity ban was imposed for a number of years. The first English edition was published by Olympia Press in nineteen sixty five and Vidar said it was one of the most exciting books he had read for years.

I read it as he asked and found it depressingly familiar. The story derived most of its erotic power from the ultimate objectification of a woman.

At about the same time he acquired a copy of the Marquis de Sade's *'Justine'* which he found equally stimulating and again, directed me to read, telling me I would learn something about life if I did.

The book had been written in the late seventeen hundreds and concerned a virtuous twelve year old girl who sets off on a journey through France during which she learns a lot about sex, always inadvertently, going from one unfortunate situation to the next and being confronted with rapes and orgies on a grand scale. Justine never forsakes her virtue, however, but her bad luck continues. Her sister, Juliette, on the other hand, who is rather less than moral, has a much easier life and is blessed with better fortune all round. Finally, the unfortunate Justine is killed by a bolt of lightning.

The story of Justine's misfortunes amused Vidar a great deal and he never failed to convulse into helpless laughter when describing the story to those who had never come across it.

During these years both his mother and his brother came to stay with us, each on separate occasions. Before his mother arrived he told me again the story of her childhood and her upbringing and warned that I should be wary of her because she was a dangerous woman and would try to influence me. He said that over the years she had met a number of his girlfriends and had heartily disliked them all. I waited with a sinking heart for the visit.

Marie-Josephe von Carlowitz was a formidable looking woman in her late seventies. She was almost six feet tall and stood very straight. It was clear that she had once been very good looking. Throughout her stay she was unfailingly courteous and considerate and I began to cautiously like her. On the last day of her visit she told me that the previous evening she had advised her son that in her opinion he should marry me because she found me in every way suitable for him. I was hugely flattered.

Predictably, Vidar was angry, not just with her, but also with me because he said I had somehow bewitched her and that ability in me he found most disturbing. It was the first time I had heard of this particular ability and I was merely intrigued.

A few weeks later she sent a trunk filled with family possessions that had originally been in her home in Saxony. Together we unrolled linen banqueting cloths together with napkins for eighty guests all monogrammed with the von Carlowitz insignia, and more silver than I had seen in my life before. Bit by bit we unpacked the items then somehow or other got the huge trunk up to the top floor, packing everything up again.

Some time later, his brother came to stay, fresh from one of his solo yachting trips that had brought him so many accolades. Vidar was half proud and half resentful.

'My brother has always chased after fame and fortune,' he told me. 'Now it seems he has more of it than he bargained for.'

Rollo was surprised to find that on his arrival he was asked to speak on two radio programmes and make a television appearance. Chauffeuring him to and from these engagements clearly irritated his younger brother.

He began to demonstrate how much power he had, particularly over me, by being rude to me and ordering me to do certain things, berating me if I did not make coffee quickly enough or was gone too long when grocery shopping. When Rollo suggested that they drive me to the supermarket Vidar laughed and said that shopping was a woman's work and he wanted no part in it. So Rollo said he would walk with me and help me carry the bags back which annoyed him even more.

The day before he left he asked me why I stayed with Vidar.

'Because I love him I suppose,' I said.

'I don't think he has the same regard for you,' he said. 'He treats you very unkindly a lot of the time.'

I could only agree. Rollo asked me to go to Germany and stay with him for a holiday. I would have loved to be able to agree but I knew that it was impossible. He told me that his mother had liked me very much and that he, too, liked me very much.

'It seems that my brother is the only one who does not like you so much,' he said and both of us laughed.

Again and again I turned my attention to finding a solution for the absurd situation I found myself in, living with and supporting a man who cared nothing for me, daily becoming further enmeshed in a vortex of emotional distress and disturbance.

From time to time I visited Shelagh, now at last a contented sole parent to Virginia, a solemn and round baby with a mop of blonde curls and cornflower blue eyes. Virginia's father was no longer in evidence, and indeed as far as Shelagh had been concerned he was merely the donator of sperm because she was quite convinced that she could bring up a child alone.

'Perhaps a baby is the answer for me,' I said half to myself.

She looked at me sharply. 'Did I actually hear you say that a baby might be the answer?'

I nodded and immediately I did so, I realized that a baby was perhaps the only answer even if it was definitely not the most sensible solution to the dilemma.

Later, when discussing the events that then took place, I invariably maintained that I did not actually set out to deliberately get pregnant, that it happened accidentally and because I had been told I was infertile and needed a hysterectomy. That was more than half true. I had recently consulted a reputable gynaecologist because of an ongoing low grade pelvic infection. He was called Tony Woolf and he said that my fallopian tubes were blocked and I was almost certainly infertile.

'You need a hysterectomy,' he said and even I, knowing little about these matters, was a little surprised because I was only twenty-six years old.

'Are you certain I couldn't have a baby?' I had asked him tearfully as he rocked back and forth on his heels, showing off in front of his students.

'Well pigs might fly I suppose – think about it, and you should stop taking the pill if you're to have the operation,' he said and he walked away still posturing.

The diagnosis of doubtful fertility had not surprisingly come about as a direct result of the years of indiscriminate sexual behaviour and it was not something I had given much thought to previously because modern medicine appeared to provide the answer to a multitude of minor ills. There was a pill for almost any problem.

'How is having a baby going to improve matters?' Shelagh now asked. She handed me a mug of instant coffee and waited for me to speak.

'I'm not totally sure – at least, I can't really put it into words. I just feel that if I had a baby to think about I could see a way through the mess I'm in…'

She looked at me incredulously. 'I don't think you're too clear about that at all. I think you're hoping that if you get pregnant he will suddenly have a change of heart and start planning a wedding – well, we both know that's not going to happen don't we?'

And we did.

She thought she understood but I knew that things were not exactly as she perceived them to be. I was totally aware that there was no way that the thought of a baby would make any impression upon Vidar L'Estrange except to make him further enraged. I did not at any stage imagine, as some have since suggested to me, that his heart would soften on account of it. I knew better than that.

No, the baby, should it eventuate, was to be my departure permit. Its very existence would ensure my passage out of the relationship. With a child inside me I would not be able to stay no matter how much I yearned to. I would be forced to leave him, but I would be taking a part of him with me. I would not lose him totally because I would have his child. It was the assurance of a loss that would not be total that would sustain me.

Half-heartedly I attempted to explain but Shelagh merely shook her head in disbelief.

'First you have to become pregnant,' she said.

Of course I did and if Tony Woolf was to be believed, that was not going to be easy. I stopped taking the contraceptive pill immediately and determined that I would keep myself only unto Vidar for as long as it took and I fervently hoped it would not take long.

Shelagh remained resolutely doubtful and said that in her experience these things did not usually happen overnight.

'Just look at how long it took me,' she advised but I didn't want to for obvious reasons. I now envied her the baby Virginia, already growing towards toddlerhood and desperately trying to walk.

'I've decided to consult a fortune teller,' I said in what I imagined was an off-hand manner but instead of laughing Shelagh said she would come with me for emotional support.

Madame Sandra worked on the very top floor of a building close to Tottenham Court Road tube station, overlooking Oxford Street. We giggled a bit as we climbed the stairs because although we were curious we were also more than half wary, mistrustful of fortune tellers.

I could not totally rid myself of the image of two of my mother's younger sisters, Aunts Phyllis and Rose, both of whom did stints at Kentish fairgrounds from time to time when I was a young child taking turns at reading palms.

'And Rose can no more look into the future than fly to the moon,' my mother had announced derisively.

We reached the top landing and pushed our way through several bead curtains, Shelagh hissing that I should take care not to give her any clues.

Madame Sandra looked true to type with lots of colourful scarves and silver jewellery. She welcomed us cheerfully.

'It's a guinea for the right hand, a guinea for the left – and a guinea for the crystal ball,' she announced.

'I'll have the lot,' I said decisively and carefully handed over three pound notes and three shilling pieces which she at once stowed into a heavy metal cash box, locking it with a key that hung around her neck amidst the rattling silver.

She took my right hand in hers and said, 'You're not a very happy girl are you?'

I remained resolutely silent because how often do happy girls visit fortune tellers?

'And it's about a man... And he's causing you a lot of pain – a lot of pain. There have been so many tears shed. Yes, it's definitely about a man.'

She looked at me questioningly.

I said nothing because unless I was a lesbian it was hardly likely to be about a woman.

'You wear a wedding ring dear – but you're not married, are you. You are certainly concerned about your future – and so you should be dear, so you should be. You're considering which path to take and you're confused...you wear this ring but I cannot see a wedding...there's been no wedding has there dear?'

I was wearing it that day although I didn't always do so. My thoughts wandered to how many women in London wore wedding rings whilst still unmarried.

Madam Sandra gave me a look that indicated in no uncertain terms that I was making the job of a psychic more difficult than it needed to be. She began to speak more sharply and her beads and chains rattled their frustration in jangling unison.

'You're going to leave this man soon but there will be a great deal of acrimony between you which will last a very long time. It's good that you leave him. He looks as if he's a very nasty piece of work to me – you should have walked out long ago!'

I felt tears pricking the back of my eyes and blinked rapidly. I must not cry.

She examined my left hand and then rested her own on the crystal ball saying nothing for several minutes. I still remained completely silent.

Her irritation subsided and she spoke in the more acceptable tones of a clairvoyant once more.

'Although you are entering a time of great conflict it will pass... by Easter next year you will have a son who will be a great comfort to you.'

I did a rapid calculation and gave Shelagh what I hoped was a brief questioning glance. It was mid-October and Easter usually occurred during the early part of April. A pregnancy traditionally lasted for forty weeks so if I was to have the comforting son she spoke of by Easter, I would have needed to be pregnant for a number of months already, and I was most decidedly not in that happy state.

I elected to speak.

'That's not possible,' I said, 'because I'm definitely not pregnant.'

Madam Sandra looked into the crystal again and went back to her rather more than determined voice, 'I can only tell you what I see dear – and I see a son and I see him in your life just before Easter next year – that is what I see whether you like it or not.'

'All I'm saying is that it doesn't seem possible to me – given that I'm definitely not pregnant.'

I sounded just as angry as I felt and she looked at me with obvious dislike.

'Look dear – I'm not your doctor. You'll have to take that up with him. There's no point you arguing with me about it. No point at all. All I can do is tell you what I see. Anyway, as I said, you're going to leave this man you're with and when your boy is a few years old you will marry a man you already know. Yes, you've already met him – and his initials are...G...H... and you'll go and live in a land of sunshine and white buildings.'

She looked at a fob watch hanging from one of the numerous neck chains. The consultation was obviously over.

I thanked her and we went down the long dark stairway again and headed into Soho for sustaining cups of real coffee.

'Well she was right about some things,' Shelagh said comfortingly. 'You are unhappy after all – and what she said about the man with the initials G H might still come true.'

I wondered who he was and where I'd met him. Apart from the Saturday party group and the men I sat with at the club, I met very few people. I quickly pondered the party group, trying to find someone with the correct initials, someone I might possibly consider marrying.

'Madame Sandra was a moderately inexpensive charlatan,' I said and Shelagh nodded adding that nevertheless it had been a bit of fun.

We parted as the street lights began to come on and I reluctantly returned to the Clerkenwell flat, more determined than ever to achieve the state of pregnancy.

To my very great surprise it happened almost immediately. So quickly and so effortlessly in fact that it took me completely by surprise. A week or so later upon waking feeling nauseous and trying not to even think about roasted coffee beans, I was incredulous that Madam Sandra might have been half correct after all.

'The timing's all wrong though,' Shelagh said doubtfully during one of our long telephone conversations

After a further week or two I went back to Tony Woolf who grew exasperated and told me that of course I couldn't be pregnant and he had never heard of such nonsense in his life. Then he added quite kindly that a lot of women think they have become pregnant when they have recently been told they are infertile.

'But I *feel* pregnant,' I said and he told me that of course I did because that was how the mind worked.

So I went home and got on with dealing with morning sickness and sudden aversion to coffee and all things containing tomatoes.

Vidar had greeted the news of my possible hysterectomy with attentive awareness bordering on cheerfulness. Still keenly interested in all things medical he liked to be kept fully informed of such developments.

'It's going to be such an advantage for you not to be able to conceive,' he said. 'You should be both grateful and happy.'

I said nothing and made yet another appointment with the gynaecologist who looked exasperated when I said that I had now quite decided not to have a hysterectomy because I still believed I was pregnant. He referred me to the hospital psychiatric department. I obediently went to see them on a weekly basis and initially even took the pills they gave me but they made me feel so weak and helpless that I soon stopped doing so.

In those first few weeks I was ambivalent about whether I should actually have the baby that I knew was growing inside me and this was possibly because it had come about so precipitously I had almost been caught unawares, ambushed by the reality of it. Then, quite suddenly I concluded that as the odds had been so very much against it, the probability of it happening so very small, it must be what was meant for me. It was Fate, I decided, or Destiny, or Providence – whatever you cared to call it.

And of course I discussed it in depth with the ever patient Shelagh.

'If Tony Woolf is actually to be believed,' I said, 'This might be the only child I will ever have. It would be foolish not to have it.'

'Although we both agree don't we that there is little chance of Vidar having a change of heart and becoming a family man....' She was looking at me intently, eyebrows raised.

I nodded. 'Absolutely.'

'Well then you need to leave as soon as possible before he realizes.'

I knew that was the sensible thing to do but because there was now no chance at all of him considering for a moment that I might be pregnant, and because he had suddenly become so solicitous at the thought of the hysterectomy, I was reluctant to leave. I would stay with him for a few more delicious weeks, weeks in which I would harbour a special secret. I felt calm and almost peaceful, emotions that had eluded me throughout the previous years with him. When he drove off into the night on a whim to visit Christine I no longer felt spikes of fury rise within me but instead reveled in her surprise when she learned, as one day she undoubtedly would, that I had given birth to his child. He had from time to time shared with me the fact that what Christine had wanted more than anything in the world was to bear his child and on one occasion she had told him that she did not mind if she had to bring up the child alone.

When I insisted that I was now sixteen or seventeen weeks pregnant the psychiatrists sent me for an X-ray of the baby's spine in order to prove to me there would be none to be seen. I was both fascinated and thrilled to see the skeletal evidence on the film and wondered if the child slumbering there was male or female and what names I should begin to consider. The doctor looked first horrified and then embarrassed and said well it did certainly look as if there was a baby after all. I lived the remainder of that week in a golden bubble of euphoria, whenever Vidar left the flat, having long conversations about pregnancy with Shelagh.

'You really must leave him now,' she repeatedly urged, 'because when he finally finds out he's going to be very angry and that will be much easier to deal with if there's some distance between you.'

Less than a week later I had cause to wish I had taken her advice.

Fairy Tale Babies

It is not easy to resign oneself to enduring bouts of excruciating pain and I had never been particularly good at pain in the first place so when the spirals of agony woke me in the middle of the night, I was only too happy to agree with Vidar that he should take me to hospital. He, invariably a more than compassionate friend when he could become involved in the ill health or hospital admissions of those around him, drove me in haste to St. Bartholemew's.

It is now quite difficult to accurately remember the sequence of the events that followed not only because it all happened a very long time ago, but also because when I examine the details the only thing that emerges with any clarity is his extreme rage which was both hypnotic and terrifying.

I was given a pain-killing injection and told that the agony I complained of was probably due to a damaged fallopian tube as it stretched to accommodate the fetus. I stayed for several days and feared leaving. When I did go back to Northampton Square the house was ominously quiet and Vidar was upstairs in his studio half attending to some work. He stopped what he was doing and turned to face me. He spoke quietly.

'You have deceived me. I will never forgive you.'

I had not expected forgiveness. I tried to explain to him that this child might be the only one I was ever likely to have and he ignored me because he was not in the slightest bit interested. He said in quite a patient voice,

'Apart from the fact that I most definitely do not want a child, surely it must be obvious to you that I cannot have a child with someone like you?'

He was looking at me almost helplessly. 'That at least must be obvious.'

I shook my head because it wasn't and he went on to explain that I was not a suitable person to be the mother of his child and no matter how many changes I made I would never become suitable.

'If you do not get rid of the thing inside you,' he told me, 'you will force me into actions I am most unwilling to take.'

So then of course I became fearful but foolishly I still asked him why I was not suitable and what would make me suitable.

'One of the things that makes you totally unacceptable is the fact that you are unable to tell the truth.' He looked at me without emotion. 'You are a persistent liar.'

I knew what he referred to in particular. At some stage I had finally told him the truth about my mythical daughter, Sarah, the child whose parentage I shared with Stan Douglas. I struggled now to remember why it was I came to tell him that particular story in the first place. It was several seconds before I recalled it had come about because before introducing us Michelle had told me he was only prepared to carry out an abortion on a woman who had already experienced childbirth. I tearfully explained that to him now and he told me that my motivation was of no consequence because it was still a lie, which of course it was.

'Not only that,' he said after a moment or two, 'what about all the lies you have told me about your family? One untruth after another.'

Again, he was correct, and there appeared to be no way of explaining that the wild inventions concerning various relatives that he would never have to meet amounted to nothing more than infantile daydreams. The mothers and stepfathers, the siblings I created with such ease and the houses they lived in were mere reveries and fancies, a habit that had begun as a child and was now hard to break.

'All monstrous lies!' he insisted, 'as if such a monumental liar could be allowed to bear a child of mine – the thing inside you must be destroyed.'

'But I can stop telling these stories – I will never tell another lie,' I was weeping now and fervently wishing I had put more effort into abandoning my fantasies.

'It's not just that though,' he said. 'Even if I could believe what you now say, it would not make you the kind of individual worthy to be a mother to my children. I pity any child forced to put up with you as their mother because you are repellant. And I pity any man foolish enough to become involved with you at any future stage.'

He managed to sound quite regretful when he then said, 'There is now no way out for you because if you do not destroy that fetus I will destroy you both.'

'No – I will go – I will leave,' I told him. 'You will never have to see me again.'

He said that leaving was no longer an option and for that matter I should have left long ago.

I wished I had.

I began to wail and was unable to stop so he went downstairs in disgust and sat cross legged on the bed, pulling idly at the pattern on the duvet. I followed him and tried in vain to control my hysteria.

'It's far too late for me to have an abortion,' I told him at last when I had managed to pull myself together enough to speak sensibly once more and he said that was no concern of his and how I got rid of the child was up to me but it had to be done.

'What will you do if I don't get rid of it?' I ventured to ask. Surely he did not propose to commit a murder in the midst of a Clerkenwell winter afternoon with snow like a carpet in the square outside. A killing whilst children played within earshot.

'If you do fail to do my bidding then I will curse you and your child into Eternity. I will place a demon on your shoulder that will never leave you. You will have ill luck wherever you go. You will never rid yourself of my curse.'

It was a promise he would repeat hourly during those next days, often whispering it in my ear as I tried to sleep. In that time we twisted and descended into a place of horror within which I seemed incapable of making rational decisions because I was so paralysed with terror.

I suggested I could protect myself with prayer and this threw him into a new dimension of frenzy.

'Your fucking Virgin Mary will be no help to you for she is powerless against those I can conjure up. That whore will be as defenseless against me as you will be. You will never, ever escape for if you try to get away on a vessel as big as the Queen Mary the fucking thing will sink.'

He began to pack to leave on a short pre-arranged visit to his mother in Munich. Although I realized that part of his towering rage was theatre in order to immobilise me with fear of the consequences if I did not obey him, I was unsure of the magical ability he claimed to have and if indeed any part of it had substance. This uncertainty was something I held close to me and could not even discuss with Shelagh.

I was afraid enough to promise to kill the baby. I would do it while he was away. I think I may even have told him I had contacted an abortionist.

Puddles, the poodle, so firmly above me in the pecking order, was clearly deflated when it became clear that he was not also to go on the journey to Munich and looked at me uncertainly when I told him to go to his basket. He was no longer accustomed to doing anything I asked him to, although he obeyed Vidar immediately.

Now, he padded slowly towards the basket and instead of settling down in it, he chose to sit beside it, ears down and cringing.

Vidar was ignoring both of us and so I hissed to the dog that he had better watch out for the duration of his absence. He understood immediately and so he got up and flopped into the basket and stayed there even after Vidar had clattered down the stairs and banged the front door behind him.

Later when he tentatively emerged and began to give my bare leg cautious licks I told him I detested him. I meant it and he knew that. He whined miserably.

What followed was remarkably imprudent and as I now re-examine my actions from the security of a humid Auckland summer day nearly five decades on, I can see how improbable they sound. I even have to remind myself that things really did happen this way and I am not applying some kind of writer's license to the events simply because it is unlikely that there is anyone left living who would be able to challenge me.

I remained frozen for several hours, lost in meandering thoughts about what I was about to do and when the telephone rang I did not answer it because I thought, correctly as it turned out, that it might be Shelagh who would not approve of my plan. It was after all the plan of a woman who was half mad and perhaps I was suffering from a form of temporary madness at that time. From time to time the dog whined more assertively but I reminded him that he had made it impossible for me to regard him with the love he now seemed to crave.

In order to protect the child inside me for a little longer I decided to fake an abortion. I realized that the plan was not a solution to the problem, it was simply postponing what might well be a personal catastrophe, but that was the decision I had come to. I have never been in the habit of making life's important decisions on the basis of what the majority judge as being 'right' or 'wrong', but only on what feels correct for me from where I stand at the time. Therefore I am largely protected from the feelings of guilt or remorse that so often plague others because if an action feels wrong, generally speaking, I refrain from doing it in the first place. The plan can therefore only have seemed right to me at the time.

I bought the hare the following evening from the game butcher in Chapel Market and he was surprised when I asked him not to remove the entrails, telling me they were not good to eat. I carried the newspaper parcel home with me in the early dusk, blood dripping from it and through my fingers. I felt a little like Lady Macbeth and was able to smile at myself in the mirror by the kitchen sink, holding the blood-soaked hands up before my face. The smell was disgusting.

I placed the parcel in the refrigerator and made a pot of tea and drank three cups whilst staring down at the square below where snow still lay. The lights from the windows around where people, ordinary people, could be seen going about their early evening business, boosted the sudden sensation of a community warmth from which I was excluded. What perfect bliss to be an ordinary woman, in an ordinary family, having an ordinary pregnancy. I would even happily settle for no husband if there could also be no threats of violence, no forced abortions. I yearned to reach out and be mystically fused and melded into the routine and convention of the life around me.

I sat stock still until it was quite dark outside and the lights in the windows began to go out one by one and the sound of traffic from nearby Goswell Road grew less and less until there was almost silence. Through those hours I contemplated and deliberated and meditated upon what I was about to do and implored God himself, if he indeed existed, to help me. And if it transpired that there was no God, then I called upon any spiritual force willing to be of assistance. I felt a little like Faust. At the same time I was certain that what I was doing was ultimately for the good because now I wanted the child with the kind of desperate longing that is more akin to animal than human experience. Then I was overcome with fatigue and slept for ten hours.

When I woke I decided to spend the day cleaning the flat and did so slowly and methodically whilst listening to the early recordings of Menuhin. I was almost content and daydreamed about what life might be like if good fortune should befall me and allow Vidar to die whilst in Munich. A road traffic accident perhaps. Tragically mowed down by a tram as he crossed the road. Or a sudden heart attack. I saw him half falling and clutching desperately at the wall, a little like Dr. Zhivago at the end of the movie when he frantically tries to follow Lara in the street. How delightful it would be if the remainder of my pregnancy could be spent cleaning and tidying the nest into which my child would be nurtured and in the evenings knitting tiny garments in bright colours rather than pastels.

I imagined carrying the child down into the square to feed the birds, then perhaps on to the library to look for picture books. I would turn the studio upstairs into a nursery with shelves for books and a stripped pine cupboard for toys. Later, I began to draw detailed nursery plans so I knew exactly which walls would be lined with shelves and where the child's bed would go as he or she grew older. I even wondered what I might decide to recount in years to come about the sad fate of the absent father. Would I perhaps invent a nicer person and give him a more heroic death? After all it would be a strange child who would really applaud such terrible truths about their entry to life and with Vidar safely dead it would not be necessary to reveal the actual facts.

After a further period of sleep I dissected the hare, carefully preserving the innards and contentedly turning the flesh into one of Vidar's favourite meals, a red wine casserole similar to those served by Clive or Mariella at the best of the Saturday night orgies. It would be left to develop extra flavour and then reheated for his return. It simmered away in the kitchen filling the whole flat with a comforting aroma so that even Jessica called up the stairs to comment on it.

'That smells divine! What is it?'

'Jugged hare for when Vidar comes back,' I called back. 'He loves it.'

'Lucky man,' she said and I could not help but agree because I thought he was indeed a lucky man to have someone like me so attendant upon his every need, but then I was so fortunate to have conceived the child of this unique individual. I tried to visualize what it would look like when it was born and whether the father's unique qualities would be obvious. Then I pictured it at three or four years old. As it grew would it resemble its father? Should it be a boy I realized that the greater part of me wanted him to reflect his father as much as possible. Though hopefully minus the negative aspects.

An intelligent and compassionate child.

A musical and curious child.

A child who would love his mother.

An hour or so before Vidar was due to return I took the entrails of the hare from the fridge and draped them artistically across the bathroom floor. I ran a warm bath into which I added a bottle of red food colouring. I stepped into the bath when the dog began to bark joyfully as he heard the familiar step on the stairs. And that is how he came upon me looking tragic, and I thought just a little like The Lady of Shallot.

He stood uncertainly in the doorway and said, 'Oh goodness me – oh goodness me… how are you feeling?'

His voice expressed genuine concern and for the briefest moment I felt almost guilty at the immense deception that would now take place because now there could be no turning back.

I spoke weakly, 'I feel reasonable but I hoped to be able to clean up before you arrived.' I gestured fleetingly at what had once been the throbbing life force of the hare, now gently re-heating in the kitchen.

He told me not to worry about a thing and that he would do the cleaning up and he did so as I lay in the warm water. Then he made a pot of coffee and handed me a mug, sitting beside the bath as we both drank in silence.

At last he said, 'I am very relieved you know because neither of us need the drama of eternal curses.'

I could only agree. He asked me what the tempting smell from the kitchen was and when I said Jugged Hare he leapt to his feet and said he would go at once to the off license on the corner and buy a really good bottle of red wine, which he did.

I had no appetite for the fetus-preserving hare but he ate a great deal of it and drank two glasses of wine whilst I sipped on a half glass and felt the confidence of triumph rise within me. I marveled at how easily duped this Fully Enlightened One was. Then a brief rush of remorse as he urged me to sleep.

I did sleep but at some stage during the night as he lay beside me looking strangely at peace, I quietly rose from the bed to execute a further measure of the deception by slashing my genitals with a razor blade in order that whenever he should wake he would find a reassuring issue of fresh blood on my pristine white cotton nightgown and in the bed. I had been apprehensive contemplating the blade but in the end it was surprisingly easy to do and scarcely hurt at all.

I slept for hours, mentally exhausted now and he allowed me to do so. When I finally woke I was dazed and confused and could scarcely believe that I was on the other side of a strategy that had initially seemed insurmountable to implement. My baby was for the moment safe again.

There was no doubt that he had seen on the floor of the bathroom, what I intended him to see and what he wanted to see and he even commented on the size of the aborted fetus. It was, it his opinion, approximately eighteen weeks. He told me gently for the second or third time that I had saved myself a lot of pain and grief and that he would now remove from me the deadly structures for the curses that were to have been placed on both my person and that of my child.

Of course I should have used the next week or two appropriately. I should have looked for a place to live and made preparations to leave but predictably, I did not do so. At that stage I could have left with impunity and he might even have vaguely regretted my leaving. He would have kindly lectured me upon the matter of my destructive nature and how it had fractured the close bond he had once hoped we would have. I could have cried and he might have comforted me. But I stayed and once or twice even allowed myself to imagine how different life might be should he have an unexpected change of heart. What might it be like should he for some reason come to see that it was cruel to deprive me of his child? What if he felt the stirrings of paternal affection within him? Might it be possible somehow to persuade him that this child was Meant To Be? Could he then be swayed to re-assess our relationship?

Embarrassing though it is now to relate, these were the extraordinarily unbalanced thoughts that paraded across my consciousness.

It then became too late for me to continue as Controller of my own Destiny. That power was abruptly snatched from me some weeks later as I approached the twenty-fourth week of my pregnancy. With more than a small degree of triumph I saw that he was still quite ignorant of what was taking place in front of him as he told me more than once how well I had done to rid us of 'that demon fetus'. It was possible to pretend to be almost content until searing pains again tore through me in the middle of the night and I feared for the child's life and prayed. So it was that we found ourselves at the hospital once more this time with Vidar importantly explaining that I was recovering from a recent miscarriage.

The anger that exploded when he was told that I appeared to still have a 'pelvic mass' was like a nuclear blast but I was only to feel the full effect days later when I was sent home again, the pain having abated and no real cause found for it.

This time, thankfully, his fury was directed more towards Cruel Fate rather than myself because he had with his own eyes seen the evidence of my obedience to him in the form of the dead fetus on the bathroom floor. He did no work and did not answer the telephone but instead sat on the bed hugging his knees and swaying slightly. He spoke to himself sometimes in a low voice and when he turned his gaze towards me I was in no doubt as to the depth of his rage.

Eventually he told me, 'We must now act.'

I asked him what he meant. It was impossible to swallow because I was so frightened of what he might instruct me to do.

'There were more powerful forces afoot than I first imagined,' he said, crushing a cigarette into the already overflowing ashtray before him.

I briefly thought it might be possible to argue that the child's destiny was so vital to mankind that significant measures had been put in place to preserve its life but before I could begin to travel down this track he said, 'There were twins – can you believe it? Fucking twins!'

He had almost begun to accept a degree of the argument and so I simply nodded and said something vague about the child clearly was meant to be born because it was now far too late to destroy it.

'Oh no,' he said, 'it must be destroyed.'

Although he accepted the premise that a Divine Force was protecting the child, he did not for one moment accede to the idea that it might be ultimately for Good. In his world it could only be for a truly terrible Evil and what is more one that was mercilessly intent upon destroying him, Vidar Gebhard-L'Estrange. He must now depend upon all his mettle and his inner resources in order to fight it. My faint hope that he would see a Divine Providence had decreed that the child should live, was not given the slightest consideration. He began to believe that the annihilation of the baby was part of his own Divine Purpose

'This thing is a test for me,' he told me.

It was then as if we became prime players in some malevolent folk tale where we re-enacted processes that had been set down in a dark history that was predestined to be played and replayed throughout centuries. I became increasingly afraid of him and could neither eat nor sleep over the following days. In my terror I first sought help from the Police, anonymously at midnight from the telephone box that still stands outside Sadlers Wells Theatre. Even as I dialed the number I knew that the Police Department was not going to be of any assistance to me. The theatre-goers were long gone and the façade of the building was bleak and forbidding. No-one was out walking on the streets and even the traffic seemed to have come to a halt. Time stood very still for a moment or two. 999 responded unemotionally and when I said I wanted to speak with someone about a crime that was about to be committed, the voice became at once fatherly. I explained that the father of my child wanted it aborted and that I was anxious to preserve its life. Was it possible for the would-be killer to be arrested if I gave more details of him? The fatherly voice reassured me and kept me talking and then within minutes, or so it seemed, the kiosk door was wrenched open by two police officers demanding to know more. 'I'm making it up,' I sobbed, 'It's a joke – just a joke. Then before they could ask more I ran away through the warren of narrow streets behind the theatre. They did not pursue me. Perhaps it was a narrative that was not completely unfamiliar to them because men frequently urge women to have abortions they would rather not have. To cast an even darker shadow there was in those days no procedure for legal abortion. Abortion was against the law and abortionists invariably went to prison which is where, of course, I had been hoping to send Vidar. I had for a while happily contemplated the idea of him languishing in a prison cell.

I next sought help from the Catholic Church. I consulted Vivien Godfrey-White, an erstwhile friend who was an ex-nun and therefore treated with some caution by Vidar. She lived with a cat called Phryne above the Catholic Book Shop in The Strand and in the daytime worked in the shop below. Her free time she devoted to the study of orthodox religion and the study of less orthodox beliefs such as Magic.

Now she listened attentively to my half-truths, because of course I did not dare to reveal the whole story, especially the chicanery with the hare innards. She gave me a bed for the night and said she would speak to someone at the Cathedral for advice and I should come back the following day. It was raining heavily when I returned to be instructed that the following afternoon at four o'clock I should go to Westminster Cathedral, to a particular side door and ask for Canon Gonzelli who would advise and counsel me.

'You must tell him the whole truth,' she said. 'He's an Exorcist and a very powerful man – he can only help you if he has all the facts.'

She told me he could cast out any Demon set upon me by Vidar and I imagined a giant of a man.

He turned out to be a rather small person, shorter than average, bent over with a wizened and leathered appearance so that it was quite impossible to tell what age he might be. What was left of his hair was gingery and he had the most surprising cornflower blue eyes, as sharp and keen as those of an eleven-year-old boy. He opened the door I had been directed to himself and led me through a number of corridors to a small, windowless and cell-like room where the walls were lined with rows of dusty books that appeared not to have been opened for years. He bent to switch on a small bar heater and sat on one side of a wide wooden desk, motioning me to sit on the other. He spoke perfect English with a slight foreign accent.

'Tell me your story,' he said and so I did so, leaving out nothing this time. The telling of the story took longer than I imagined it would and was exhausting. He did not say anything until I got to the part about Vidar's hatred of the Church and the Demons he had conjured up to plague and pester me into Eternity if I did not ensure that the child died.

'You have been playing a very dangerous game,' he observed and then the tears began to spill down my face and drip onto the ancient carpet beneath my feet, faster and faster until I found it impossible to stop the flow. As I wept he emphasized the risks I had taken and said that I had placed myself in very real danger.

'You must understand that the Demons this man speaks of are not merely figments of his imagination – they are the agents of Satan himself,' he said and caused me to become ever more terrified until he assured me that he could help to rid me and my child of their influence.

Canon Gonzelli took me back through narrow corridors until we finally found ourselves inside the Cathedral itself, huge and quiet but for the background murmur of a priest somewhere speaking with a group of visitors. In a small side chapel he lit candles and placed his hands upon my head, reciting prayers as I knelt still in terror before him.

But slowly, as he spoke above me, I began to feel calmer and realized that although I would have told anyone a week or two before that I was not wholly religious, that I no longer had real faith that God existed, at that moment kneeling in the chapel I experienced the power of something entirely spiritual.

Before I left he gave me newly blessed Rosary Beads, small black beads with a simple silvery link chain.

'Hold them to your heart when you feel the Demons coming closer and you will find they have the power to protect you.'

The rain had stopped by the time I left the comforting safety and security of the Cathedral building and as I moved into the street I was aware of the possibility of harm hovering in the air about me.

I left by a different door and quickly found myself in Francis Street, heading in the general direction of Victoria Station where I knew I would be able to search for the familiar Underground sign. The wet pavements glittered eerily and street lamps sent a procession of demonic dancers to accompany me as I hurried through home-going Londoners, not daring to breathe too deeply for fear of the pursuing spirits. I clutched the black beads hard inside the right-hand pocket of my rain jacket and said several Hail Marys and as I reached the entrance to the tube station and began to descend the escalator, the shimmering inky dancers were left behind, howling abuse in a language I could not understand. But the underground system as everyone knows, is a perfect habitat for unfriendly apparitions and once on the platform I was again under attack as shadowy fiends played games of biting and pinching my lower legs.

Vidar was sitting in the kitchen when I returned to the flat and when he asked where I had been I told him. There was even an edge of triumph to my voice. He said that my Virgin Mary would not be able to help me no matter how hard I prayed to her and her envoys would be of very little assistance and support against the demonic forces he had invoked to hunt me down.

'Don't even begin to think of running away,' he said with a strange lack of acrimony. 'The time for escape has long gone because no matter how you try to flee they will always catch up with you. Wherever you might go in the world they will always hunt you down. They will always find your hiding place.'

My teeth began to chatter with such panic that I could not form sentences. Wordlessly I brought the Rosary Beads from my pocket and placed them on the table between us.

He leaned across, chuckling faintly and touched the beads with his forefinger and it was as he did so that the silvery chain immediately broke in two places. We both drew back, me in further panic, and after a few seconds he said, 'They do not have much power to protect you for I have already shattered them.' But he spoke uncertainly.

Later Vivien, who could always be relied upon to be fey, told me that it was her opinion that the beads had in fact absorbed the demonic force, deflecting it from its target and rendering it impotent. But I was much less sure and in any case I had already stepped down into terror once more and Vidar quickly realized this and was able to turn it to his advantage.

Over the next days and nights he expounded in terrifying detail what my life was likely to entail if I did not now do his bidding. He advised with chilling brevity that the simplest way forward from the point we now found ourselves at was for him to kill the child in my womb. I sat and listened, absorbing the words and somehow failing to analyse what they meant, forcing him to repeat himself endlessly but strangely patiently.

So it was that Vidar, with a long bladed kitchen knife within reach should I happen to have a change of heart, performed upon me the second abortion procedure of our six-year relationship, almost within the presence of the fractured Rosary Beads that lay still on the kitchen table.

Of course it's true that I could simply have pretended to agree and taken the first opportunity to escape down the stairs, heading directly to the nearest Police Station. It's somehow doubtful that he would have entered into a pursuit, knife in hand, in order to make me return. Years later I can look back and query the absurdity of my behaviour.

'WHY didn't you run away?'

'WHY did you cringe in the corner like a whipped animal?'

'WHY were you such a pathetic example of sniveling cowardice?'

There are no encouraging answers because things were the way they were and I was simply the person I was, readily succumbing to fear and effortlessly crushed, vanquished and subjugated. Decades later he was to describe the pressure he put me under as extreme and voice significant surprise that I seemed to withstand it for so long but that is not how it appeared to me, either then or now.

Then, although my greatest desire was to protect my child, it appeared to me that I easily ceded to the fear he instilled in me and rapidly capitulated into a place from where there seemed no escape. Now what I feel is extreme anger, not simply towards him for the unforgiveable extent of the pressure he placed upon me, but also a burning rage towards the person I had become.

He was jubilant when just hours after the procedure, the infant appeared to have been successfully dislodged from within me as the obvious and certain signs of a terminating pregnancy began.

He asked that I should give him a signed cheque for the next month's rent on the flat plus enough to cover power, telephone, etc and he thought that a hundred pounds should be enough to cover the basics and leave a little for cigarettes and petrol. This of course I did, although resentfully. Then with a kind of weary triumph he dropped me at the hospital without allowing the car engine to stop for a second. He said, pressuring the accelerator as he explained, that if I told them the truth then he would unfortunately have to ensure that my life came to an end. He managed to make this sound as if it would hurt him more than it would hurt me. I agreed to lie.

I was treated for a 'threatening miscarriage' and sent up to a ward for several days where I slept most of the time and became confused about the passing of time. It was astonishing to realise that somehow or other the baby appeared to have survived this determined attempt on its life.

I asked the staff not to give Vidar any information about me if he happened to enquire because I knew he would want to reassure himself that the work had been completed. As this happened at the first glimmering of the dawn of The Rights of Patients, they acquiesced and he was told nothing which he later complained was unnecessary and secretive.

So I left their care amazingly still pregnant and went to stay with Shelagh and Virginia, dazed and bruised and unable to make much sense of the recent events, returning to Northampton Square only to collect a few personal belongings. This I did, fearfully and at a time when I knew him to be absent from the place. And when I did, I paced through the hollow rooms as if on slippered feet, apprehensive of the muffled echoes from stairs and walls that still reverberated from the years of sorrow and unfulfilled hopes.

Despite Shelagh's warmth and support and constant reassurances that finally and at long last I had acted rightly and properly, I mourned the loss of all the wild expectations I had for so long nurtured.

In spite of his behaviur toward me, regardless of the fact that he had told me plainly that he did not want me in his life, closeted away there was a very small space in which to fit the odd occasion when I still embraced the hope that one day things might work out well for us. I knew better than to discuss this with anyone, even Shelagh, because it sounded not merely foolish but irrational.

Always Blessed

So began my life without Vidar L'Estrange and after the first ten days when I simply sat motionless and at times crying, I found the new freedom almost unnerving and was at a loss to know what to do with it. If I wanted to visit the nearby Portobello Road Market I no longer had to almost beg permission and calculate to the quarter hour when I would return. I could wander between the stalls for hours if I so wished and this liberation began to feel exhilarating and so I walked longer and further than I had done for years. I sauntered the streets of West London stopping to admire the lines of dilapidated Victorian terraces as if I was seeing them for the first time and daydreaming that possibly one day I might become a protected tenant of a ground floor flat where the garden would be transformed into a blaze of colour with a lawn and borders of spring flowers or a playground with perhaps a sandpit or even a swing. Dreaming on I banished the tenancy and instead became the owner of first the ground floor flat and later the house itself. It would sit in one of the more desirable streets nearing the top of Ladbroke Grove, definitely not those close to the tube station where the exterior paintwork was less pristine and the present tenants within usually black.

As I walked at times I ruminated in helpless circles of tangled thought as to how I had reached the point at which I found myself, reflecting upon the consequences had I made different decisions. I hugged in my heart more than a small measure of contentment. I was six months pregnant, unmarried, with little money in one of the harshest cities in the world with no place of my own to live, and I had no business to feel in any way satisfied with my lot; yet surprisingly there were many times when I did.

Shelagh expressed her own surprise.

'I thought you'd be in a much worse state emotionally,' she said.

'So did I, but my major emotion at the moment feels something very like happiness,' I told her one morning when the sun was shining and a conglomeration of thrushes and sparrows seemed to be singing like nightingales.

'Perhaps it wasn't love that was keeping you with him.'

There I could not agree because my love for him had been and still was, completely overwhelming, so much so that I still saw the growing child as the entity that would replace him, almost perhaps become him and these thoughts were an even deeper, darker secret.

'It would have been much wiser for you to have left him when he first demanded that you leave,' she observed unnecessarily.

But I had more than half convinced myself that when he had first told me he wanted me to leave it had been part of his sadistic game and he had never intended that I should actually do so.

'I don't think he really meant it,' I said. 'If he had been serious he would not have continued to take my money and ask me to buy materials for the business – and pay for the car.'

She did not look convinced and said that if a man demanded she leave him she would do so and what is more if he made subsequent requests for money she would have packed even more hurriedly.

'But if I had done that I would not now be pregnant,' I argued and she said that I could have become pregnant at some time in the future with a different, possibly more worthy male.

'But it wouldn't be this baby – his baby.'

'Maybe an easier child to bring up though,' she postulated. 'Remember that the one you have at the moment might not be plain sailing if it's anything like its father.'

I did so hope she was right though this was a time when genetic inheritance held less substance than now because environmental factors reigned supreme when raising children. Infants could be taught to read in the cradle with the aid of flash cards and in some cases were said to also master Hebrew and Calculus by the time they were two years old. If you wished your child to become a classical musician you simply paved the way with recordings of Verdi operas in the womb and the rest was easy.

It was her total confidence in the fact that a nurturing environment was the one over-riding consideration for the lifelong emotional security and well-being of any child that in the first place brought Shelagh to the conclusion that a father's input could be relegated to that of a sperm donor. I kept an open mind on these matters and continued the long daily walks, once finding myself as far away as Covent Garden, and then, exhausted, giving in to the prospect of a bus ride back to Ladbroke Grove.

I decided that it was all the unaccustomed exercise that promoted the labour pains that came to pass almost three weeks to the day after I left Northampton Square. Shelagh maintained that it was Vidar's final abortion attempt despite the lengthy interval of time. I had been baby-sitting the three-year-old daughter of the people in the house next door while they celebrated their wedding anniversary. Shelagh urged me to do so because Anne was a splendid cook and always left her baby-sitters very tasty suppers. She was right and I was left a Gorgonzola soufflé with a herb salad. When the niggling pain first began just before eleven pm I almost thought the Gorgonzola might be responsible. At first the pains were mere twinges though thirty minutes apart but by the time the couple came home at one o'clock they had increased in intensity.

I left, complimenting Anne on her soufflé and went directly to the main road and hailed a taxi that delivered me to Charing Cross Hospital in record time when I told the driver I thought I might be in labour. It was a grim place at that hour filled with little light, muted voices and every corner of the place seemed chilly. I was put into an empty side ward while someone searched for an on duty doctor who knew something about labour.

I began to believe that perhaps the child had been murdered after all, and lay there planning wild reprisals. The fetal stethoscope was prodigiously uplifting when the thunder of an infant heartbeat was discovered.

'It sounds much too fast,' I said.

'That's normal,' but the doctor looked ill at ease and had beads of moisture trickling from his hairline to his eyebrows.

I attempted to sound less distressed than I was. 'Will the baby die?'

He said, 'If your dates are correct it's very premature.'

A conversation took place about whether I should be given pain relief when the contractions grew stronger and somebody talked about depressed breathing so I was left without it.

I rang Shelagh who came at once and sat with me during the long morning and afternoon and tried to be cheerful. Then at five she had to leave to collect Virginia from the Daycare centre.

Daniel was born at last just before seven pm in the evening, abruptly and following a bout of searing pain and increasing agitation as those attending us came and went muttering things about gestational development.

Suddenly he was there, purple and screaming.

'Don't let him die,' I sounded like a schoolteacher issuing instructions to a class of noisy students.

'He sounds very lusty at the moment.' The sweaty doctor, still inexplicably on duty, looked relieved, almost jovial; job over!

He asked for an incubator and when one was found frantic minutes went by while they asked each other where the wall socket was and finally someone hurried off to find an extension cord. Daniel was deposited in it and whisked away.

Later that night, on the ward of newly-delivered mothers complete with their infants, the new-fangled notion sweeping through maternity wards at the time, I was visited by an earnest female doctor.

'Your baby has been taken to the Prem Unit in Fulham,' she said, 'and he's doing quite well though of course he's very premature.'

So completely saturated in euphoria was I that I heard little but the fact that he was doing well and all the information about birth weight and breathing difficulties went to the four corners of the ward and never for a moment penetrated my consciousness. It was to be some days before I quite realized that my son's birth at twenty-seven weeks gestation was, for the time, critically premature and at just under two pounds his weight was very low.

There were two of us on that ward minus our babies, mine because of prematurity and Mandy's because he was going to be adopted and her parents did not want her to become attached to him. Her mother visited daily and fussed and propped pillows and promised to buy her a new swimsuit just as soon as she came home, because then she could go back to school and go swimming with her mates at The Oasis and put all this nasty business behind her. Her father stood at the end of the bed and looked uncomfortable.

Mandy and I drifted rapidly into a powerful though short term friendship.

'What's your baby called?' she asked.

'Daniel Patrick,' I said.

'My baby is called Kevin,' she told me, 'I've named him after his Dad – he's a pop singer and he's in a band and everything. He's gorgeous but he doesn't know I've had Kevin.'

She began to cry and went on to tell me that although her mother would probably let her keep Kevin if she pushed hard enough, her father was dead set against it and that was that. She had to go back to school and get her exams and become a Telex Operator. She thought I was lucky to be able to keep Daniel; I thought I was lucky too.

A red-faced social worker with slight asthma came to the ward several times over several days to speak to both of us, doing so without a hint of privacy. The woman in the bed on my right was American with a husband at The Embassy and had just given birth to a nine-pound boy called Tom. She listened to everything that was being said to me with great interest. The woman on my left was not English and she at least pretended not to understand what was being said.

'What have you decided for Baby's future?'

I replied as impertinently as I could manage that I thought it was probably a little too early to put his name down for Eton and she wheezed a little as she scanned my face with obvious distaste.

'You perhaps should show some responsibility and give his future some thought,' she advised, adding that if I declined to do so she would be forced to recommend he remain in the Premature Baby Unit until I came to my senses. So I told her I might well decide to remove him from the unit the moment I was released from the ward and added that I assumed she didn't actually have him under lock and key. Having done so I felt pleased with myself, like a fourteen-year-old schoolgirl who has just been rude to a teacher and amused the whole class. Then I was a little fearful that she might actually have the power to decide his future without my consent.

She sighed and glanced at her watch.

'We need to know what kind of home you will be taking him to,' she explained. 'Whether in fact it will be suitable for a low birth weight baby.'

That outraged me and I asked if she would feel the need to ask such questions if I was married. I told her I could not help noticing that those on the ward claiming to be in that happy state were not subjected to the same level of interrogation. What if I should be in an abusive marriage? What was it exactly, I demanded, about the marriage ceremony that turned a woman into a good and responsible parent?

She sighed again and turned her attention to Mandy who simply cried and nodded and so she was able to comfort her and reassure her that she was doing the right thing.

When she had left, Mandy blew her nose and said, 'I think you're ever so brave to stick up for yourself but you want to be careful because social workers can really stuff you up if you're not careful.'

She went on to explain that her family had been in their clutches once or twice when her twelve-year-old brother started pinching stuff from Woolworths so she knew what she was talking about. So then of course I worried and thought I should backtrack a little but having established myself as the ward rebel in so far as authority was concerned it was rather too late to become reinvented as more compliant.

A day or two later, Mandy was white faced and melancholy saying, 'Kevin goes today – off with his new mum and dad. I really hope they don't give him some awful new name like Norman or... Gordon or something....'

She began to cry once more, quietly, huge tears dropping unheeded on the new yellow sweater her mother had knitted. Neither of her parents visited that day so she and I sat together in the newly established Smokers' Room and I introduced her to the joys of nicotine which she assured me was helping her to keep calm. She talked to me about Kevin the pop singer and showed me a creased photograph of him saying that his son had the same red hair so nobody could accuse her of inventing their relationship. She said that she and her best friend Sheryl had gone to every one of Kevin's London concerts and Sheryl had been jealous because Mandy was the one who got pregnant. I found this confidence surprising because she seemed so young yet I might have been more than likely inclined to behave similarly at the same age.

The next day her mother came to take her home and hurried her from the ward, reluctant for her to spend time on extended goodbyes, clearly seeing me in my unmarried state as somehow threatening her daughter's ability to put the baby incident behind her.

As the mothers who remained kept their distance I was able to withdraw once more into my bubble of euphoria because whenever I thought upon my newborn son I became suffused in exaltation simply because he actually existed and he was of the flesh and blood of Vidar and I was his mother. Never had I felt such passionate and all-consuming emotion and nothing that had happened to me previously could compete with the feeling of ecstasy. The rapture that these truths generated was so immense that at times I became anxious that it would somehow be torn from my grasp and so I woke in the middle of the night apprehensive that it had all been a dream. At these times I panicked and thought that in reality I was back in the Clerkenwell flat with the aborted remains of my child about me and Vidar hissing profanities in my ear. So during the weeks that followed his birth I still hugged close to me that extraordinary feeling of bliss, somehow imagining myself to be among the luckiest women in the world to be so blessed with the thing I had wanted with such desperation, the son of the man I thought I would never cease to love.

Because the baby was so very premature, he needed to remain in the hospital unit for many months and I found myself in the strange position of being a mother at a distance because although I visited the unit most days, I was not able to actually touch Daniel until he was four months old and had gained sufficient weight to make him, presumably, more 'normal'.

Often in those first few months, I mused upon the fairy tale aspects of his entry into the world and tried to determine if there was some way of convincing his father that this birth had been inevitable. Could he be persuaded that as in the best of fairy tales, he had simply misread the signs and that the existence of the child had come about from innate good rather than evil and, furthermore, was Meant To Be.

'Just as your own birth was Meant To Be,' I could hear myself explaining, 'after the termination your mother had….' and I might then pontificate a little on the mischievous inter-generational spirit that had worked enchantment on both Vidar and his father. Though unlikely, this scenario might well contain an extraordinary though improbable Truth because the behaviour of L'Estrange the Elder was, within the parameters of the time in which it occurred, very similar to that later re-enacted by L'Estrange the Younger. A tangible scientific explanation might even emerge some day and fact may then be allowed to lie somewhere alongside genetic memory.

I visualized a moment when Vidar would abruptly realise that I was correct, that he had simply been misdirected in his thinking by a malign spirit. Would he then embrace both Daniel and myself and beg our forgiveness? No matter how many times this scene played deliciously across my imagination, it always did so without much conviction.

The closer the time came for Daniel to leave the hospital, the more I dwelt upon the matter of how his existence might be revealed, not just to his father, but to others I had relationships with including my own family. If we continued to live in London it would be impossible to keep the child a secret and at present only Shelagh and Virginia knew about him. The day of his hospital discharge was delayed several times, on one occasion because he needed an urgent operation for an inguinal hernia, but by the beginning of October we were able to collect him. Virginia was very excited indeed and referred to him as her brother.

As with many dramatic break-ups of relationships, those we knew had been obliged to take sides and Vidar, true to form, had demanded of most that if they wished to remain his friend they could no longer be mine. Unreasonable though that is in itself it is still played out in various guises and in varying degrees between intelligent people who should know better. I was aware that it might happen and pretended that I did not mind very much though of course I did. The only surprise was with my brother who lived with his wife and small boy in Camden Passage, Islington. As a couple Vidar and I had been in the habit of seeing them once or twice a month.

'Janice and I have decided that for the time being we won't be able to see much of you,' he had said self-consciously after I left Northampton Square.

'Why not?' I demanded. Possibly they were leaving the district.

'Well we've been seeing quite a bit more of Vidar since you left and now we invite him to all our parties – and with you two breaking up and all...' his voice trailed off.

My heart thumped uncomfortably because now I was a mother I had already decided that I needed a family and I should endeavour to see more of them if I wanted my child to grow up knowing what a family was. Already I had rehearsed conversations introducing Daniel to his Uncle Bernard and Aunt Janice and little cousin Merlin, only a few months older. I had even seen them playing together in the sand pit at the park, saw myself taking both of them there.

'Hi Jan – don't worry, I'll take the boys this morning,' and off we would go through London squares to the play facilities in squares and gardens.

But of course as I had not yet revealed the fact to Bernard that he was an uncle he was unlikely to jump to any sensible conclusion as to why I now sniveled down the phone something about it being very unfair.

'What on earth's the matter?' he sounded genuinely puzzled. 'You know yourself that with Vidar always being right, it's impossible to have you both in the same room at the same time and in any case you'll be likely to fly off the handle if he brings his latest girlfriend with him.'

'Brings her where?'

'To a party.'

'How many bloody parties are you aiming to have?'

'Look, I don't want to argue about it,' he said in his 'this is final' voice, 'I'm just explaining that's all.'

'Who is this latest girlfriend anyhow?' I was now feeling very aggressive.

'Christine,' he said. 'He's living with that skinny bird Christine again – they both came over last weekend. She's quite nice when you get to know her.'

So he was living with Christine. She had finally wormed her way into my place in his bed. If she had appeared before me at that moment I think I would have strangled her with my bare hands, thoroughly enjoying every second of the act. I felt murderous for hours.

'I'm going over to Clerkenwell this evening,' I told Shelagh. 'What's more, I've decided to tell Vidar about Daniel.'

'Do you think that's wise?' she looked and sounded very doubtful as she watched me applying make-up and choosing what I should wear.

With the thought of Christine to the forefront of my mind I cared little if it was wise or not and rang him on the pretext of picking up mail, and being in the district. Then I added that in any case there was something important we needed to discuss.

'All right,' he said.

It was as I was walking up the stairs behind him that he half turned and casually told me that Christine was now living with him. I affected nonchalance whilst savouring her disquiet when she heard about Daniel.

When he opened the door to the living room she was sitting in the middle of the carpet looking wraithlike and otherworldly. He said he hoped what I wanted to discuss was not too personal and I said that of course it wasn't and that as Christine was living with him now, she had a right to know in any case. He looked slightly confused, I thought.

She sprang lightly to her feet, her white muslin skirt swinging against her pale legs and her untidy blonde hair escaping its many slides and clips and tumbling over her shoulders. Though inelegant she looked composed and natural and aloof. My heart was pounding and my hands were clammy because my hatred of her was so intense and it was tiring trying to force my face into a brighter than was natural smile. I heard my voice echoing back to me like that in a dream.

'How lovely to see you Christine. What a lovely skirt! Hasn't it been warm lately? Our flat is like an oven....'

It all sounded very artificial but I babbled on, walked to the window and looked out over the darkening square before turning to face them both again, slipping my jacket off as I did so and dropping it over a chair. She half smiled but said nothing except to offer coffee. I told her I would simply love one – white, no sugar – and she went off to make it. I hoped she was not lacing it with cyanide and almost laughed at the absurdity of the idea before wondering how likely it was that she detested me as much as I detested her. I tried to remember the names of all the poisons I had read about that were tasteless and impossible to trace at autopsy. Thalium seemed to ring a bell so then I thought she might have some and wildly followed her into the kitchen to 'help'. She was standing by the kettle, waiting for it to whistle. My whistling kettle, the very one I had made his morning coffee with for years. My kitchen was now her kitchen. And how I had loved this kitchen. It was me who had adorned the walls with Moulin Rouge posters. The homely peg rug on the floor was mine, bought at a library craft fair because it reminded me so much of my childhood.

I bent to touch the rug, then felt embarrassed. How often I had watched my mother, aunts and grandmother, busily engaged during winter evenings, making their own peg rugs from narrow pieces of cast aside clothing, socks, shirts, skirts, jackets. Items that had no wear left in them, that were too shabby and bedraggled to pass on for another round of wearing to someone smaller, painstakingly cut into strips of the right size. The cutting was often delegated to me and my female cousins once we reached an age deemed responsible enough, never to the boys, and as we grew to be eleven, twelve or thirteen years of age each of us had made our very own rugs.

'I love these rugs,' I said to Christine and she looked at me uncertainly though with a degree of triumph because my kitchen rug was now hers and I was aghast that I could have abandoned it so carelessly when I left. Maybe I had thought it would simply wait for my return, for the time when I would come back to this place to resume my real life, with my son and his father.

She asked how much milk I wanted and I told her, watching her pour it carefully into one of the chipped brown mugs. I stretched out my hand and asked if I should take Vidar his and she snapped that she would do it herself. Well of course she would. She swung his favourite Denby mug out of my reach, deftly, not spilling a drop and her pale eyes looked directly into my smiling, terribly aching face. 'You really hate me don't you?' she observed.

Perceptive Christine. Her observations spot-on.

'Of course I hate you – nothing is surer. I hate you for your composure, your willowy slenderness, for knowing Vidar years before I did, but more than any of those things I hate you for standing in my kitchen, opening my fridge, holding my mugs and looking so very much at home as you do so. I hate you for stealing my life.'

Of course that is what I did not say.

'Heavens, you mustn't think that Christine. I don't hate anyone. It's such a negative emotion isn't it?' I spoke far too loudly as I led the way back to the living room where Vidar lay slouched across the day bed idly looking at an old copy of The Times as if he was reading it, which he was not. He did not look up at me until we were all seated. I noticed that she sat beside him, just a little too closely, her hair snaking over the red and blue sequined Tibetan cushion that I had found in the Emporium in Kings Road.

I dropped as nonchalantly as I could manage with trembling knees onto the rug in front of them both, sipped my coffee for a bit, then hugged my knees. I was wearing a short tweed pinafore dress and under it a black polo neck sweater that matched my tights. All very up to the minute stylish for nineteen sixty eight so, confidence slowly mounting I began to fantasize that I looked just a little like Jean Shrimpton on the cover of the latest Vogue magazine. An effect lost on both of them probably as Vidar concerned himself little with fashion trends and from the look of her so did Christine. Though to be honest she looked far from her usual dowdy self on this particular evening and I decided that was probably because she now had her man firmly in her grasp once again. Regaining he whom she so coveted had made her bloom from within the way pregnancy affects some women. I abruptly remembered why I was actually there, in the Clerkenwell flat at that time, drinking coffee from a Denby mug and seated on the floor attempting to resemble a fashion model dawdling between photo shoots.

At the same moment Vidar said, 'Why are you here?'

Christine nodded and edged still closer to him and although he did not appear to notice, I did and drained the coffee in long, deliberate gulps wishing it was rum, or brandy or even whiskey which I hated.

'I came to talk about a most extraordinary thing that happened a few months ago – something that concerns you and me Vidar, and ultimately you too Christine as you are now an important presence in Vidar's life....'

She sat just a little more rigidly, both hands clutching the mug of coffee, knuckles white. There appeared little red spots high on her cheek bones. Both of them were looking at me expectantly, unflinchingly.

'Three weeks after I left this place, I gave birth to a live child,' and as I said this I could not help but allow a small smile of triumph just for her and she could not help but say decisively, 'No – that is not true....'

He laid his hand on her forearm to silence her and jerked more upright, asking me what exactly I meant. I wondered what it was he failed to understand about the precision of the language I had used and so I repeated it, pausing slightly between each word.

'But you had a termination and I know that for sure,' he said quietly. 'I did it myself and so I cannot possibly believe you.'

Christine was not heeding his hand still on her arm and now she jerked herself free and turned to face him, 'You told me she had two terminations… one when you were in Germany, another when you returned – twins you thought. How on earth?'

He nodded. 'Yes, yes, yes… that is all correct. I know for certain she had the first one because I saw the evidence with my own eyes. It was all most regrettable, a twin pregnancy and somehow the second fetus remained… and that is the one I terminated later myself.'

She allowed herself to half smile but it was the smile of someone who harboured a doubt. 'So how could you possibly have given birth to a child three weeks after you left? It's not credible is it Vidar?'

He sat quite still, saying nothing.

I shrugged, rocked back and forth just a little much the way he was inclined to do himself, and tried to look sombre. Then quite suddenly I wanted to laugh.

'Triplets maybe?' I ventured.

She gasped and her eyes widened. 'That is quite impossible. I find I am totally unable to believe that.'

Her voice was now sharp, school-mistressy. The words bounced off the once white, now nicotine stained walls until I almost fancied they danced about my ears. I wished he would order her to be quiet but he still said nothing and so I said nothing further. She demanded to know what she called 'the truth of the matter' and even if I had wished her to become more informed, which I did not, I would not have been able to reply because that same truth of the matter was itself deeply hidden inside the convoluted events of the past year and now difficult to prise from the quicksand of deceipt.

I had more recently romanticized no further than the glorious moment of revealing the birth to a first amazed then gradually more accepting father. This was not quite the scenario I had imagined so now, I just sat still and was vaguely aware that as usual I wanted to cry.

At last Vidar asked almost wearily, 'What has actually happened to this live child – this third fetus?'

What indeed? I explained about the extreme prematurity, the long months in hospital and the growth to robust good health of the enchanted triplet. Vivien had told me, 'Fairy Tale babies are always blessed.' I now fervently hoped she was right.

He was very still, sitting in a stooped position, eyes fixed somewhere at the point of my knees, exuding an air of total exhaustion. She was straight and upright, hands twisting together, radiating a great deal of doubt and disbelief. Several times she said that it was not possible. She did not believe it.

Then she said in a voice that was far too loud, 'You are known to be a habitual liar. Everything you say should be treated with the utmost caution.' A great deal of time had clearly been spent in discussion of the worst facets of my character. I found this gratifying.

He murmured more to himself than to either of us, 'There were some very powerful spirits at work in those last terrible months we were together.'

I congratulated myself for the inspired purchase and use of the hare, the flesh of which he had so readily consumed. It was satisfying in itself that a fresh hare could be purchased on that day in Chapel Market for had I been forced to settle for a mere rabbit some of the underlying symbolism would have been lost. I once more began to enjoy the fairy tale.

He was still speaking quietly. 'I went into battle against them but I underestimated their power.' He then looked directly at me again. 'I underestimated you – and your ability to withstand the pressure I placed upon you.'

'Well I guess that's often the way where fairy magic is involved,' I said and even thought I might be correct.

But Christine did not for a single second believe any aspect of the fairy tale although she was reluctant to say as much in his presence. I made brief reference to his mother's failed termination all those years ago which he had over recent years been more and more inclined to view as a magical attack upon himself even as he lay defenseless in the womb.

She did not quite laugh but looked as though she felt the urge to. I was a little aggrieved that she was prepared to overlook the strange repetition of events deep in his past now linked forever to my own experience. Why was it she ignored both Destiny and Fate? I could not determine how much she took into account my relentless determination to hold on to the baby regardless of outcome. We might have more in common than seemed obvious. In my position she might have done the same.

Vidar said several more times that he found it impossible to accept the possibility of a live child.

'Do you want to see him?' I asked hopefully, willing him to say yes.

Christine closed her eyes and wildly claimed that a divine communication was telling her, 'It is not...it is not...'

'Show me the child,' he said.

To my surprise he began to lead the way down the stairs and she got up to join us but he turned and told her that this was something he had to do alone. She shot me a look of undiluted hatred as he and I together stepped deeper into the territory of myths.

It was the only time he came willingly to see his son, lying peacefully asleep in his makeshift cot in Lancaster Road, unaware how alert and cautious I was, hovering above him ready to tear out the heart and eyes of his father should he make a wrong move.

But he did nothing except almost whisper, 'This thing is not human.'

Astonishingly he now seemed almost to fear the supremacy he perceived in the tiny child and briefly I tasted victory.

In the days that followed my prime emotion was relief because the fear of Vidar finding out about Daniel's existence was now removed. I was free to enjoy the baby, take him out and about and show him off to people who would be totally uninterested as most people are when the baby belongs to someone else. I was overcome with delighted satisfaction when contemplating how poor Christine might be feeling and how she and he would set about untangling the tightly woven fairy web. The fantasy had now become so adhered to truth that I could no longer rely upon myself to know what was accurate and what was invention. Significantly, Vidar had now seemed to entwine himself into the fabric of the fable. So it was no great surprise when two or three weeks after this time of revelation he rang and told me that he would like to meet up with me for a cup of coffee if I was willing. He had some mail to hand on to me and there was also a matter that he would like to discuss. Was I willing? Of course I was. I could hardly get to the meeting point, Farringdon Tube Station, quickly enough.

Might this be the moment when he would ask me to return to live with him? He had undoubtedly by now had time to think through the earlier events and there had been a moment of awe-inspiring realization when it dawned upon him that he had completely misinterpreted those omens of myth and fable and now knew that he had to be part of Daniel's life. He might even admit to feeling foolish because it would perhaps seem to him almost irrational that he had doubted me. He was Fully Enlightened after all.

I determined to reassure him, telling him that even those who are Enlightened are entitled to make occasional errors of judgment and he had long realized that those demons were formidable.

As I got ready for the meeting I considered what he might actually say and hoped that his opening strategy would concern Christine. Perhaps even, 'After a great deal of thought I have asked Christine to leave....'

'Oh really? Why are you telling me this?'

He would fidget a little and light a cigarette. 'I have come to the conclusion that I cannot abandon the mother of my child, no matter how imperfect she might be. The child needs two parents.'

No doubt he would elaborate and tell me how he had not been able to rid himself of the image of the sleeping infant, flesh of his flesh, the infant that was Meant To Be. After some silence he would awkwardly ask me to return to live with him. Should I perhaps at that point hesitate and demand time to think? Unwise with Christine still lurking in his life. No, better by far to agree immediately. What bliss! If I was allowed to return to him I vowed to work harder than ever at becoming a 'real woman' and my future sexual appetite would be prodigious, encompassing both males and females and possibly also an occasional animal. We would still attend the Saturday night orgies at times if it proved necessary because perhaps Jessica from downstairs would babysit, and the other attending males would be astounded and say things like, 'Great Scott old chap – we all really envy you that slave of yours. My word, hasn't she come along beautifully? Motherhood suits her.' Then he would glow with pride and perhaps even tell me that he loved me.

Shelagh said she would take care of Daniel and added that I looked stunning. I was wearing rather a lot of make-up, high boots and an old trench coat, dressing down in order not to look as if I had taken too much trouble about my appearance.

'Don't hope for too much,' she warned. I did not bother to argue with her. What did she know after all?

There was a kind of glow about the old Metropolitan line that afternoon as the equally elderly train rattled and rocked out of Ladbroke Grove station towards Farringdon. Westbourne Park, Royal Oak and Paddington seemed bathed in golden sunlight and even Great Portland Street and Euston Square, normally shrouded and lacklustre, strived to appear cheerful. Farringdon, although unkempt as usual, itself had an air of anticipation about its shabby environs as if waiting with baited breath for the outcome of this momentous meeting between the parents of a Special Child.

We met in an adjacent workmen's cafe of the kind that no longer exists. A place that then always seemed to be open, selling strong tea and fried egg sandwiches eighteen hours a day to the usually crowded tiny formica-topped tables in its equally tiny interior.

He was already there with a cup of suddenly increasingly popular Kona coffee in front of him, smoking. I thought that he smoked too much and as soon as we were living together again I should make efforts to encourage him to cut down, not just for his own health's sake but because now of course there was Daniel to consider. The hospital paediatrician had told me on more than one occasion that Daniel who already wheezed from time to time, might develop the occasional lung problem as was common with low birthweight babies. He didn't actually call it asthma but then this was a doctor who was reluctant to name any condition as though by doing so he made it more concrete, turning it from a possibility into a reality.

Vidar began to speak quite briskly and told me that he had now had time to give a great deal of thought to my pregnancy. He now believed that the very fact that it had occurred at all was due to some outside force working for Evil.

'Or perhaps for Good?' I tried to look diffident. This was not the way the conversation was supposed to start.

He looked gloomily up from the coffee but began to stir it. 'You only think that because your thought processes have been hijacked,' he said. 'What little innate ability you once had to process information has been altered by the meddling of a very dangerous spirit.'

He did not look like a man on the brink of accepting fatherhood and I felt panic rising from within and threatening to spill onto the table between us. But I persisted.

'How do we know it is dangerous? It could be the very opposite. Perhaps we only think of it as dangerous because this entity, whatever it is, wants us to think that way.'

He looked and sounded totally exasperated.

'I do think I am in a slightly better position than you to interpret such matters. I have studied the power of magic for years and you are at this moment within the clutches of something very nasty indeed. I tried to save you from it but you would not listen. If only you had listened to me months ago things would never have got to this stage.'

The sky outside began to darken and the former warmth and sunlight of the journey was abruptly hurled into a void of despair and despondency. Without much enthusiasm I asked him to explain. There was going to be no reconciliation.

'If you had not hesitated to abort that pregnancy in the first place when I ordered you to, you would not be where you are today.'

Well that at least was true. I would not be the mother of Daniel, gift from all the Gods.

'I knew that the longer it went on, the harder it would be for you – that is quite understandable of course. What I did not understand was that the Thing growing inside you was endowed with three heads...' he stopped to light another cigarette and offered me one which I accepted because although I had almost given them up, I began to fear what he would say next.

'Now you are in an unenviable position because in order to rid us of this Beast you will have to have great courage. You will have to assume the mantle of a Warrior Woman.'

He suddenly took my hand in his and looked directly into my eyes. The eyes of my baby son looked back at me and I ached with a pulsating passion for them both.

'You will have to have the courage of Artemis,' he was saying, 'Be as bold as Boudicca.'

There began a familiarly tight feeling in my throat and my heart thumped painfully. I asked him what I was to do, imagining it might just be possible to achieve. If standing inside a circle of daggers reciting the Lord's Prayer backwards whilst my flesh was pierced by demons was going to win him over then I would certainly give it a go.

He lowered his voice. 'I want you to rid us of that child. Neither of us can move forward with our lives while it lives. I do not want you to look upon it as human because it is not. It is as foul a creature as it is possible to be. It spews filth into our lives and it must die.'

He went on to instruct me how to suffocate Daniel using a plastic bag and how and when to remove it from his face, how long to wait before dialing for an ambulance. He intimated that if I had the courage to carry out this act he would be forced to reassess his feelings for me because the act in itself would indicate a change within me of gigantic proportions.

I began to feel frozen. I asked whether he would prefer to carry out the murder himself and said he would not because I had given birth to the creature and therefore it was only right that ridding the world of it should fall to me.

We both drank what was left of the coffee. I idly speculated on what the café clientele of men in blue overalls would think if they knew I was being detailed to murder a helpless infant with the aid of a plastic bag.

We sat together in silence for a long time. At last I got up, feeling stiff, all my muscles now aching as if I had been involved in a great deal of sudden and unexpected exercise.

'I don't think I'll be able to do so,' I said, 'I do not have that kind of courage.'

He told me he was very sorry indeed to hear that and said, 'Because of your ineptitude that disgusting fucking thing will be on my tail for the rest of my life and I therefore will curse you both through this life and into the next. You will have no luck – I will make sure of that.'

His voice had begun to rise and then the blue-overalled together with a woman whose hair was tied up in a bright red scarf, looked at us in a half interested way.

Somehow we both walked from the café, he in the direction of St. John's Road and me back into the station once again where a Hammersmith bound train thundered onto the platform almost immediately. In my despair I briefly contemplated throwing myself under it but, predictably, lacking the necessary daring, did not do so. Instead I nursed the misery closer and stepped inside the carriage.

Somebody Has To Do It

Shelagh thought that the time had come for us to seek advice about having some kind of charge brought against him. In fact, she elaborated, that time had long since passed.

'Can't you see that it just isn't right for him to continue to get away with this kind of behaviour?' she asked angrily.

I agreed with her and I wanted to report the latest incident to the police but I felt prevented from doing so, petrified at the mere thought of the process, of what the demons he had placed about me might do. I visualized them lingering in a half light but ever vigilant.

'He gets away with this sort of thing precisely because people are too scared to do anything to stop him.' She was sitting on a floor cushion, brushing Virginia's blonde curls into a fashionable topknot to be secured with the French clip she had been allowed to choose herself from Harrods the day before and now clutched possessively in both hands.

Virginia looked anxiously at each of us, finally venturing, 'You and Jeannie don't like Vidar do you Mummy?'

'Don't be silly,' Shelagh began to brush more vigorously and Virginia lapsed once more into silent watchfulness and tried to look less silly. She began to turn the clip over and over.

'You realise that if you do nothing it almost gives him permission to continue trying to persecute people, forcing them to do his bidding?'

'I suppose so.' I was brooding upon previous examples of similar behaviour, similar though in no way as extreme, conduct that he had related to me with a degree of something like self-satisfaction.

'I explained to my mother that I could have nothing more to do with her if she continued to have a relationship with my brother now that he and I no longer see eye to eye.'

'I told my cousin I would not be able to see her again if she refused to drop her association with my aunt. I have discovered that my aunt is a poisonous bitch.'

'I made it very clear to Christine that she must never see Joy again – certainly not if she wants me to continue to be her friend.'

Clearly in most cases the support of demons had not been an essential ingredient, those instructed perhaps being more easily compliant than I had been. But had they been wholly acquiescent regarding these orders, I wondered? Had Marie-Josephe Gebhard-L'Estrange communicated immediately with her older son telling him that sadly she was unable to see or speak to him again because it would greatly offend his brother?

It seemed doubtful.

Had his cousin hastily written to the aunt: *'sadly I have been advised by Vidar that I cannot have any further association with you..'*

Not very likely.

Did Christine have one final conversation with her good friend Joy informing her that their long friendship was now over?

In her case, possibly.

In those next few weeks I dwelt a great deal upon the fact that Daniel's father had asked me to commit an act of murder. Each time I gave thought to that meeting in the

Farringdon café it was with shock and distress. Could it be possible I had exaggerated the whole episode? Did he really offer such detailed advice as to how the killing should be carried out?

Then I began to worry that by ruminating upon it so much I might be aiding and abetting the demons he had threatened to send to pursue us, making their job easier. I would then feel compelled to rush to the baby's side to reassure myself that he was in no imminent danger and that he still breathed normally. Common sense dictated that the demons his father spoke of with such keen passion existed largely in his imagination and that I must not give them substance and begin to believe in them myself. Such counsel is sensible and even painless in the middle of a sunny autumn day, pushing the child through Holland Park with the routine activities of human endeavour about us. In the silence and darkness of night it was more challenging. Then I became fearfully uncertain and more than half accepted the existence of his mystical power. My belief was substantial enough to prevent me from making any report to the Metropolitan Police.

My ambivalence to do so lay within what remained of my spiritual beliefs. I was not totally convinced that God really existed yet I would have hesitated before claiming to be a non-believer. I believed in Something but was at a loss to know how to adequately describe what it was. I did not label myself as Agnostic because among the loose ends of a Roman Catholic upbringing there still lingered a robust thread of real Faith, a conviction in the existence of something Divine, even Mystical that did not quite fit into any religious classification. Not a typical Deity, not necessarily all-knowing. Not bathed in syrupy righteousness but a manifestation that worked for the ultimate benefit of mankind, sometimes against enormous odds.

This God that I had constructed was never in any doubt that Vidar had been vehemently against personal procreation and as it had later transpired, most particularly so if I was to be the mother. My God was totally aware of my subterfuge and each and every machination of my duplicity. More importantly however, my God recognized that Daniel, the result of all the spiritual chicanery, was simply an innocent victim of circumstances and should be protected. My devotion to the baby was self-evident, unmistakable maternal passion for all the world to see, infinitely more extreme than the unmitigated paternal hatred.

Although in those days I sent up frequent prayers to remind the Deity of our difficulties, at the same time I had only a small doubt that we would ultimately be protected and that remaining small vestige of uncertainty only made its presence felt as I have said under the cover and darkness of the night. In those prayers I frequently proposed bargains.

'If you protect us I will go to Mass every Sunday – even though I know that Mass isn't really your thing – it's the closest way I can find to show my appreciation.'

'If you don't allow any harm to come to us I will do good deeds for the rest of my life and I will train Daniel to do good deeds also. We will live exemplary lives.'

'If Daniel grows up unharmed once he is a man I will again become a nun and I'll be the best nun you could ever ask for.'

I regressed once more to the child who made frequent pacts with the Virgin Mary.

'Holy Mother please, please allow me to get Friday's spelling test mostly correct and I will never tell another lie….Holy Mother I beg you to help me with long division and if you do I will do the washing up every day for a whole week.'

Now I tried to negotiate more appropriate incentives on a daily basis, then as time passed and Daniel appeared to suffer no long term damage or injury, my pleas and prayers subsided to a more manageable, less frantic level. I gradually clawed my way towards adulthood once more.

Later that year for some odd reason or other Vidar told his mother about the child and she valiantly travelled to London and demanded to see him. Predictably he waited until she arrived before telling her that he had no intention of preventing the meeting but she must understand that if she did meet Daniel he would be unable to have further contact with her himself. It was a game he knew well, played to perfection and clearly enjoyed. After some days of hesitation she admitted defeat because she loved him dearly and by that time she was old and lonely, and then he managed to extract a further undertaking from her that she would never reveal Daniel's existence to Rollo. He did not wish his brother to know about him. She kept this promise over the years and when as an adult Daniel finally got in touch with his uncle he was astonished that the secret had been kept from him.

Strangely, although she clearly feared her younger son yet desperately desired to maintain a close connection with him, at the same time her grandmotherly instincts remained strong and at one point she wrote me a letter telling me that her greatest wish was to meet her grandson before she died. Because she had been left in no doubt as to the extent of the many curses placed upon him she enclosed a piece of lucky heather to place over his bed. I vowed to keep the letter for him but sadly somehow or other over the years it was lost.

I was totally in love with my baby and saw my life as infinitely less complicated than had been the case when I lived with his father but it was a strangely disquieting time when I mostly elected to keep away from those friends who had known us both, largely because I knew it was most unlikely that they would display much loyalty towards me.

Clive had kept in touch with me during this time, half as a friend and half as a client and often taking me out for mid-week dinners. I assumed from his general conversation that he was still organizing the occasional Saturday orgy although he was careful not to dwell too much upon them because it appeared that Vidar was a regular attendee with his new girlfriend, a teenage runaway called Jenny, joyfully discovered by him in an all-night café on Christmas Eve.

Instead he made strenuous efforts to introduce me to an establishment he frequented on a regular basis, a deviation house run by a Madam called Connie. His efforts came at a time when I was acutely aware that I needed to return to work of some kind but dithering about what it might entail.

I was now at a point where I could completely abandon my previous life of sin and depravity since there was now no-one urging me to delve deeper and deeper into it. There was no pressure to continue for the titillation of the man I loved, not to mention for the added bonus of the remuneration involved. I now had the perfect opportunity to discard a life of immorality and return to shorthand and typing. I might even find a job in Tin Pan Alley once more and Stan Douglas, calling by one afternoon to chat, made various suggestions and offered introductions.

'Why typing?' I asked him, slightly confused since it was he who had so persuasively urged me to enter the night club lifestyle years previously.

'Just thought now you've got a child you might want to do something different – you can't work in a night club for ever after all.'

Did he now think I was now past my prime, over the hill?

'It does pay better,' I said and he agreed.

The sensible option as seen now from a twenty-first century vantage point would have been to have investigated a career in journalism. I knew I would enjoy the journalistic life and I would probably be good at it. Daniel's hospital specialist obviously thought so too and had introduced me to the editors of magazines called 'Health Visitor' and 'The Nursing Times' who asked me to write articles for them on various topics – mothering a premature infant, coping with life as an unmarried mother, etc. It had been very exciting initially to see my name in print in real magazines, bought and read by real people. There was something, however, that was quite disengaged about the experience and almost as if the person who wrote under my name was not actually me at all. I bought at least half a dozen copies of each edition bearing my name, feeling enormously pleased with myself. They paid reasonably well too but not as well as what I might have received for sexual favours and I began to see with a shock that I was actually craving a return to more exotic part time work. It was disturbing to admit then and now that I actually hankered after a return to life as a showgirl, possibly even at Murrays Cabaret Club if Pops would have me.

Daniel was now nine or ten months old and for the past several months both Shelagh and I had applied for what we both called National Assistance although the National Assistance Act 1948 had recently been replaced by the Supplementary Benefits Act. This meant that because we were both unmarried with children to support we were entitled to have our rent paid and also a small sum to live on. Theoretically we were supposed to name the fathers of the children the State was now supporting which was fair enough because then some of the money might be recovered from them. Shelagh had named Tim who was an actor she had a brief relationship with and who was quite unaware that as a result of the relationship he had become a father. He could now not be found.

I was very reluctant to name Vidar because I felt that by doing so all the unpleasant business regarding magic and demons and curses would be stirred up once more and in any case I believed it most unlikely that the State would ever be able to retrieve any money from him. Instead I made up a barely believable story about going to a party and not being able to remember what happened to me there. For the same reason when I registered Daniel's birth I did not name his father on the Birth Certificate. These decisions were made hastily and I came to regret both of them in later years.

Although Virginia was nearly four years old, Shelagh had never previously applied for any state assistance but instead had gone to work as a clerk in a city office as soon as possible after the baby's birth saying it was because she feared any invasion into her privacy. From six weeks of age Virginia had been placed in Daycare. She had always been a sickly child, pale and often bad tempered with a strangely swollen abdomen and frequent unexplained high temperatures. Eventually it was found that she had Coeliac Disease in an extreme form and her diet needed to be closely monitored. The Daycare centre seemed unable to cope with her new dietary requirements and so Shelagh decided that the best option would be to abandon her job and apply for help. I decided to do likewise but we both found that state assistance gave us barely enough money to survive on, living as we did in central London. In the nineteen sixties, London might have been swinging but women who had babies out of wedlock were still treated as social outcasts. Welfare had to be a short term measure.

For some reason, probably because of the tales we told about those who did or did not father our children, we were allotted a Visiting Officer whose name was John Vincent. We called him JV and he seemed to visit far more frequently than should have been necessary. At first we thought this might be because we were thought to be unstable and possibly even bad mothers, but it turned out months later that he simply liked us. We made a change from the rest of his case load and so he took to popping in for cups of instant coffee on a reasonably frequent basis, on one occasion bringing us a second hand TV set as a gift. We suspected that his home set must have been recently updated and we were very grateful.

Clive clearly thought that it was a pity Daniel had been born at all and couldn't understand when I told him that the baby was definitely wanted.

'He's going to cost you a great deal in the end,' he said, sounding a bit like a maiden aunt. 'How on earth are you going to ensure that he's properly educated?'

There was no adequate answer to that question, or at least not one that Clive would see as adequate. He had no children of his own, saw suitable education in terms of Eton and Harrow, and did not understand maternal instinct.

'You need to earn some money dearest,' he said, not for the first time, one evening when he picked me up to take me to his current favourite restaurant in Notting Hill.

'You'd have the opportunity to earn quite well with Connie,' he stated, reluctant to leave the subject as we sank our teeth into roast duckling with cherry sauce. 'She's in Pont Street – and she has an impressive client list.'

'Impressive?'

He poured more wine and looked at me sharply. 'She doesn't deal with no-hopers darling – people stick with her for years because she provides a bloody good service and she never gossips. Connie's as safe as houses.'

He managed to make her sound a little like a Swiss bank.

I was cautious because working in Pont Street for Connie sounded a long way away from working in the floor show at Murrays and also because a brothel catering to those with sexual deviations was not something I had any experience in. Perversions sounded unsavoury.

'I'm not sure I'd be good at it.'

'You'll pick it all up in no time,' Clive assured me, 'I'll take you to meet her darling – you can have a chat and then make up your mind about it.'

So a day or two later I met her, having been instructed by Clive, who accompanied me, to wear demure underclothes in pastel colours. I dropped into Marks and Spencers at Marble Arch to make the special purchase, bra, panties and underslip in palest lavender, trimmed with lace and most definitely not what I would normally have selected.

Connie's establishment was above an antique shop that appeared to be run by two elderly gentlemen who looked as if they had been there for decades, as dusty as the stock over which they hovered. She operated out of what was in fact quite a large apartment in which every room except the kitchen had been given over to the specific needs of sexual deviants.

She was a woman in her late sixties, not exactly motherly but looking more like an aunt you didn't see very often. She wore a tweed skirt and fawn twin set, sensible flat shoes and pearl ear rings. Her mid brown hair was permed in a short and practical fashion and she wore very little make-up. She was precise in her movements and stood erect, smelling of Mitsouko by Guerlain. She briefly appraised me, taking in every detail of my modest blue pleated skirt and the new cream sweater that could easily be mistaken for cashmere but wasn't.

'How are you dear? – I'm Connie.'

I had already decided to become Bernadette which my family always considered to be my real name. My father, Bernard Joseph had been unyielding in this respect and initially I was to be Bernadette Josephine which caused my mother sleepless nights.

'I want just plain Jean,' she had repeated. 'A name you can't shorten and after Jean Harlow. A sensible name.'

An hour before the baptism ceremony at the distinctively austere Roman Catholic Church on The Hill at Northfleet, he conceded that Jean might be adopted instead of Josephine which she thought was only a minor victory. I was told later by several aunts present at the time that when the priest, dripping holy water above me asked what my name was to be my parents both spoke at once, she firmly stating that it was to be Jean, just plain Jean and he just as definite that it must be Bernadette Jean at which point my mother is said to have burst into tears. The baptism certificate, long since lost, turned me into Jean Bernadette which my father never forgave her for and for the first ten months of my life he determinedly called me Bernadette and for the sake of peace my mother did not argue. When he finally got his Calling Up papers and disappeared to Italy and North Africa with the Royal Engineers, I finally became Jean and later still Jeannie. Nevertheless, at times in my life when asked my real name I always felt I should be Bernadette and for some reason I decided to adopt it once more with Connie.

We shook hands warmly. Clive had clearly talked to her about me in advance of the meeting and so after more pleasantries during which we drank tea and nibbled on Bourbon biscuits, he demonstrated how competent I was at my chosen occupation.

We had moved into a tiny sitting room at the centre of which was a small raised dais and upon it a sturdy wooden post with a number of restraining devices and chains attached to it.

Clive said to Connie, 'Chain her up' to which she replied, 'You do it dear,' and so he did only a little resentfully because what he really wanted to do was observe us both from one of the armchairs.

Later, when I got to know her better, she told me that some clients, like Clive, tried to get her involved on the periphery of their fantasies but she was not going to have that at all because at her age she was beyond all that kind of thing and what's more she found some of their requests quite disrespectful.

He then ordered me to lift my skirt which I struggled to do because of the security of the restraints and shackles but eventually the pale lavender lacy garments were displayed to his satisfaction.

'Just look at her beautifully clean underclothes.' He was definitely getting into character now, adopting the mantle of the hobby sadist. Connie looked and agreed with him.

'I'll show you what a good slave she is,' he said. 'Fetch me some canes – I think I'll have canes today.'

So from one of the cupboards Connie produced a cylindrical container presumably designed for umbrellas and walking sticks, now filled with a variety of canes of various thicknesses and lengths. Clive selected one and then released me from the chains.

'You realise I'm going to punish you don't you?' he said, stroking my chin with his left hand.

'Yes Master I do.'

'And you understand you must thank me for every stroke don't you, no matter how much it hurts?'

'Yes Master.'

'Why must you thank me Bernadette?'

'Because the pain is good for me Master and you only inflict it because you care about me.' With Clive I was word perfect.

So I was required to lower the lavender panties just sufficiently for the exercise and he proceeded to inflict ten strokes of the cane, rather more severely than was his normal practice. However, I steeled myself not to wince too much and thanked him profusely for every stroke. Following the final one I was instructed to watch attentively while he masturbated and he told me what a wicked slave I had been to encourage such behaviour from him.

'I'm so sorry Master – so terribly sorry – but don't beat me again Master....'

And then it was all over and he went to freshen up whilst Connie led me back to the kitchen and poured more tea, her face betraying no emotion whatsoever. She offered another biscuit.

'Yes dear,' she said at last, 'I think I can use you, probably two days a week to begin with. How about Wednesdays and Thursdays? How would those days suit you?'

They suited me very well.

'Now I start at about midday – mid week we get quite a few on lunch breaks. I finish sharp on six as often as possible because of my train.'

We agreed that I would drop by the next day without Clive and she would show me the rest of the establishment and explain a little about the clientele.

Clive had returned looking pleased with himself and placed some five pound notes on the coffee table to which she said there was no need, no need at all. However, they were allowed to remain.

'Well, what do you think?' he asked when, half an hour later we were sitting in a coffee house in Kensington High Street. 'Funny old duck isn't she?'

I agreed but said there was something likeable about her. I didn't really find her terribly likeable at that stage but was at a loss as to what else to say.

'I've known her for years of course,' he said, biting into a caramel slice, 'She comes up from Brighton each day on a first class season ticket and shares a carriage with Larry Olivier. She runs a very good show, very efficient and she's as solid as a rock. Been in the business for thirty five years to my knowledge and never been raided.'

In those days London Madams like Connie lived in fear of being raided and eventually they invariably were so the fact that Connie had so far flown under the radar was impressive. In the nineteen sixties it was not actually against the law to be a sex worker and you could in fact happily work in your own home and you might be largely left alone. However, soliciting was an offence and running a brothel was most definitely forbidden, brothel keepers being harshly treated by the legal system.

The next afternoon Connie outlined my job description and showed me around the premises. Although some of the rooms contained beds, she said they were not routinely used. Her clientele was made up for the most part of sadists and masochists but she also catered to a number of other more specific sexual deviations such as necrophilia.

'Though I've only got two at the moment,' she said, 'And the older fellow never uses the coffin.'

She had thrown open the door of a room that contained a small four poster bed with heavy velvet drapes and a plinth at the foot of it on which was a darkly polished coffin with satin lining and elaborately decorated handles.

I swallowed and said in as normal and level a voice as I could manage, 'So I just lie in it do I?'

'If he wants that dear,' she opened the nearby wardrobe door, 'And here are the wedding dresses he might want.'

We examined two ivory silk dresses, one with a long train and leg of mutton sleeves and the other knee length with short sleeves. I made suitably admiring noises.

'Is it a bride fantasy then?'

She looked at the dresses as if seeing them for the first time. 'Well you could say that dear but I'm of the opinion that the poor fellow's wife died on their wedding day – he's never really got over it. The other one is quite different, he's just your average necrophile.'

I couldn't help wondering what might be average about necrophilia.

'We'll look at the dungeon now dear.'

I followed her along the corridor to the room behind the kitchen that had clearly once been intended as a maid's room. The one small window was covered with black hessian and the walls were adorned with a number of mechanisms obviously intended for long or short term restraint but what dominated the room was a huge wooden crucifix.

She followed my glance and half chuckled. 'Again dear not a common request but having said that we have one or two of them. One of them is a lovely chap – never takes too long, just hang him up there and in next to no time Bob's your uncle but the other two can be real sods at times....'

'Oh – what do they want then?' I was beginning to think I might not be totally suitable for this particular part time job. The floor show at Murrays became ever more enticing.

'Well old Henry really does think he's Jesus and of course you might have to be Mary Magdalene – but look it's not the end of the world and he pays well.'

She brushed an imaginary speck of dust off her shoulder and looked at her watch. 'It's the third one you have to be careful of – not that he's ever been a problem to me but I inherited him from somebody else because she just couldn't cope with him anymore.'

With a little encouragement she explained that he paid very well indeed but that some girls just did not like being up on the cross themselves and I said that I could completely understand that.

'Sometimes we don't see him for months on end,' she said comfortingly.

She showed me the rows of rubber and bondage regalia and outfits neatly hanging in the hall cupboards together with the assorted apparel for the leather fetishists and warned me never to get them muddled up.

'A rubber man will get very upset indeed if you muddle him up with a leather man – they like to feel they're special as you probably realise.'

I said I could understand that and we moved on to the large marble and gold bathroom and I wondered vaguely if there was such a thing as a bath fetish.

She pointed to the round glass table beside the bath.

'There we are dear – and I do have quite a few of them.'

'Oh.' I had no idea what she was talking about so I just nodded because if she had quite a few they might indeed be the backbone of the business.

'I think I've got most of London's now,' she observed, 'because naturally enough they're not popular.'

I agreed that they well might not be and remained mystified.

'Somebody has to do it,' she said, 'but it's not always a pleasant job is it dear?

I nodded with more enthusiasm and was still perplexed.

She then showed me the various costumes for those who did not request either rubber or leather attire and explained that she thought it tidier to keep them completely separately, though some of the girls could be remarkably untidy.

There were a number of school uniforms, nurses' uniforms, police uniforms, nuns' habits as well as a range of demure Victorian and Edwardian day dresses. A row of shoes with impossibly high heels stood neatly in a row, erect as soldiers.

'It's better that you come here looking as ordinary as possible,' she said. 'Don't wear anything that draws too much attention to you – and not too much make-up. Don't arrive in a taxi or if you do, make him drop you at the corner, never in front of the building.'

We went back to the kitchen and drank more tea. She asked me how long I had been doing 'this kind of work.' I decided not to tell her about my previous experience in night clubs and said instead, 'Not long at all really but I've got a little boy to support – he's nine months old.'

'Don't tell any of the clients you've got a child dear – they might not like it.'

She asked how old I was and when I said I was twenty-eight she obviously felt that was getting on a bit and said I was to tell the clients I was nineteen. Finally she talked finance.

'What happens with money is that I'll pay you at the time whenever possible of course and always in cash. I only deal in cash and with one or two exceptions they all conform. There are different rates for different services and I take a cut from all of them – you get the rest.'

It sounded fair enough to me.

'How about starting next week,' she suggested and I agreed at once though I felt just a little uneasy.

Once in the street again I hesitated before deciding that Knightsbridge was probably marginally closer than Sloane Square and headed that way trying to shake off the odd feeling of regret that my life as a showgirl would now appear to be well and truly a thing of the past.

A House of Deviation

'So how would you describe yourself now?' Shelagh asked, 'Now you're an employee of Connie? There must be a proper name for it.'

We sat in what passed as the living room but doubled as her bedroom, in the Lancaster Road basement flat where the layout was the opposite of what now might be called 'friendly' or possibly even 'intuitive'. The flat was entered via the side of the house, down a flight of uneven stairs that were proving pushchair-unfriendly in the extreme. The miniscule galley style kitchen in those days for some reason called 'an American kitchenette' was jammed to the right of the entrance-way and Virginia slept in what had once been the wine cellar, to the left. What she proudly called her room was separated from all those who entered the place by a heavy curtain donated by our landlord's wife. As it was the first separate personal space she had experienced in her almost four years of life she was inordinately proud of it, endlessly re-arranging books and dolls and boxes of Lego. The bedroom occupied by Daniel and myself faced the rear garden and led directly into the bathroom which meant that anyone wanting to use those facilities day or night had to do so by passing through it.

When the sleeping spaces had been decided upon Shelagh had said that she didn't want to shove me into the back room but she did think that with a small baby it would be much more convenient if I was the one closest to the bathroom. This had been some months before

Daniel was released from the Premature Baby Unit and by the time he was I had become accustomed to the inconvenience of the through traffic.

We were sipping strong instant coffee. We always made it with evaporated milk and it was our non-alcoholic beverage of choice at that time. I considered what being an employee of Connie now made me.

'Well definitely not a showgirl,' I allowed the final remnant of the dream to flutter away into the ether with more than a little unwillingness.

'Not a hostess either,' she agreed, adding, 'Well in a kind of a way maybe you are a sort of hostess.'

I considered this, thinking back to the hostess years. Strangely even that work, reasonably tasteless as it had been, was beginning to look attractive as it receded. I corrected her. 'Strictly speaking Connie is the hostess. I'm sure she would see herself that way.'

'Definitely not a call girl…' she was sitting on the floor, her back resting against the bed where Virginia now lay pretending to read a book called 'Little Bear', her current favourite and one she was most definitely intending to read for herself before too long. She looked from one to the other of us with interest and asked what a call girl was.

'Never mind,' we said in unison.

'I'm not keen on call girl,' I said.

Shelagh advised that 'fallen woman' was more descriptive and I said that if we were going for descriptive I'd always fancied being a harlot.

'What about strumpet? Or floozy? – even hussy.'

We were both now becoming helpless with laughter and Virginia got tired of asking what these new words meant and wandered away to see if the overweight three-year-old boy from next door, known as Nosher to all and sundry, was available to play.

'I'm settling for courtesan,' I said at last. 'It has a ring of chic to it – after all let's never forget that Lillie Langtry was described as a courtesan at one time.

'You bear no resemblance to Lillie Langtry.' Shelagh got up from the floor and made a fresh round of the evil-tasting coffee.

Despite the forced humour with which I cautiously approached the topic of my new employment I was distinctly nervous when the following Wednesday I prepared carefully for my first day. After a great deal of indecision I wore a grey twinset hurriedly bought from Whiteleys with a tartan skirt of indeterminate clan tradition in muted charcoals, greys and reds. My black shoes with kitten heels had been polished until they glowed and teamed with a black shoulder bag, carelessly slung across one shoulder. The Burberry trench coat, a gift from one of my former club customers, Dennis, completed the ensemble and I must admit I was more than happy with the effect. I looked respectable and easily overlooked.

'You look like someone applying for a job at MI5,' Shelagh told me approvingly.

'Is Jeannie going for a new job as a harlot?' Virginia asked with interest.

'Don't use that word,' we were speaking in unison again, to her always a bad sign and she looked confused, opened her mouth to ask why not and wisely closed it again.

It was a beautiful sunny early December morning when I turned towards Pont Street from the tube station, strangely mild for the time of year. Even the plane trees, now devoid of their usual plumage, nevertheless looked slightly bewildered as if contemplating the notion as to when or whether they might prudently begin to think about Spring.

The two elderly men in the antique shop were engaged together in attending well to an American with natural voice projection who wanted a writing desk shipped to Baltimore because it was the most delightful piece of furniture she had ever come across in all her born days. I pressed the bell and waited while she invited them to call her Bonnie and told them the glass in her windows at home was nearly two hundred years old. I could not hear a word of what they said though they seemed both to be animated. It was possibly a very expensive desk.

As I pressed the upstairs bell for a second time Connie appeared at my side saying her train had been delayed by a whole half hour and it simply wasn't good enough. She might even write a complaint to British Rail. There had apparently been a points failure somewhere and I nodded in what I hoped was an interested manner although I did not have much clue as to what a points failure might be, even after years of using suburban trains in my teenage years.

The American exited the shop, the narrow door held open by one of the proprietors. Connie bid them both good morning and commented that it was a really lovely day for the time of year. We ascended the stairs and she began to take off her headscarf and said that she only spoke to the 'old fellows' when it was impossible, or impolite not to. She warned me to keep my distance also.

She urged me to take my coat off and hang it in the entrance hall, then we went into the kitchen and she immediately filled the kettle.

'At times dear, you'll be here by yourself,' she said. 'You'll be locking up by yourself – what you must remember to do before you leave is empty the kettle – completely empty it, do you understand?'

I said I did and she added, 'If it's not completely emptied you get a terrible lime scale build-up inside and I can't abide it.'

I would be very careful to make sure it was empty I told her.

'I don't like to turn down custom,' she said as we sipped our first cup of tea of the day, 'but I don't like to miss my train either so there will be times when you will have to lock up. Now today you'll be working with Kiki and Margo and they will both be here soon.'

Almost as soon as she spoke they arrived, within a minute or two of each other, neither ringing the bell to be admitted as they both seemed to have keys. Kiki appeared to be several years younger than me and later I found that she was twenty-four. She was very blonde in a Nordic way, tall and slim and fashionably dressed in a navy and beige woollen mini dress and jacket and soft boots from Anello & Davide. However, she wore no make-up and carried an umbrella which considerably toned down the first impression. Margo was probably in her mid-thirties, small and dark and sensibly dressed like me. She lived in Folkestone, she told me later, and was married with two little girls. It was her second marriage and her husband was younger than her, and trying to build up a business as a plumber in the area but it was uphill work. When I got to know her better, a week or two later, she told me that her family thought she worked part time in an antique shop because the two owners were old and didn't want to run the place on a full time basis.

'Like the couple downstairs?'

She laughed. 'They gave me the idea.'

It seemed a good idea and I employed it for myself which worked out very well indeed just as long as no-one was interested enough in antiques to try to locate the premises. This is in fact is precisely what happened three years later when the man who was to become my husband, on a whim decided to find the place. Suffice to say, Margo's electrician did not belong to the ranks of the curious and merely said from time to time that he wished she would find employment closer to home.

'He's not much of a cook,' she said, 'and he hates having to get the dinner ready for him and the girls, even though I prepare most of it in advance.'

Kiki said that her boyfriend with whom she lived 'most of the time' was not curious really about what she did and anyway she told him she was a model, a photographic model. That was why, she explained, she took the precaution of leaving home each day looking as much like a model as possible.

The jaunty red telephone on the kitchen table began to ring and within twenty minutes of arriving, both Margo and Kiki were dispatched into the depths of the apartment to await clients, both regulars and both it seemed, called John.

When the phone rang for the third time Connie said, 'No – Kiki is busy I'm afraid but I've got a new girl here today – Bernadette. Would you like to try her? Yes, she's a very nice girl – very young – only nineteen. Just left home I think'

He obviously agreed and she replaced the receiver, turning to me again. 'He's called Peter and he wants a school girl – ideally he'd like you to be fifteen but of course that's not possible. Now let's find a uniform for you.' She led the way to the cupboard containing the vast array of costumes. 'He's very fond of the maroon gym slip and cream blouse but underneath you have to wear red satin panties.' She began rummaging through the various options until she found an ensemble that satisfied her.

It was by no means cold but as I dressed as instructed my teeth chattered. No bra, red satin panties, gymslip, maroon and yellow tie, straw boater with a yellow band around it. I looked every inch the schoolgirl. Connie had left an array of canes on the bottom of the bed, laid out in order of circumference and length. I sat on the bed in the middle bedroom and studied myself in the large gilt framed mirror opposite and tried not to think about them too much. Would he perhaps be more punitive than Clive?

Peter turned out to be quite an elderly man, smartly dressed in a dark suit. Connie introduced me.

'This is my new girl, Bernadette – now treat her nicely won't you?' Then she closed the door behind her.

He smiled at me a little stiffly and asked me to stand up and face the mirror which I did at once.

'When I ask you to do something I expect you to say – Yes, Sir,' he admonished as he chose a cane, picking up first one then another, examining each as if this was the first time he had come across such items. Finally he made a choice and swished it through the air two or three times.

'You know what is going to happen, don't you Bernadette?'

'Yes, I do Sir,' I responded meekly, looking down at the floor and wishing I had been told what kind of accent I was supposed to have. Was I perhaps an East End schoolgirl – or a girl from a boarding school? He provided the answer almost immediately.

'How old are you now?'

'I'm nearly fifteen, Sir.'

'You have broken bounds yet again,' he said in a weary voice, and reminding me of the Mother Superior who years ago prevented me from becoming a nun.

'Yes, I did Sir.'

'You went into town didn't you?'

'Yes Sir....'

What had I done in town?

'Are you wearing your school knickers?' he asked me and I noticed a bulge in his trousers increasing in size as he spoke.

'No Sir – I don't think I am,' I replied honestly.

'What are you wearing instead?'

I now began to enter into his fantasy with a little more enthusiasm. 'I don't want to tell you Sir....'

'Why don't you want to tell me, Bernadette?' His voice became more animated and he straightened his shoulders.

'Because you'll be angry Sir and you might beat me.'

'Yes, I am going to beat you – I'm going to cane you... but I want you to tell me what you are wearing instead of your school bloomers.'

With not too much effort, I began to cry. 'I'm wearing red satin panties, Sir – I threw my school knickers away.'

'How dare you throw your school bloomers away? I want you to show me – lift your skirt.' The cane whistled a little as he made practice strokes, slowly encircling me two or three times.

Connie had told me that he would be entitled to give me ten strokes. He asked me to lower the offending red panties and I prepared for the first of them. It was surprisingly moderate and so I relaxed a little.

'They won't all be as gentle as that one,' he said. 'I have been kind to you Bernadette – you must agree surely?'

'Yes Sir – you have been very gentle....I don't deserve your compassion.'

'That vulgar item of apparel you are wearing instead of your regulation bloomers is disgusting – I would expect to see it covering the private parts of a hussy rather than a girl from this school. What will your parents do when I inform them of this further breach of rules?

'My father will beat me, Sir.'

'Exactly – and I'm beginning to think you like being beaten.'

'I know I need to take my punishment, Sir.'

He ordered me to lower the panties further and gave me three more strokes of the cane in quick succession. They were much harder than the first one and I winced and cried harder.

'Just stop snivelling,' he ordered, busily releasing his now erect penis from the smart trousers. The buttons were small and rubber and difficult to navigate under the circumstances.

The final strokes were delivered with increasing severity and between each he masturbated, telling me what a filthy little hussy I was and how he longed for the day when his school would be rid of me. I was, it appeared, a bad influence on the other students. I apologized and told him that it would not happen again but agreed that I was indeed a filthy little hussy.

This seemed to be exactly what he wanted and he thanked me politely before disappearing into the bathroom. A few minutes later I heard him speaking pleasantly with Connie in the kitchen.

I changed back into my own clothes, being careful to hang the school uniform back in its rightful place before returning to the kitchen.

'Go and freshen up a little dear,' Connie advised, 'There's a lovely young man on the way who wants to try my latest girl. He's a regular and his name is Hillford – we all call him Hilly.'

I wondered if Hillford was his first name or his family name or perhaps even an assumed name.

'Years back I knew his father,' she elaborated, 'and I think Hilly is just trying to prove he's a grown up boy – he'll give you a couple of strokes and then it's just straightforward – I don't think his heart is really into sadism to be perfectly honest.'

Kiki came into the kitchen at that moment and said, 'Oh lucky you – Hilly is lovely.'

If he was quite so lovely why did he make appointments with Connie in the first place? But when he turned up a few minutes later, he proved to be a charming and well mannered, very good looking young man looking for all the world as though he had just emerged from the corridors of Eton. He could not have been more than twenty-three years old. Exactly as Connie had predicted, he chose what he termed an implement of torture, this time a leather strap, and applied two or three strokes to my bare backside in a half-hearted fashion. Then we chatted for a bit and he told me that his 'folks' were putting a lot of pressure on him to make his mind up about what he wanted to do in life but he didn't have very much interest in the paths they suggested. He wanted to know all about me and I told him a long and involved story about leaving home in Wales only a month or two ago.

'You don't have much of a Welsh accent,' he commented and I said that might have been because I went to an English boarding school, well aware that my vowel sounds were such that this was unlikely. However he didn't seem to notice and asked me which school.

'Cheltenham Ladies College,' I said and then wished I had chosen somewhere less prominent because the only thing I knew about the place was the name.

'Gosh – fancy that – my sister went there,' he told eagerly. 'Which house were you in?'

Oh dear. I said I really did not want to talk about school because it had been bad enough going to the place without having to talk about it all this time later. He laughed loudly and said that was exactly what Charlotte would say.

'What I would really like to do,' I said lowering my voice in what I imagined was a very seductive manner, 'is to get into bed with you – now, before Connie comes in and tells us that time is up.'

'Oh she won't do that,' he said, 'Connie's an old friend and a good egg.'

However, he began to remove his clothing and move toward the bed.

I found myself wondering what his mother would say if she knew where he was at that precise moment. He turned out to be as routine as any girl in my position could possibly ask for and his love-making took approximately a minute and a half.

'You can probably leave early today, Bernadette,' I was told after he left. 'The only others coming are booked in for Kiki and Margo. On some Wednesdays it can be a bit slow... I'm sorry I've only been able to give you two today.'

I did not mind only having two as long as I could be sure I hadn't inadvertently done something wrong but in the next breath she said, 'I'm very happy with your work dear – they both said you were very good.'

She then gave me thirty pounds in five-pound notes and I left the place with a spring in my step. Outside in the street I turned when someone called my name to find to my surprise that Hillford was loping towards me carrying a huge bunch of roses which he thrust into my arms.

'Why?' It was quite the most unexpected behaviour from someone I had only known for just over an hour.

'Oh I don't know – it's a lovely day. You've made me feel happy. Flowers for a pretty girl – seems like good sense to me...' then he kissed my cheek, turned and walked briskly away.

'Thank you,' I called after him and he turned for a moment, walking backwards and called back that I had made a lovely day even better.

I could see why everyone in the flat above the antique shop said they really liked young Hilly.

The lovely day was now deteriorating into early darkness and some of the street lights of Belgravia had already sprung to life and were illuminating the street. Now the sun had vanished the customary chill of December began to penetrate in a familiar fashion.

I quickened my pace and headed towards Sloane Square station stepping onto a Circle Line train towards Notting Hill Gate where I planned to walk at a leisurely pace back to Lancaster Road. It was just before five o'clock and even the normally busy Circle Line trains were only half full, not yet with office workers but middle-aged women and mothers with push chairs getting home before the rush really started. A number of them looked inquisitively at my overly large bouquet of roses and I realised that hindered by this accessory I should have been in a taxi. I stared back at the curious, attempting to look hostile, thinking about their surprise if they knew I was on my way home from my part time job as a courtesan, a hussy, a harlot and had just been caned by a man who yearned to become Headmaster of a girls' school where some of the students broke the rules on a regular basis. I visualized the five pound notes in my wallet and thought that to celebrate my first day as a truly fallen woman Shelagh and I might ask Nosher's mother, Judy to watch Virginia and Daniel so we could take a bus to Queensway and have an early Italian dinner.

Emerging from Notting Hill Gate less than twenty minutes later darkness had descended absolutely and early carol singers intoned an unenthusiastic version of Silent Night and blocked the pavement as they did so.

'What's with the roses?' Shelagh asked when I finally arrived at the flat shortly before six. I told her about Hilly and gave Virginia one of the blooms for the top of her bookcase. Judy said she couldn't babysit because her mother was taking the whole family out for 'a Chinese tea' and so I went up to Ladbroke Grove for wine and fish and chips and strawberry mousse in cardboard cartons.

'So far it's not such a bad life,' I reflected as we delved into the chips still in their newspaper whilst sitting on the floor with the bar heater on.

'It's certainly not bad pay,' Shelagh agreed, 'and the hours are short.'

'You should think about doing it yourself,' I said.

She looked doubtful and said she didn't know about that. She didn't think she would be good at the caning part of the deal. I said that it probably didn't have to be part of the deal, there were very likely other openings in the trade that were more straightforward. She still looked unconvinced.

'You're much better than I am at trying new things,' she said at last. 'I keep thinking about what people would think if they found out – you know, the gasps of horror.'

We looked at each other and I assumed a posture of nonchalance whilst she sighed. Virginia took advantage of the moment and crammed several of the now cold chips into her mouth and waited to be reprimanded.

'The first time is the worst,' I said. 'Luckily I was drunk the first time – but it's strange how quickly it just becomes work like anything else.'

She looked sceptical, drained her glass and held it out for a refill repeating that I was better than she at risking the unknown.

'There's an art to dealing with risk,' she said. Perhaps she was right.

Not Clothed In Scarlet Garments

I have never found out if there actually is an art to dealing with risk or if some people are just better at dealing with it than others, but I do know that I took to life as a part time sexual deviation professional with interest and energy. Night club customers seldom varied in regard to their sexual preferences, most being of the 'get your clothes off, let's get it in, let's do it if we can', variety – and often they could not, being worse the wear for alcohol and when that happened a few could become slightly belligerent. Their demeanour frequently seemed to imply that it might, after all, be my fault. At those times they had to be spoken to very gently and persuaded out of asking for their money to be returned. I had in the early days even discussed the ethics of this with other hostesses but as one they advised that if a punter couldn't 'get it up' it was not my responsibility because I was fulfilling my part of the bargain. Michelle even claimed that Contract Law supported our position so with that in mind I concentrated hard on developing the skill of speaking agreeably with all and sundry. Most of the time this strategy worked and I discovered that those so afflicted found it easy to like me.

Deviants were infinitely less complicated to deal with, most having long uncovered and emotionally dealt with their particular predilection. They arrived promptly at the time agreed, in a sober state and knowing exactly what they wanted of the individual they had hired. Usually Connie allotted each of them an hour and they were free to use the time as they wished, often having cups of tea and chats either before or after embarking on their sexual fantasy. More time always cost more money. Most were not in the first flush of youth and some were in their seventies, Hilly being something of an exception. With all of them there existed more than a little scope for drama.

By the end of my second week, Connie decided that my trial period was now over and I was given a set of keys and promoted to the status also occupied by Kiki and Margo. Although the majority of clients were what could be described as run of the mill sadists and masochists, Connie was careful to ensure that when we staff were on the receiving end of the beatings, we were not caned or whipped with any vigour more than twice a week.

'The clients don't like to see the evidence on your backside,' she explained to me when I asked why. 'It puts them off if they can see that somebody else got at you recently – I like to give you time to heal a little.'

This was concerning because by the time I became a proud key owner, my rear end sported a multitude of marks in various hues that could only have been caused by the application of a cane or something similar.

'As time goes on you'll heal quicker,' she said knowledgeably and gave advice about lotions and ointments that could be applied to speed up the process and make-up that could mask the evidence.

'Eventually the skin becomes more resilient anyhow,' she added.

Margo said that Connie knew what she was talking about because she had it on good authority that she had been a Ward Sister in a prominent teaching hospital years before. When I asked who the 'good authority' was she had forgotten or didn't want to say.

Kiki thought that Connie had always been in the deviation business and that as a younger woman she had participated at a personal level, still attractive enough to earn a great deal of money during World War Two.

'She might have started off as a nurse,' she conceded, 'but that career didn't last long enough for her to become a ward sister in my opinion.'

Margo said Connie's appearance in the nineteen forties was beside the point because good service was much more important that good looks in the sex industry.

She added, 'She's had some nursing experience though – she's quite efficient at stuff like taking blood pressures and giving enemas. She taught me how to do it.

We both looked at her and Kiki shivered. 'I really do hate those enema types – I said I didn't want to do them.'

'I don't mind,' Margo's voice lacked any animation, 'I'll do anything I have to.'

The mysterious 'enema types' worried me a bit and I was anxious about what dealing with them actually entailed and whether I would be capable of taking them on in as an emotionless fashion as Margo.

Finding out enough about our employer to make her more human was testing because when we sat in the kitchen drinking tea with her the conversation revolved mainly around banalities. She repeated instructions regarding the emptying of the kettle on a daily basis and talked about the journey from Brighton to Victoria a great deal.

'I had breakfast with Sir Larry today,' she said one morning, shaking the rain from her umbrella and folding her silk headscarf carefully. 'We both had the kippers.'

It took a few seconds before I realized who she was referring to.

'What did you talk about?' I was truly interested having seen him in a cameo film role very recently in which he played a police inspector. Despite the fact that he had very little to say or do he had been brilliant and turned a mundane movie about a missing child into something memorable.

'Well we talked about what we were going to do for Christmas of course,' she said, 'and complained about British Rail and how unreliable the timetable can be. He's just come back from Italy and says the trains there are wonderful.'

'Does he ever ask what kind of business you are in?' I felt courageous for some reason asking this question.

She gave me a searching look before deciding that the question was less invasive than it appeared. 'I tell everyone I'm an antique dealer dear.'

Well, it seemed that the world of antiques was plagued by the world of whoring. What would the Antique Dealers' Association, if there was such a thing, think of that?

'Good idea,' I said.

That afternoon I was earmarked for Barry the Butcher before realizing that he was one of the so recently discussed 'enema types' and perhaps it was because I had asked one question too many about Sir Larry. I reminded myself that paranoia was not attractive and cornered Margo in the bathroom to elicit more information about what was in store for me.

'None of us like Barry very much,' she admitted, 'mainly because he's a bit smelly but don't worry because he's relatively straightforward and he's usually only here for half an hour. He's always worried about getting back to Smithfield because it takes forever to get across town after three o'clock.'

She gestured toward the mysterious glass top table that graced the centre of the bathroom. 'He just lies underneath and you have to squat on top and try not to lose your balance. It's best if you have your feet as far apart as possible.'

I began to feel distinctly uneasy, still largely oblivious as to the details of what was to come.

Connie was sweeping crumbs from the kitchen floor with a soft brush when I approached her for further information.

'I do wish you girls would be more careful when you eat those crumbly Rich Tea,' she said reproachfully, 'I'm not going to buy them in future if you make such a mess with them.'

I urged her to tell me a little about The Butcher and she sat down and leaned onto the table. 'You have to understand that I've known him a long time,' she began, 'and to be perfectly honest with you none of the girls are too keen on him.'

'Tell me why not.'

She pushed the previously offending plate of Rich Tea biscuits toward me and continued, 'Generally speaking I like to give you notice of his visit – for obvious reasons.'

'What obvious reasons?' Hopefully this question did not sound too naïve.

'Well dear if you can hold on until his visit it's all the better for everyone. What he likes best is that you don't go at all that morning – you try to hold on as I've said. But look, I give you an enema beforehand so that makes it a lot easier all round. Did you have a big dinner last night?'

I tried to remember and my mind was blank. She said that I would be as right as rain and not to worry so I tried not to but it was difficult. She poured boiling water in the teapot and gazed at it contemplatively.

'The biggest problem with him is that he comes straight from work and is often covered in blood,' she said, 'animal blood I mean dear – he's a butcher as I said and by the time he gets here it's all a bit smelly,' she poured us both cups of Assam and I noted it was stronger than usual.

'Coprophilia is never popular,' she looked into the cup and then straightened her shoulders, sitting back in the chair as far as possible. 'But you have to take the good with the bad and realise that it's all part of the job. Girls who won't do it are a nuisance and I have to think carefully about how much they are worth to me as employees really – you do understand don't you dear?'

I thought I did. In any event this was a time for positive thinking. A real live coprophile would be thought-provoking though not in any way appealing. After all you didn't meet them all that often, even at places like Connie's.

When The Butcher arrived he was a short fat man in his sixties, wearing overalls that appeared not to have been washed for weeks and that were liberally splattered with layers of what I earnestly hoped was indeed animal blood. His finger nails were filthy and he smelled as if he had run a marathon and had yet to step into the shower. It was clear, however, that he was not the kind of man who went in for much exercise. I supposed his wife had over the years become accustomed to the smell.

He seemed friendly enough and waited patiently in the kitchen whilst Connie escorted me to the bathroom and searched for the purgative paraphernalia. She told me to remove my clothing and deftly administered what appeared to be a soap and water solution.

'Now just hold on won't you?' she said, 'I'll send him in.'

The Butcher entered the bathroom and whilst I sat on the edge of the bath, holding on for dear life, he removed his overalls and underclothes agonizingly slowly, chatting to me about how long he'd known Connie and how bad the traffic had been from Smithfield to Belgravia. His stoutly pallid body was predictably pungent and I caught drifts of his aroma as he squeezed himself beneath the glass table. For a man of his physical stature it was not an easy feat. Having positioned himself to his satisfaction he beckoned me to do likewise above him and I had to leave the relative security of the bath edge itself. I did not at this stage have much control left and as he began to tell me how he loved to see 'little brown turdies' he got something that must have been substantially different.

He did not complain though and seemed happy enough amusing himself beneath the table. Perhaps he was a man whose sexual preference did not lend itself to complaint for it must have presented some difficulties throughout his life. Imagine having to explain the situation to those you were hopeful of entering into long term relationships with. How had he broached the situation with his wife – or was he yet to do so?

When he had paid up and left Connie thanked me for my co-operation and said that next time she would give me a day's notice in order to try and give him what he paid for, but then on the other hand if he didn't give her similar notice what was she to do? She could only do so much after all.

We had a few days off in which to celebrate Christmas and New Year and on my last working afternoon beforehand I took the Piccadilly Line into the heart of the West End and headed up Regent St towards Hamleys. I bought furniture for Virginia's dolls' house and a red plastic racing car exactly the right size for Daniel to sit in and pretend to drive and then instead of struggling on bus or tube, hailed a taxi back to Lancaster Road.

Shelagh and Virginia were going to Manchester to visit Grandma and Grandpa and so Daniel and I were left to our own devices which at first I thought would be fun but when the time came realized was terribly lonely. On Christmas Eve I wheeled him in the push chair to Portobello Market where there was an attempt at a Christmas Market in what seemed to be Jamaican style. We ambled through the crowds listening to one group of singers after another and watching clowns on stilts do amazing tricks with balloons. He was now old enough to pay attention to anything lively and he did so with delight, from time clapping his frozen hands together having completely discarded his mittens.

I wondered what Vidar was doing at that moment, recalling the half dozen Christmases we had spent together, all except the very first one fraught with tension. Life as an unmarried mother might equate to life somewhere near the bottom of the social heap but the daily difficulties were less stressful than those I had tried to cope with whilst living with the man I loved. For a moment or two I thought about boarding a number twenty-seven bus and heading in the direction of Clerkenwell, considering what it would be like to stand in the square and look up at his windows. But instead we returned to the silence of Lancaster Road and Daniel went to sleep immediately whilst I slept fitfully and was awake still when the first signs of daylight appeared.

Christmas alone in London is not to be recommended. The pulsating heart of the vast city seems to slow down and the hours drag. It is unnaturally quiet because the streets are largely devoid of vehicles and in the inner suburbs where normally children can be relied upon to be in evidence on the streets strangely there is little sign of them. It is as though the Pied Piper has lured them all away for it is not until Boxing Day they return in fits and starts sporting new skateboards and trikes and even the occasional puppy.

I played with Daniel, watching his delight as he examined his new toys and at some stage I roasted a chicken, of which we ate little although Daniel was greatly interested in the individual size plum puddings from Sainsburys, first simmered and served with ice cream. At last the day came to an end with us both watching a TV Spectacular where Bruce Forsyth reigned supreme. I vowed that as my son grew older I would organize Christmas better and perhaps even make intense efforts to re-establish contact with my family.

Connie went back to work during the first week in January and as Shelagh and Virginia were still in the north, Nosher's mother Judy agreed to babysit for a moderate fee when I told her about my part time job in the Belgravia antique shop.

It's generally quiet just after Christmas,' Connie said, arriving just after me on a day that was so cold our breath blew clouds into the icy kitchen.

I asked what kind of Christmas she had and she said it had been quiet although she'd had a telephone call from her daughter.

'I didn't know you had a daughter,' I said, pleased to find out something more about her.

'Oh yes dear,' she said looking as if that had been a very odd observation for me to make.

'I've just the one daughter. She's in South Africa – been there for years she has and she's got a really lovely home out there.'

She told me that Sonia, for that was the daughter's name, had recently married a man she had been engaged to for some years and they were deciding whether or not to have a child. It appeared that he had been married previously and had two teenage children who lived with their mother but Sonia, understandably enough, would like a child of her own.

I longed to ask her if theirs was a close relationship. Did she exchange intimate chit-chat with Sonia? Did Sonia perhaps know of her mother's chosen profession and was she quite blasé about it? Or would she be utterly shocked if by chance she found out?

But of course I did not ask any of these questions and Connie ventured nothing further.

'You're the only one here today dear,' she said, 'I didn't think there would be a need to call the other girls in at this time of the year.'

And indeed the red telephone stayed silent for the first hour or so. I sat and read a book whilst Connie produced her knitting; a sweater for Sonia long overdue for completion.

'This was supposed to be finished in time for Christmas,' she complained, 'but this Arran pattern is quite complicated so I've been slow.'

I said I hoped the South African climate would be cool enough at times for her to wear it and Connie said that funnily enough it could be surprisingly chilly out there at certain times.

There were only two clients that day, Mr. Cohen an elderly sadist I had not met before, but who was to become something of a regular, and a younger man called Simon who was a masochist of the tediously time consuming variety.

I never learned Mr. Cohen's first name because Connie addressed him as Coney which I could not believe was his given name, and referred to him as Old Cohen. A few months later when I had got to know him reasonably well, he provided accommodation when Shelagh and I were unceremoniously thrown out of our Lancaster Road flat because it was needed for a family member. He was a property dealer with a shady reputation but he produced as if by magic the top two floors of a house in Marylands Road which we said was in Maida Vale but was more properly in Paddington.

He liked to spend most of his allotted time talking to Connie and it was only when I was despairing that we would ever get around to what he came for that he suddenly rose to his feet and ordered me to get into the big bedroom and get my backside ready. He then gave me ten sharply administered strokes of the cane and ordered me to fellate him and I said that before I would do so he had to wear a condom.

'You girls are so bloody fussy these days,' he complained, trying to get one on before his erection disappeared. Despite all that it was over and done with just before the hour was up.

'I'm quite fond of old Cohen,' Connie said when he had left. 'He's a harmless old soul and he's got a heart of gold. He's not had much luck with his daughter and she went right off the rails at one time and got into drugs. He's trying to marry her off but isn't having a much success.'

I asked why not.

'I think he's setting his sights too high,' she said. 'He wants her to marry well but with her history she's seen as damaged goods in their community. I assumed by that she meant the Jewish community but did not like to ask although later it turned out he was reasonably devout.

'The next one's a real nuisance.' Connie was tidying the kitchen as she spoke. 'He brings all his own props with him and is always worried he's going to leave something behind.'

Simon the masochist was indeed fussy and displayed the costume he liked to wear with pride, taking a long time to get into it because as he got out of his clothes every item had to be folded and laid carefully on the bottom of the bed. The costume was an old fashioned maid's uniform complete with white lace cap and when wearing it he was devoid of underclothes.

He apparently followed the same pattern on each visit. Having got into the maid's uniform he became Susan and I was his uncompromising mistress with a whip in my hand, ordering him to clean up every scrap of fluff from the carpet with dustpan and brush and urging him to work faster and faster.

'You simply must work faster Susan... this is not good enough. I will have to let you go if you work so slowly. Now, come along dear you can work faster than that.'

He shivered nervously, apologized again and again and every now and again he would have the whip applied to him for which of course he thanked me and became ever more wildly sexually excited. His excitement was very slow to build but eventually became so great that the session came to an end quite naturally with no stimulation applied other than the commands to increase the pace of his work.

It all sounds comparatively easy but in actual fact his session went beyond the allotted hour and was decidedly labour intensive. I actually came to believe that I would almost rather have been the one on the receiving end of the whip strokes.

He took a great deal of time getting back into his clothes, folding the maid's outfit up carefully, and counting his dustpans and brushes to ensure nothing was lost. I was delighted when he finally left.

The following week both Margo and Kiki returned to work and the phone began to ring as regularly and reliably as ever.

It became briskly busy and I was required to work for an extra day each week. The steady stream of sadists and masochists was occasionally punctuated by shoe fetishists who wished to have their outspread hands almost punctured by high red or black patent leather heels. Now and again those on short morning breaks popped in demanding only anal intercourse. The latter were not popular but at least they were quick and the use of Vaseline was helpful.

At about this time I met the Cardinal who had fantasies about teenage girls plagued with impure sexual thoughts who in despair approached him for advice.

'Is he a real Cardinal?' As a lapsed Catholic I was shocked.

'He claims to be,' Connie sounded suddenly doubtful, 'But you never know do you? Possibly he's only an Archbishop.'

'I don't think there's much difference,' I said. Clearly Connie's knowledge of the hierarchy of the Roman Catholic Church was vague.

She added, 'I wouldn't go so far as to say he was one of those responsible for electing the last Pope but they can't all be there when they're needed can they?'

She proceeded to tell me what the Cardinal required of me.

'He's quite uncomplicated – no canes or whips, nothing like that at all. You must dress down – a simple cotton dress, white knickers, bare legs, sandals that sort of thing. What he really wants is you to talk dirty to him – but don't go too far – no four letter words. If you go too far he backs off completely. It has to be gradual and you have to let him take the lead and judge the next step.'

I thought I could easily manage that. I had at one stage considered life as a nun after all.

'It will help a great deal if you know some Catholic prayers,' Connie added and I assured her that I did.

He was an elderly genial looking man, tall with a surprising shock of white hair. He said his name was Raymond. When Connie introduced us he shook hands with me. Disappointingly he was not wearing scarlet garments.

Without too much ceremony we went into the small bedroom together and he sat on in the wing chair by the bed and made me kneel in front of him.

'Why are you here today child?'

'Because I feel I need guidance Your Eminence'

This was something I could do well I decided and entered into the spirit of the procedure with no problem whatsoever.

He asked what kind of guidance I needed and with considerable hesitation I told him it was a difficult matter to discuss because it concerned those things that were for the sanctity of marriage only – did I have his permission to name them? He said I did.

'It concerns sex, Your Eminence,' I said in a low voice.

'What is it about sex that puzzles you child?'

'The feelings I have Your Eminence – feelings that I yearn to act on. But I know if I do I will be doing wrong.'

'Tell me about these feelings,' he urged, becoming obviously very interested indeed.

'Terrible feelings that involve wanting to ask men to describe to me the act they take part in with their wives in order that children shall be born....'

We were heading in the right direction I could see that he was pleased. He asked me if I had ever had a boyfriend and I said I had not because my parents would not allow it – I was too young. He asked me how young and I decided I was just fifteen. He agreed that I was much too young for a boyfriend and told me I had sensible parents.

He asked if I understood anything at all about the mechanics of sex and how wanton women aroused men and were responsible for them taking part in lewd acts. I shook my head.

'Would you like me to demonstrate to you what sometimes happens between men and women?' he asked and I told him I would be very grateful if he did, as long as he thought it would be right to do so because I was fearful of committing a sin.

He then produced his erect penis. 'This is the male organ,' he told me. 'This is what is put inside the woman...how do you feel when you look upon it?'

'Your Eminence – looking upon it makes me want to touch it,' I ventured, hoping that was the correct thing to say and he said he would allow me a small touch but no more and I had to ask him nicely, say please in fact. I did so.

I touched it tentatively.

'How do you feel now?' he asked.

'I feel that I want to say words that Your Eminence would greatly disapprove of,' I admitted and he said I should say one or two of them just in order to demonstrate to him what I was thinking.

I chose one or two reasonably tame pseudonyms for the penis and he then added one or two of his own which were considerably more descriptive.

He then asked me to show him my breasts and when I did so he said he would have to give me a warning.

'A warning?'

'Yes my child,' he put his right forefinger under my chin and lifted it so he could look directly into my eyes. 'You know what men might call these beautiful breasts?'

I shook my head and he beckoned me closer and said in a low voice, 'Men may very well call them tits...'

I gasped and lowered my eyes once more. I knew he was happy with our progress and before too long he said that he would penetrate me – for my instruction only of course and I must thank him and God for it. I thanked him profusely and shortly thereafter he was making preparations to leave.

'A very pleasant young lady,' I heard him tell Connie as he paid. 'I like her very much – a nicely brought up girl – not in any way vulgar.'

Then he left as quietly and unobtrusively as he had arrived.

'He was very happy indeed,' she said. 'Sometimes the girls go too far and then it upsets him but you had just the right touch.'

She added that sometimes those from the Church could be demanding though the Cardinal was a lot less trouble than the Bishop who wanted four girls at once for his lesbian fantasy and always complained that their hearts did not seem to really be in it. I did not ever meet the Bishop she spoke of although lesbian fantasies were common enough among Connie's clients.

It was in the first few months of nineteen sixty nine that I met one of the necrophiliacs whose activities had been described to me on a number of occasions. Connie was, predictably, quite matter of fact about him, simply laying out the wedding dress I was required to wear on the bed in the coffin room and maintaining, not for the first time, that it took all sorts to make a world.

'Don't give it too much thought,' advised Margo as she bit into a cream cracker on which perched a large hunk of Cheddar cheese. 'Apart from the wedding dress fixation he's not too much trouble and you don't actually have to have sex with him because he just plays with himself.'

She was right as it happened. His name was Humphrey and he arrived looking for all the world as if he had stepped out of one of the City of London's finance houses, complete in dark overcoat and bowler hat. He was a mild mannered man, polite and very eager to meet 'a new young lady' and noting that he thought I would fit the dress much better than Margo because she was rather shorter.

He removed his clothes, donned a dressing gown that I was not even aware was among the rows of costumes, and helped me into the pale satin gown, telling me how beautiful I looked in it. I stood in front of the long mirror by the bed and for an instant looking at my reflection I had to admit he might be right. It was a lovely dress.

He knelt in front of me and kissed first my hands and then my feet, encased in white satin slippers that were a fraction too small and squashed my toes uncomfortably.

'It is my privilege to be with you today,' he said and then he gestured toward the coffin and indicated that it was now time for me to lie down inside it.

The situation being new to me, the first problem I encountered was how to place myself into it whilst maintaining a degree of elegance. Humphrey steadied me and when I was safely inside, arranged the white dress artistically around me. I was surprised to find that the confines of the box were extraordinarily claustrophobic, the satin lined walls of the interior seeming so much higher from within than without. I closed my eyes and tried not to think too hard about it. Instead I would think about the party Shelagh and I had been invited to on Saturday, at the mews house of a group of New Zealand doctors, at least one of whom I had met several years previously on the evening of Christmas Day nineteen sixty five at Clive's Christmas party which I attended of course with Vidar. I experienced a sudden painful memory jolt of misery when I recalled that day, a time when I still lived as part of a couple.

Humphrey was slowly encircling me talking softly about how much he loved me, how he would never find another woman to equal me. He noted how pale and frozen I was in death. I thought some more about the upcoming party and tried to block his voice out as much as possible, fearful that he might say something completely unexpected. Connie had confirmed that this was the client whose wife had died on their wedding day, the man who had found himself unable to come to terms with her death. Surely though he must have started off as a necrophiliac in the first place? Perhaps not, perhaps the condition had first emerged out of love.

I pondered upon how many among the general population had the same sexual problem and whether it was relatively common as deviations go. In normal daily life it was possible to go for years without ever hearing mention of necrophilia until a serial killer such as John Reginald Halliday Christie popped out of the woodwork. It had been said at the time of his trial, that Christie who murdered eight women, one of whom was his wife, was a necrophiliac. I had been about twelve or thirteen years old when he was executed and had no idea what the term meant but sensing it related somehow to sex thought better of asking questions. When we first moved to the Ladbroke Grove area Shelagh and I had excitedly visited the scene of his crimes, number ten Rillington Place, hastily renamed Ruston Close after his death.

Turning my attention back to Humphrey, he eventually grew aroused by the sight of me and the session was completed to his total satisfaction without any further input from me and almost without me noticing. He politely helped me emerge from the coffin and I thankfully stepped out of the dress, hanging it back in the wardrobe with the utmost care because I knew Connie would examine it later and rearrange its folds to avoid unnecessary creases.

As I got ready to leave I heard her straightening where no straightening was needed and saying more to herself than to us, 'look at this, Kiki's put a rubber suit in with the leather ones again – was she never made to tidy her bedroom at home? I sometimes ask myself how you girls were brought up.'

Sweet Love Remembered

There were times when I was filled with anxiety about how well the work with deviants seemed to sit with me because after the first few months of emotional initiation I began to realise that it suited me admirably in every way. Not only did it largely remain part time, I enjoyed meeting the mixture of decidedly different people. The added bonus was that at least half of them did not want any type of sexual intercourse. At the same time I did not disassociate myself from life in the mainstream and as I had more than enough time for writing, I continued to do so. I began to have moderate success not only with childcare articles where I wrote about life as an unmarried mother interested in the development of her child, but also with short stories for lightweight women's magazines. All the stories also reflected how life revolved around women and small children and some of them were even picked up by similar French and Italian magazines and published in translation. The pay for this work was passable but not enough to make me contemplate giving up the sex work and again the initial thrill of seeing my name in print wore off much quicker than I had anticipated.

Daniel's hospital specialist, Dr. Barnes who still saw him regularly because of his low birth weight and the ongoing lung infections he was plagued with, was keen to rehabilitate me. In addition to pointing me in the direction of quasi-medical magazines, he also found me part time secretarial jobs with people he knew in private practice. I worked for a paediatrician in Harley Street while his secretary was away on holiday and then for several months for his brother, a dermatologist who was semi-retired and worked only two mornings a week, starting at eight am. I was able to go directly on to Pont Street afterwards so it was all very convenient. At the time it all seemed most satisfactory but I now realise it might have been more judicious to have developed the writing side of my many-faceted working life. I was remarkably lucky with regard to what I wrote, most of which went into print immediately without any major hiccups and this was due in the first place to Dr. Barnes who worked diligently on my behalf. He, however, maintained that it was because I was a 'natural writer' which was flattering.

It seemed that during this time I was presented with a number of opportunities, none of which I was motivated enough to hold on to. One of my clients, a well-established script writer responsible for a number of television series that had been sold worldwide was also interested in my writing. He introduced me to his agent and I recall going to see her in her very grand office overlooking Regent Street and being told I had a definite 'ear for dialogue'. I failed to take hold of that particular opportunity largely because I thought I might have to commit too much time to it. From where I sit now that seems a remarkably stupid decision. However, that was then and this is now and nothing is more complex than trying to unravel the reasoning behind decisions made in a different era. Possibly a part of me still believed that I would be reconciled with Daniel's father and in that case there could be no question of me following a career in writing although naturally enough, a career in the sex industry would be perfectly acceptable.

There was one occasion during the early stages of my relationship with Connie when Vidar and I met and had coffee together in a place very fashionable at the time in Knightsbridge and the name of which I have long forgotten. I cannot remember the reason for the encounter but there would undoubtedly have been one because we did not at any stage meet simply for social reasons and in fact by that time rarely met at all. I recall sitting at a window table, clutching my cappuccino in both hands, shaking a little and nervous that perhaps he would fail to turn up. I longed to see him.

He was ten minutes late and I was already feeling almost desperate, once again hurtled into agonizing memories of the depth of my devotion to him.

'You look nice,' he said pleasantly, sitting down opposite me and smiling as if we were a quite ordinary couple, devoid of history that hung between us like a heavy curtain of misery.

I smiled in what I hoped was a casual fashion and we conversed for a moment or two in a civilized way. He told me that Christine was still living with him and the information sent a spear of violent resentment through me so that in that moment I pictured slaughtering both of them as viciously as it was possible to imagine.

'How lovely,' I said, 'How is she?'

'She's fine – she's just got a new job working on a magazine that does restaurant reviews – she starts on Monday.'

With little prompting he told me the name of the magazine and where the office was. Because I still found her to be responsible for stealing my life, the following Monday I got up early and staked out the office, near Marble Arch, watching her arrive on her first day. Her fair hair was styled elegantly and she wore a new grey suit, shoes with moderate heels and a bright red scarf. She looked stylish and I loathed her with a newly ignited passion. I tried to think of some reason to follow her up the stairs and enter her workplace, confront her at her desk saying, 'Hello Christine – fancy seeing you here…' but it was impossible to dream up a plausible reason for doing so.

'I hope it will still leave her enough time to help me with the business,' he was saying. 'She has been my rock since you left. I could not have managed without her.'

I said I hoped so too and when he asked me how things were going for me I told him about working for Connie and during the telling made it sound much more exciting than it actually was, throwing several crowned heads of Europe into the list of clients as well as a plethora of Cabinet Ministers.

He looked at me sorrowfully. 'Why is it you could not get a job like that when we were together?'

'I suppose it is well paid,' I agreed cautiously but he told me I was deliberately misunderstanding.

'You know how much I would have loved it – to think of you having sex with all those kinky men – but you wait until you leave me before you do so. Do you understand now how determined you were to fracture our relationship?'

I resisted the urge to tell him that it wasn't too late, that I could return and we could live happily ever after. Instead I got up saying, 'Well you certainly know me very well don't you?' and walked out of the place with as much dignity as possible, which wasn't much because I was almost incandescent with rage and misery and jealousy of Christine.

A little after this incident Shelagh finally decided to also embark upon a life of sin though she initially told me she drew a line at deviants and would concentrate on the occasional uncomplicated rendezvous with those simply looking for early afternoon encounters whilst Virginia was at pre-school. In her case the decision was primarily because there were so many opportunities she wanted to give her daughter that involved cost far beyond her current reach. Even ballet lessons in the local church hall did not come as cheaply as one might have wished. Visits to Covent Garden to see The Nutcracker were simply out of the question without a boost in income. The velvet dress and black patent shoes, a compulsory uniform for those in the audience under the age of ten, just an impossible dream. However it has to be borne in mind that she would never have made the decision she did if it had not been for my influence. But then neither would Virginia have had the various treats and indulgencies in the years that followed. It was not a conundrum that either of us examined too much at the time.

The most memorable of all those who frequented the Pont Street premises was undoubtedly Clement, the man who died on the cross. There seemed to be two regulars who required to be crucified though of course for each it was a much scaled-down version of the real thing involving bondage materials rather than nails. Clement was a regular, attending about once a month, usually on a Friday afternoon which was not normally one of my working days. He hired two girls on each occasion and this particular Friday I was simply filling in for someone called Rhiannon whom I had never met and who was apparently unwell. The other girl was Renee, known to be an extreme leather and bondage specialist and I had met her once or twice. Fridays, I discovered, was in general the day for those with desires and needs that were excessive. Connie did not normally come into London that day but merely allowed her premises to be used on a rental/fee basis by a couple of women she knew well and totally trusted. On this particular Friday she was only present because she was intending to go to the theatre in the evening, invited by an impresario client to an opening night. She was already complaining that being almost forced to attend in order not to offend him had ruined her weekend and she did so look forward to her long weekends.

Renee and I both dressed in leather cat suits, waited the arrival of he who was to be crucified and she told me a little about what would take place whilst Connie sat in the kitchen and complained about people who insisted on doling out theatre tickets and how they had little consideration for others. Later we had reason to be very grateful to those inconsiderate theatre ticket dispensers.

'First of all we humiliate him and take turns to whip him – only across his back and don't let the ends curl round the sides. Masochists hate that,' said Renee. 'Then we tell him that it has been decreed he is to die and he will in fact die like the Lord, on the cross. We tie him up on it and just leave him there for half an hour or so – we need to spin it out a bit because he pays for two hours. After a while we say we are going to make him fuck us both and he pleads with us not to but we insist. We take him down and he has to choose which of us is to be first and we argue with each other about who he chose and say it isn't fair. We still tell him it has to be both of us. Sometimes he actually does but usually not – and he'll probably end up with you because he's not met you before.'

She asked if it was clear or if I wanted to ask questions.

I said it seemed clear enough.

Clement arrived, a round man of middle years, wearing casual clothes which he told us was now permissible on Fridays at work and that his company was quite progressive in that respect. I tried to picture him at work, signing cheques at his desk, making telephone calls.

The humiliation routine went very well with him leaning obediently over an armchair in order that we could each apply strokes to his back and none of the strokes curled so he began to relax. He even told us that he felt today his punishment must be ultimate.

'We have decided you must die on the cross,' Renee told him and he at once began to weep and begged her to reconsider. Renee said we would consult with each other once more and we went into the kitchen where Connie asked if we were ready for a cup of tea.

'In five minutes,' Renee told her and we returned to him.

'I am sorry to say,' I told him as he lay quivering on the floor, 'that you have to be crucified. There can be no mercy shown to you.'

He complained, pretended to struggle but between us we tied him to the cross and went back to the kitchen where we stayed for twenty minutes chatting to Connie, still in our leather cat suits which were becoming uncomfortably hot.

Eventually Renee said she would go and have a look at him and returned within a moment or two looking ashen.

'What on earth's the matter?' Connie looked only half surprised for some reason. 'What's happened?'

'I think he might be gone,' Renee managed to say.

'Gone? What do you mean – gone?' Connie got up from the table and strode down the corridor.

Renee looked at me helplessly. 'He looks like he's dead.'

After several minutes we both went after Connie, hesitantly cramming ourselves together in the doorway of the room as if actually stepping inside would somehow contaminate us. Connie was still trying to find his non-existent pulse and shaking her head.

'He's gone all right,' she said and clasped his hand in hers for a few seconds. 'Poor old bugger.'

'But that's the point...' Renee was stuttering a little. 'He's not all that old – fiftyish probably.'

We went back to the kitchen and sat for a few minutes then Connie made a telephone call to someone called Duke who would come with a friend and get him down from the cross and dressed.

'It's probably his heart,' she said. 'He carries too much weight of course.'

She suddenly became galvanized.

'You girls get every whip and cane back in the cupboards – and get out of those stupid cat-suits and properly dressed.'

Connie issued orders mostly about tidying the bedrooms and throwing dust sheets over the coffin and cross and other incriminating objects, which we did. Then she told us to go home and leave her to deal with the matter and we went, gratefully, though not directly home because Renee was in need of a drink. We went into the nearest pub and ordered double vodkas and hovered over them still horrified by what had happened.

'Has anything like this ever happened to you before?' I asked at last.

Renee looked at me as if seeing me for the first time, 'No – never. I've been in this business for more than fifteen years and this is the first time – I've heard of it happening to other people though.'

'Shouldn't we have tried to resuscitate him?' I was beginning to feel guilty. We had done nothing concrete to try to help Clement.

She gazed ahead, helplessly and took several gulps from her glass. 'I wouldn't know what to do.'

It occurred to me that we might at least attend a basic first aid course in order to be better prepared for the future but didn't like to voice the thought.

Instead I said, 'What do you think she's doing? – Connie I mean.'

'Well the guys she rang will come in and dress him, then prop him up on the loo – then I guess she'll call an ambulance and the police.'

'Why the loo?'

She said she didn't really know why but that was what you were supposed to do if a client died under those circumstances and two other girls she knew had told her that. When it had happened to them they didn't have a Duke and his mate to help and had to get the customer into the bathroom by themselves. It had taken hours and they both ended up with disc problems. It was a situation everyone dreaded because the police were almost certain to become involved. Connie might well be charged.

'What would we have done if Connie hadn't been there?' I said into the sudden silence.

Renee looked at me in horror and did not reply.

'Charged with what?' I said at last. 'What might Connie be charged with?'

'Running a brothel of course.'

'Not with causing his death then?'

She shook her head. That was a great relief because we had all been implicated and in a flash I had seen myself giving evidence at an Old Bailey trial, photographers waiting outside like vultures just as they had for Christine Keeler and Mandy Rice-Davis several years previously. I had already decided not to make the mistake of wearing anything too flashy. For me there would be only twin-sets, low heels and demure hair styles. Definitely no make-up. The general public reading the headlines and scanning the images would gasp at the remote possibility of such a dowdy personage actually being a perversion house whore. All would think there must have been some mistake. I felt a sudden pang of guilt with regard to Daniel's hospital doctor who believed I spent my days either typing letters about skin conditions or writing short stories with happy endings. I would not like him to witness me emerging from a sleazy court case concerning those who paid to be crucified. It would be remarkably difficult to explain.

I fully expected that we would be questioned by the police within a day or two but nothing of the kind happened. The following Wednesday when I turned up for my shift Connie looked as bright and cheerful and normal as ever.

'What happened with Clement?' I asked at last when half an hour had passed without any mention of the death on the cross.

'The lads came and saw to him,' she said, 'and then we got him taken away. Poor chap had a heart attack it turned out – on the lavatory. Sad isn't it?'

'Yes,' I agreed, 'Very sad.' And that was all that was ever said on the matter but for several Fridays the premises remained unused and Kiki said that possibly it was out of respect for the deceased man.

'But why wasn't there an investigation at least?' I was incredulous.

Kiki was examining the effect of her newly bobbed blonde hair in a hand mirror. She said that as far as she knew Connie just had access to the right people. But who exactly were the right people? Kiki said she had no idea.

She put the mirror away into her shoulder bag.

'All I can tell you is what was once told to me – that at least two of the regulars are something or other high up in the police force – Renee said one of them is in the unit that decides whether you get charged or not – lucky really.'

It was really very fortunate for all of us. It took me some time to recover my former equilibrium.

One of the occasional Friday sub-lessees was Paula Driver, a tall statuesque blonde who lived in one of the mansion blocks on Maida Vale with her small son who was somewhat inexplicably called Monet. Later I discovered that she had a passion for art and Monet was dear to her at the time when the boy had been born. Paula specialized in extreme and intricate perversions, often those involving elongated scenarios lasting several hours and a veritable cast of players. One of these was Brian Featherstone, at the time a High Court Judge.

'How are you placed on Friday dear?' Connie asked one Wednesday afternoon.

I told her I would be totally free.

'Then I shall introduce you to Paula,' she said. 'She's popping by later today.'

In fact Paula popped by within the hour, looked me up and down quizzically and said I would do very well indeed. Connie sat in the crucifix room with her knitting whilst we chatted in the kitchen.

'What I need is someone who will arrive looking as severe as possible,' explained Paula, 'and by that I mean very little make-up and hair drawn back tightly off the face. Bring some black high heeled shoes – as high as possible, and wear black stockings and a black suspender belt. We have to wear uniforms but I bring those with me because he's very fussy. We are going to be Gestapo type guards and there will be six of us in total...'

'Six?' I was surprised and told her cautiously that I knew very little about the Gestapo. In fact the sum total of my knowledge had been gleaned from Holocaust survival accounts.

'Don't worry – you don't have to know the whole history. You just follow my lead,' she said. 'He's a very good and regular client so I want everything to go smoothly. Be here by eleven fifteen on Friday morning. We will probably finish at about six.'

'Quite lengthy,' I said and she agreed. 'But he pays well as I told you and if he likes you he will ask me to get you again.'

On Friday I turned up promptly with hair tied back in the most severe style I could produce and with my black patent high heels in my shoulder bag. Paula was already there with four other girls – Margo and Renee and two others I had not met before, Rose and Jessica, both sensationally good looking Africans.

Paula introduced us and indicating the Africans said, 'Rose and Jess are the slaves so they can be humiliated and treated almost as severely as Featherstone.' I glanced towards them and wondered if they felt demeaned before we'd even started but neither showed any sign of it.

'Now for the benefit of Bernadette and Rose who are both new, I'll quickly run through the programme,' Paula continued, glancing at her watch.

She told us that as she spoke Brian Featherstone was being held on Hampstead Heath, by a colleague whose duty it was to simply hand him over. He was already manacled and blindfolded. The slaves would collect him at precisely twelve forty five and escort him to Pont Street by car. The driver was someone Paula knew and trusted, and later I learned it was in fact her husband. Once at Pont Street he would be hustled up the stairs as quickly as possible and taken into the large bondage room where he would be both humiliated and interrogated. At her direction his clothes and the blindfold would be removed, but not the handcuffs. He would be made to perform cunnilingus on both Margo and Renee and if his performance was satisfactory he would be unshackled and given a glass of champagne and allowed to drink it. Later he would be further interrogated and beaten and threatened with guns. As part of his humiliation I would be required to urinate into his empty champagne glass and he would be ordered to drink it. She looked up sharply and said, 'And make absolutely sure you can go because you have to piddle in front of him. If you're in any doubt you'd better start drinking now.'

I obediently began on a litre of water.

At all times we were to take guidance from her and to speak to him in severe terms though never raising our voices or using coarse language. Every step of the way we were to behave in an ultra-controlled and unemotional manner. There must be no raised voices or unacceptable displays of emotion. He would address all of us except the slaves as 'Mistress'. At some point the behaviour of one of the slaves would displease Paula and she would be taken into the bathroom and shot without any further ceremony. From then on she would retire to the kitchen and prepare the refreshments because Featherstone liked to finish the afternoon with smoked salmon sandwiches and more champagne. During the elaborate play acting, if it went to his satisfaction, he would become more and more sexually aroused and finally he would be required to penetrate one of us and the choice would be his.

'And after that,' she smiled around at us, 'it's just a drink and a sandwich and polite conversation before he departs. He'll be gone by six thirty.

The two slaves, now dressed identically in Prussian blue uniforms with matching caps, were dispatched to Hampstead Heath, each sporting an alarmingly realistic looking revolver in her shoulder bag. I did not, however, query the authenticity.

Paula re-arranged Margo's hair more to her liking, in an austere style, and issued us each with navy blue uniforms comprising of tight skirts, masculine style jackets each with a row of gold buttons, white blouses and navy caps with gold trim. She and Renee had revolvers, Margo and I only whips.

The guns had unsettled me. I nervously hoped they were not real and apprehensively reassured myself that Paula and her colleagues bore no resemblance whatsoever to the Kray brothers.

We heard the trio on the stairs forty minutes later and when the door was sharply rapped, Renee flung it open revolver in hand and ushered the group into the hallway.

'Featherstone – you are here to be interrogated once more,' Paula said clearly and crisply.

He appeared to be about sixty, moderately distinguished in appearance and standing very straight.

'I realise that Mistress,' he replied in the enunciated tones of a man who was used to being listened to and what's more having his words heeded.

He was steered into the bondage room where a chair had been prepared for him, set before a semi-circle of four others for the use of Paula, Margo, Renee and myself. However he was not allowed to sit down and for the first half hour he was mercilessly questioned about a catalogue of mystifying misdeeds. The penalties were apparently grim.

It was the first time I had taken part in an extended masochistic fantasy of this kind and although in parts it was distasteful such as the drinking of the glass of urine, the situation itself was intriguing. I found myself wondering how he first came to the realization that his sex life would involve much more than most nicely brought up girls from good homes could be expected to handle. From the information Paula gave, it seemed to always involve a cast of six and that did not allow for the peripheral players such as the driver and whoever held him prisoner on Hampstead Heath. It surely must have been simply too much for any prospective wife to cope with even if she could occasionally rely on enlisting the help of friends. Now presumably at the pinnacle of his career, one could only speculate on how testing it was to keep this side of his life completely undisclosed and whether or not the thought of exposure worried him unduly. He did not appear to be a man who concerned himself much with trivia and he had a supremely confident manner.

That particular afternoon I was almost, but not quite, flattered when he chose me to be the person he concluded the session with.

By six o'clock we all sat in the kitchen in a very civilized manner drinking champagne and eating tiny smoked salmon and crab sandwiches from Fortnum and Mason, and chatting about general matters that so preoccupied the newspaper headlines at the time. Brian Featherstone had very definite views on the IRA and it turned out that he did most of the talking before suddenly looking at his watch at precisely six twenty and saying, 'Well it's been a simply lovely afternoon ladies – but now I must depart.' And depart he did.

Paula and I stayed behind to tidy up so Connie would not be forced into ill humour when she arrived on Monday. Once all the chairs were back in their usual positions, the canes and whips put away tidily, the washing up done and the teapot thoroughly emptied, Paula suggested going for a drink which I was more than happy to do.

'Are you willing to take him on again?' she asked as we sat in the quiet Belgravia pub, strangely empty and echoing, sipping gin and tonics. I said I was more than happy to do so and that in fact I had found him quite pleasant to deal with.

'He liked you,' she said, 'so I know he'll ask for you again. What he really hates is what he calls Dolly Birds – though his idea of a Dolly Bird differs from the reality – any hint of curly hair or make-up, skirts above the knee and he gets completely turned off.'

I said I would be sure to remember that and briefly considered that his aberration might be a simple extension of a penchant for women in uniform such as my own father had demonstrated returning from the Eighth Army. In his case it had led him directly into the arms of Sadie the bus conductress, but for Brian Featherstone the path had perhaps been more precipitous not to mention more costly.

'He likes to meet new girls from time to time too,' she added and I said it must be quite demanding organizing it all. Paula half smiled and told me I didn't know the half of it because she had to make sure that the girls were also going to be as discreet as possible which was easy enough when they'd been at the job for a few years but when they turned out to be amateurs it was more tricky. You couldn't always rely upon them.

She looked directly at me and drained her glass. 'That's why I prefer to find people who don't also turn out to do shifts in Selfridges.'

I gave a brief thought to the reports and general correspondence I had recently agreed to do for the dermatologist in Harley Street and decided that probably didn't really count. As for the short story writing, well that could be classed as a hobby.

'Do you have any hobbies?' I asked before I could stop myself. Paula paused for a second or two before saying, 'To be perfectly honest I love to paint – landscapes mostly, watercolours but since Monet was born I've not had much time for it.'

Later, regaling Shelagh with all the details of that particular Friday I said I had been rendered speechless to discover that someone like Paula was interested in painting. She said she didn't find it at all surprising and that women like her probably were in greater need than most for something creative in their lives.

Over the subsequent two or three years I was to meet Brian Featherstone regularly, always on Fridays, sometimes at Connie's place and at other times at Paula's flat in Maida Vale. However I was never to quite forget the first time although another encounter with him probably stands out even more vividly. That was the extraordinary occasion leading up to a General Election when we waited for the Judge to be delivered to Paula's door by slaves from Hampstead Heath.

At an authoritative knock at exactly the right time, Paula in uniform and high boots, revolver in hand, with Margo and myself standing slightly to her rear holding whips, opened the door with a flourish.

'Get inside at once,' Paula ordered in a menacing but low voice.

But it wasn't Brian Featherstone and the slaves standing there. It was the Labour Party candidate for Paddington and his assistant.

There was a short horrified moment when we all stood stock still and stared at each other before the

candidate recovered his composure and simply said, 'I'm so sorry. I think I have the wrong address.'
Then he moved on.

You'll Have to Give It Up

I worked for Connie for several years, only terminating our association completely when I decided to leave London and go to New Zealand to get married. Even then we still corresponded on a regular basis which in the early nineteen seventies did not mean emails or texts but old fashioned labour intensive letters back and forth. On a number of occasions when Connie wanted to have breaks and go on holiday, as she did when her daughter finally had a baby, I ran the place for her which I found I enjoyed very much.

'Usually when I go away I close down dear,' Connie said uncertainly when we first discussed the idea, 'Because if I go for any length of time I go in August and it's a very quiet month....' She seemed to be dithering and considering how wise it would be to entrust the place into my care. Finally she decided that as she would be gone for two months in order to help with the new baby it would be foolish to close up altogether.

'I'd be bound to lose people,' she said at last and I had to agree.

'How come you've been left in charge and not me or Margo?' Kiki demanded on our first day without her.

'Probably it's because I've run small businesses before.'

I was thinking in particular of Vidar's sound recording and the dermatologist who also went on holiday, though not for two months, leaving signed prescriptions together with a great many instructions for me to fill in appropriately.

Kiki spluttered a sound that was intended to be mock mirth. 'Small businesses? Is this what you'd call a small business then?'

'Of course it is, though maybe an unusual one.'

Ultimately that was exactly what it turned out to be of course. Although she had not asked me to, and had in fact intimated that as I was doing the organizing, I should retain all money taken in during her absence, in fact I kept proper books. It was much quieter than usual during August as she had anticipated but once they knew we were open we still had a small but steady stream of regulars. The three of us, Kiki, Margo and myself, were not totally idle although we did reduce our hours.

During Connie's absence the client I probably disliked most decided to upgrade his attendance from quarterly to weekly. It is particularly inadvisable to allow emotions to rule common sense in the sex industry but in Rodney's case I had to make an exception.

He came from a wealthy family who made their money importing electronic goods from Japan and so Rodney and his brothers had gone to all the right schools and it had been hoped they would join the professions, preferably law. Rodney was not quite up to law and so finally he had gone into the family business and clearly felt that indicated he was a failure. This was further compounded by the fact that he ended up marrying the young woman assigned as his secretary.

In total I spent over ten years as a paid sexual partner of one kind or another and during that time Rodney was the only man I came across who brought his wife with him to a pre-arranged session at a brothel. Her name was Gillian and she was younger than he, probably about forty, a small red haired woman who looked exactly like a secretary.

He hired two of us, dressed in a particularly spectacularly dominating manner, completely in leather together with helmets and masks, to verbally debase and demean Gillian and finally to flog her. She was then required to watch while he had sexual intercourse with one of us.

'She's less than nothing,' he would declare as he strutted the room, 'she comes from a background of peasants. I made her what she is today.'

Gillian remained kneeling, head bent, saying not a word.

'She may sound as if she's been educated but she isn't – went to the village school. That speaking voice she has now is just a veneer. She's nothing, there's no class about her at all.'

At some stage she would begin to cry and he would tell her to stop or she would be beaten and then of course she would cry harder. Finally she would get her beating, sometimes more severe than at others and then would obediently stand by and watch the culmination of her husband's sexual bliss with whomsoever of us he happened to choose. I always hoped it would not be me.

Once she talked to me for a moment or two, hastily and in whispers.

'Are you OK?' I asked feeling stupid, in black leather dispensing tea and sympathy having just caned her harshly.

She was wiping her eyes and blowing her nose. 'Don't worry about me. I cry very easily. He's a bastard isn't he?'

'Yes,' I could hardly say anything else, 'he is. Why do you let him…?'

She cut across my questioning, 'I love him you see – I love him so much.'

'But….' I wanted to ask why but there was no need.

'He's got so much wretched money you see. It's a fatal combination you know, love and money. It can be devastating.'

Later I observed to Renee that he was a total and complete bastard.

'Yeah he is,' she agreed, 'but he's a rich bastard.'

I could not imagine that any man could be rich enough to keep me so entrapped.

She pointed out that you had to factor the love into the equation.

Rodney thanked me for arranging a great afternoon, paid up and they left. I speculated upon how many women like Gillian there were about us, most in situations where their husbands were unable to pay for the humiliation and so it was simply heaped upon them possibly in a more dangerous fashion. What might life be like for her between the stints of bought and paid for degradation? Did they behave normally to each other? Did he simply come home occasionally and say, 'By the way darling, I've booked at Connie's again this week. I'm feeling a bit negative towards you again for some reason. Do you think you can manage Wednesday?'

'I've got the flower arranging at St. Mark's on Wednesday – can we make it Thursday instead?'

'Righty ho darling I'll ring first thing and see if we can change it…'

All quite repugnant but alarmingly similar in so many ways to the relationship I had endured with Vidar for so long. It was worrying to think that it was more likely than not that this was the way Gillian chose to accept as tolerable for making her marriage work.

When Connie returned from Africa she was delighted to hear that all had gone smoothly in her absence and a little overcome that I had prepared an analysis of attendees and payments that left her with most of the fee that she would normally have recovered from the clients.

'I won't have any qualms leaving you in charge again,' she said.

We moved from Pont Street to Pimlico a few weeks later. Connie told me that it had always been her practice to avoid complacency and move the business into fresh premises every two or three years.

'You are much less likely to get raided if you do so,' she told me.

However, it turned out that the move to Pimlico was her undoing because that was where two years later, just as she was considering her next move and where it should be, that she was finally raided after so many years without incident.

'I always like to be south of the park,' she maintained. 'My clients won't go north of the park – it's too far for them.'

She was undoubtedly thinking of those who formed the spine of the business, the minions and sycophants to Ministers from Whitehall and Westminster and of course the occasional Minister himself. Ruled by schedules and diaries their free time was limited and had to be planned for. Traffic jams circumnavigating the park could not be fitted into the equation no matter how robust the desire to administer pain to a paid recipient.

Happily for me, when the raid came I was already in Auckland, respectably married to a general practitioner and pregnant with my second son, Jonah, and my life as a deviation professional fast receding.

I had first met Jack Harris at Clive's nineteen sixty five Christmas party. It was the evening of Christmas Day and of course I was there with Vidar, who was just a little dissatisfied that it was to be a completely conventional celebration with extra hired staff to attend to the sixty or seventy guests, most of whom were men. Of the handful of girls, Natasha had invited her boyfriend of the time, a New Zealand doctor practicing in London and in convivial colonial style he brought with him two or three friends. Jack was one of them.

I had the strangest sensation when I first spoke to Jack standing by the fireplace in Clive's dining room, that I would marry him. It was such a ridiculous thought that I banished it hastily and concentrated on talking about how good Clive's party food was. In any case I was with Vidar to whom I was completely devoted. We did get on well though and I gave him my telephone number. Over the next two or three years he rang me frequently and we talked together for long periods as long as Vidar was away from the flat, and on one or two occasions even met for drinks or coffee. He then represented for me an emotional escape from the horror I seemed to be living through although I don't think I discussed that with him very much. I had not for a moment considered him as a candidate when Madam Sandra conjured up the man whose initials were GH and who whisk me out of the country because his initials were JH.

When he went back to New Zealand we corresponded though sporadically as his handwriting was so poor I found it more than challenging to decipher it. Then he returned to London for a holiday and tracked me down, asking me out for dinner. We chatted for a while and agreed to meet a week or so later.

'Where do you suggest we go?' he asked.

'Let's go to Rules, in Maiden Lane,' I suggested because it was still of all the restaurants in London my most favourite place to eat.

We went there on a stormy evening in September nineteen seventy two during Connie's trip to Africa and sat near the rear of the restaurant contemplating the menu from which I chose fried whitebait followed by jugged hare. I now look back in amazement that I had such a healthy appetite in those days because a plate of whitebait, Rules style, was not insignificant and to follow it with the hare seems now like embarking upon a marathon. Jack also chose two generous courses and then as an afterthought added a bowl of soup between them.

Out of the blue he suddenly suggested that I might like to join him in New Zealand for a holiday.

'Well it's such a long way,' I replied, completely overwhelmed. 'What for?'

He spoke briskly, not quite looking at me. 'Well I thought if we got on all right together we might get married.'

'But I've got a child,' I felt as stupid as I undoubtedly sounded.

'That's OK – it might be quite nice to have a child,' he said.

I was silent because I was not accustomed to receiving proposals of marriage and Jack's was only the second ever made to me. The first had been a mere three weeks before when a sadist called Edmund said he would be 'frightfully honoured' if I would consider becoming his wife and he was anxious to introduce me to his mother. She, an ageing duchess, I felt would be less enchanted with the idea.

'I'm not expecting you to decide at this moment,' Jack was saying cheerfully.

That was all very well and Edmund had said something very similar.

He then added, 'I tried to find that antique shop today, you know – the one you're working in, but I didn't have much luck locating it.'

'Oh.'

'You said it was in Pont Street.'

The first course plates had been cleared away and the table stretched between us devoid of anything to occupy me.

'Yes it is,' I said honestly.

His soup then arrived and he gently ladled up a spoonful and held it to his lips, looking at me questioningly.

'I couldn't find it,' he said, 'I walked the length of Pont Street and I didn't see it.'

For a brief instant I thought I might substitute Pond Street in Hampstead for Pont Street in Belgravia and instead said, 'We're moving to Pimlico when my boss gets back.'

He swallowed the spoonful of soup and scooped up a second one. 'Which end of the street is it in?'

What a nuisance this man was.

In that moment I decided to tell the truth.

'I don't work in an antique shop – it's a brothel. I'm actually I suppose….a prostitute'

I watched in fascination as the second spoonful of soup did not waver as he transferred it with care into his mouth.

He said, 'Well if we do get married, I will have to insist that you give it up.'

I was both amused and bewildered, but mostly bewildered. Finally I said, 'OK – that's fair enough. If we get married I will definitely give it up.'

I had already decided that I would marry him.

Later I began to wonder if I was doing the right thing, for the right motives but Daniel was quite deliriously happy at the thought of acquiring a father. He was now four years old and I think I had critically underestimated how important having a father would be to him. All he knew about Vidar was that he existed but that he chose not to live with us and I believed at the time that as long as I was a good and attentive mother that would override the missing paternal influence. Perhaps that is the case for some children but for Daniel it was not. He desperately wanted a man in his life and threw himself into the role of the perfect stepson with enthusiasm.

'Remember Madame Sandra,' Shelagh reminded me a day or two before we left London. 'Maybe New Zealand will turn out to be the land of sunshine and white buildings she was talking about.'

I had not given Madame Sandra much thought for a long time, though I had at various times wondered if the man with the initials GH would ever turn up. On one occasion I had made life quite uncomfortable for a South African I met who was called Graham Hawkesby, ringing him far too often and trying to convince myself that he might well turn out to be the man I was destined to marry even though I did not like him terribly much.

In the early nineteen seventies Auckland actually was a city of white buildings and when I arrived in early November, the sun was dazzling and so the effect was dramatic when put alongside Madame Sandra's prediction.

I was more than prepared to leave my life in the sexual deviation business behind me but the transition from London to Auckland was not always totally easy. The lifestyle was entirely different and would have been more easily surmountable if the people had spoken a different language. As it was, Aucklanders spoke English but could not have been further from the English in every aspect of social convention. Everything about them was surprising, from the endless weekend parties where extraordinary quantities of alcohol were consumed to the unabashed advertising of tampons and the volume of fluid they could hold, on TV screens at peak viewing time. Daily it seemed I was confronted with conventions that surprised me and it took a long time to adjust to a lifestyle that differed so drastically from that I was used to. The daily grind of dealing with sadists and masochists seemed almost pedestrian in comparison.

Once Jonah was born, followed a couple of years later by Martha, I had almost become a very ordinary Auckland housewife. My past never placed any kind of emotional burden upon my marriage and was only referred to when Jack and I engaged from time to time in furious arguments when all manner of abuse was hurled back and forth. Luckily neither of us dwelt unnecessarily upon insults thrown at such times.

The greatest threat to our equilibrium has always been that I could never quite get over my love affair with London and over the years have kept returning again and again to reassure myself that everything I so passionately adore about the city is still in its place. Rules Restaurant, Covent Garden where the narrow streets remain though their function has altered, and Soho defiantly less affected by the years. Every now and again I have to make a pilgrimage to the pubs I list among my favourites, The Punch Tavern in Fleet Street, The Swan off Gracechurch Street, The Warrington in Maida Vale, The Barley Mow in Dorset Street and The Mayflower in Rotherhithe.

It would be true to say that in New Zealand I led a distinctly different life to that which I would have led had I stayed in England. I have no doubt that if I had stayed I would have continued to work for Connie and in time might have inherited the business from her and I am certain I would have enjoyed running it. I hope I would not have been raided and that the social acceptance of such places would have hastened along, allowing times to change as rapidly as possible. I would have probably continued to write to some extent.

On the other side of the world as the children grew older so I grew interested in education and found myself writing articles revolving around differentiated systems of education for children with special needs, texts in creative education for teachers and a book about home schooling. I was involved in the home education movement for ten years and taught my two younger children myself.

When they grew beyond the home classroom I became involved in running an emergency medical clinic in the city and found that although I had always felt medical politics to be excruciatingly boring, it could in fact prove to be more interesting than one might imagine.

It is only in more recent years that I have returned to writing, firstly as a response to the in-depth family research my brother has become involved in. It seemed sensible to write initially about the kind of life we had when we were children and later my early working life on the periphery of the popular music business. I resisted writing about my time as a sex worker for a number of years. Although I was reasonably certain that those who knew and liked me would be unlikely to change their attitudes simply because they discovered what I did for a living all those years ago, my husband constantly urged caution.

Whether he is proved to be right or not, possibly none of us have complete freedom when it comes to the choices we make in life. Some things may very well be mapped out for us. For example it was not until the day I married Jack Harris that I realized his name was not actually Jack at all; it was Gordon.

THE END

This story continued from

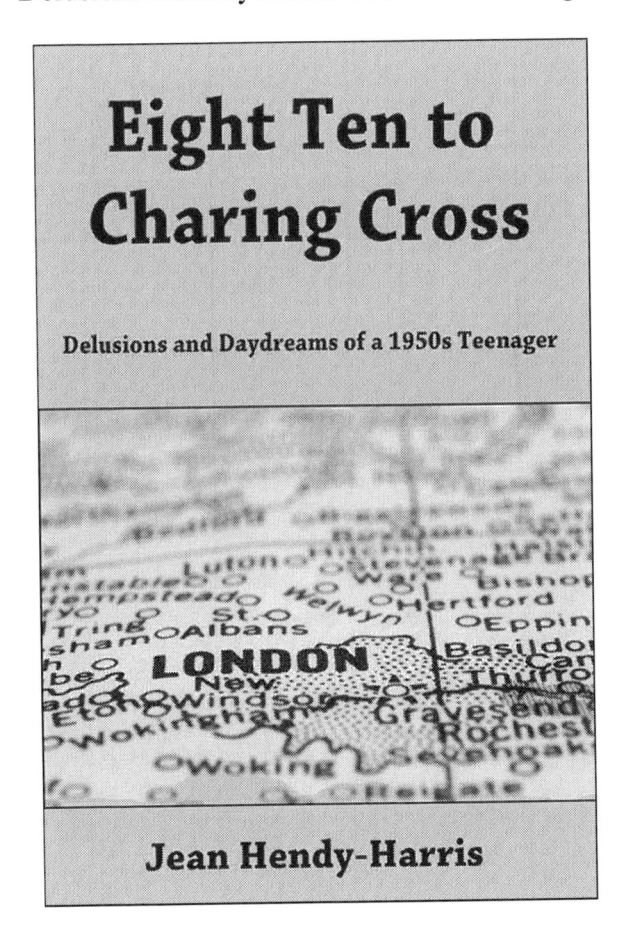

EIGHT TEN TO CHARING CROSS
Delusions and Daydreams of a 1950s Teenager

Eight Ten to Charing Cross

Delusions and Daydreams of a 1950s Teenager

Jean Hendy-Harris

and before that, the first volume,

CHALK PITS AND CHERRY STONES
A Childhood in Kent

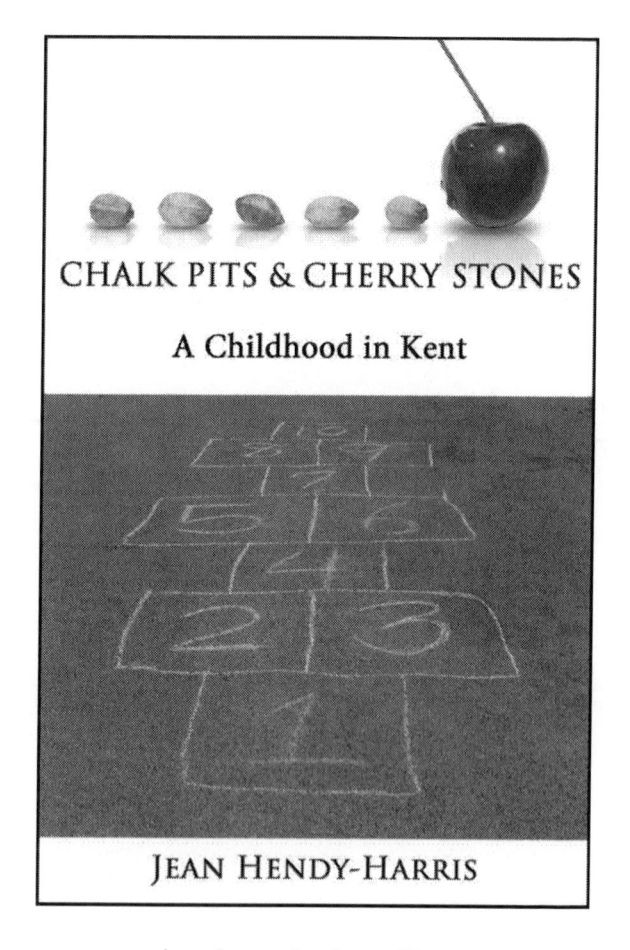

covering the author's earliest years.

All three books available from Amazon in print and on Smashwords as ebooks.

Please consider posting a review to help other readers to enjoy the author's work.

Printed by Amazon Italia Logistica S.r.l.
Torrazza Piemonte (TO), Italy